# THE ECONOMIC ANALYSIS OF TORT LAW

By

**David W. Barnes**
*Professor of Law, University of Denver*

**Lynn A. Stout**
*Professor of Law, Georgetown University*

*Reprinted from Barnes and Stout's "Cases and Materials on
LAW AND ECONOMICS" (West, 1992)*

**AMERICAN CASEBOOK SERIES** ®

**WEST PUBLISHING CO.**
ST. PAUL, MINN., 1992

*Reprinted from Barnes and Stout's "Cases and Materials on LAW AND ECONOMICS" (West, 1992).*

*American Casebook Series* and the WP symbol are registered trademarks of West Publishing Co. Registered in the U.S. Patent and Trademark Office.

COPYRIGHT © 1992 By WEST PUBLISHING CO.
610 Opperman Drive
P.O. Box 64526
St. Paul, MN 55164-0526

All rights reserved
Printed in the United States of America

**Library of Congress Cataloging-in-Publication Data**

Barnes, David W.
    The economic analysis of tort law / by David W. Barnes, Lynn A. Stout.
        p.   cm. — (American casebook series)
    Include index.
    ISBN 0-314-01089-0
    1. Torts—Economic aspects—United States—Cases. 2. Liability (Law)—Economic aspects—United States—Cases. 3. Accident law—Economic aspects—United States—Cases. I. Stout, Lynn A., 1957- . II. Title. III. Series.
KF1251.B37 1992
346.7303—dc20
[347.3063]                                                  92-20402
                                                                CIP

**ISBN 0-314-01089-0**

(B.&S.) Anal. of Tort Law ACB

# Preface

During the past three decades, scholars wielding the tools of economics have marched through the curricula of American law schools, applying economic analysis to one substantive area of law after another. Accustomed to formal theoretical models of institutions and human behavior, "law and economics" scholars often examine legal rules in the abstract rather than discussing their application to specific cases. By contrast, conventional law teaching begins with specific cases and abstracts from those cases the general principles governing decisions. The series of books of which this one is a part combines the theory of economics and the pedagogy of law by exploring economic analysis of law primarily through reported judicial opinions and agency decisions. Excerpts from classic writings have been included to give a flavor for the type of discourse in which law and economics scholars engage.

Economic analysis is becoming a routine part of the consideration of policies underlying various substantive areas of law. This series provides cases and materials to supplement law school courses in which economic analysis is particularly relevant. Three books, *The Economics of Property Rights and Nuisance Law*, *The Economic Analysis of Tort Law*, and *The Economics of Contract Law*, focus on the economic analysis of common law courses typically taught in the first year of law school. *Economic Foundations of Regulation and Antitrust Law* presents an introduction to microeconomic theory in the context of government regulation of business, including cases and materials raising issues of occupational safety and health, environmental regulation, postal regulation, cable television, and consumer protection, along with tax and antitrust cases. *The Economics of Constitutional Law and Public Choice* examines constitutional questions of equal protection, due process, separation of powers, voting rights, the police power, and judicial review, among others. All of the books in the series are designed for readers with no prior economic training.

The books exploring the economic implications of common law doctrines all include an introduction to the basic economic assumptions of rationality and scarcity and the concepts of utility maximization, wealth maximization, and allocative efficiency. They deal with the three areas of law that virtually all law students study in their first year of law school: property, torts (personal injury), and contracts. The books encourage the reader to examine the implications and appreciate the relevance of economic analysis by using the familiar case method.

*The Economics Analysis of Tort Law* traces the analytical development of tort law from negligence through strict liability for dangerous activities to strict products liability. It is designed to follow the students' intellectual progress through a traditional torts course, beginning with straightforward negligence cases and the Learned Hand characterization of reasonable behavior. The economic implications of the various defenses to negligence claims—contributory and comparative negligence, last clear chance, and assumption of risk—are then explored in detail. The book next examines the various contexts in which strict liability is imposed and the justifications for finding liability without fault as well as the economic efficiency of traditional defenses to strict liability—unforeseeable misuse, assumption of risk, and comparative negligence. The final section presents economic issues in the determination of damages, the efficiency of the collateral source rule and the problems involved in measuring future losses, hedonic damages, and punitive damages.

The case orientation of these books should appeal to those eager to escape the artificial assumptions often associated with economics, as well as those eager to explore the ethical and distributional dimensions of law. Analyzing reported decisions requires economics to come to grips with reality and emphasizes the implausibility of assumptions frequently made to facilitate economic analysis. Real rather than hypothetical factual contexts also highlight the distributional and ethical implications of economic analyses of law. Rather than gloss over such issues, the books in the series regularly raise the normative implications of particular legal rules. *The Economics of Property Rights and Nuisance Law*, for instance, considers the efficiency and distributional implications of alternative forms of property rights and of different methods of protecting property rights. *The Economic Analysis of Tort Law* draws the reader's attention to the distributional implications of alternative measures of damages. *The Economics of Contract Law* considers contract law's bias in favor of the status quo from which bargaining takes place and the implications of unequal bargaining power. *Economic Foundations of Regulation and Antitrust Law* contracts an antitrust policy that focuses on allocative efficiency to a policy that focuses on the welfare of consumers as a class. The analysis of constitutional law in *The Economics of Constitutional Law and Public Choice* focuses on the distribution of power among society's members and the distributional implications of alternative mechanisms for institutionalizing state coercion. These books are vehicles for appreciating and critically examining, rather than merely promoting, the economic analysis of law.

Most footnotes and citations contained in reported opinions and other quoted materials have been omitted without any indication. In the rare occasions where such footnotes have been included, they are reproduced with their original numbering. All other omissions from excerpted texts are indicated by asterisks.

# Acknowledgments

The authors would like to thank the publishers and authors of the following works for allowing them to include excerpts in this text or in *Cases and Materials on LAW AND ECONOMICS*, from which this text is derived:

J. Buchanan & G. Tullock, The Calculus of Consent: Logical Foundations of Constitutional Democracy 63–72, 77–78, 81 (1962). Copyright © 1962 by the University of Michigan Press. Reprinted with permission.

Calabresi and Melamed, Property Rules, Liability Rules, and Inalienability: One View of the Cathedral. 85 Harv.L.Rev. 1089, 1092–93, 1105, 1111–15 (1972). Copyright © 1972 by the Harvard Law Review Association. Reprinted with permission.

Coase, The Problem of Social Cost, 3 J. Law & Econ. 1–2, 13 (1960). Copyright © 1960 by the University of Chicago, University of Chicago Press. Reprinted with permission.

Easterbrook, Ways of Criticizing the Court, 95 Harv.L.Rev. 802, 811–16, 818–19, 831 (1982). Copyright © 1982 by the Harvard Law Review Association. Reprinted with permission.

Hardin, The Tragedy of the Commons, 162 Science 1243, 1244–45 (December 13, 1968). Copyright © 1968 by the American Association for the Advancement of Science. Reprinted with permission.

Posner, Gratuitous Promises in Economics and Law, 6 J. Legal Studies 411–13 (1977). Copyright © 1977 by the University of Chicago, University of Chicago Press. Reprinted with permission.

Priest, The Common Law Process and the Selection of Efficient Rules, 6 J. Legal Studies 65–73, 81–82 (1977). Copyright © 1977 by the University of Chicago, University of Chicago Press. Reprinted with permission.

J. Rawls, A Theory of Justice 3–4, 11, 12, 13, 14–15, 22, 60–62, 136–37, 140–41, 151–53 (1971). Copyright © 1971 by the President and Fellows of Harvard College, Harvard University Press. Reprinted with permission.

Shavell, Strict Liability Versus Negligence, 9 J. Legal Studies 1–3, 22–23 (1980). Copyright © 1980 by the University of Chicago, University of Chicago Press. Reprinted with permission.

Williamson, Economics As An Antitrust Defense Revisited, 125 U.Pa.L.Rev. 699, 704, 706–708 (1977). Copyright © 1977 by The University of Pennsylvania. Reprinted with permission.

# Summary of Contents

|  | Page |
|---|---|
| PREFACE | iii |
| ACKNOWLEDGMENTS | v |
| TABLE OF CASES | xiii |

**Chapter 1. Introduction** — 1
- A. Efficiency and Utility Maximization — 1
- B. Efficiency and Wealth Maximization — 6
- C. Comparing Utility and Wealth Maximization: The Pareto Criteria and the Role of Compensation — 11
- D. Efficiency and Equity — 17
- E. Externalities and Inefficiency — 20

**Chapter 2. The Economic Analysis of Tort Law** — 27
- A. Liability as an Incentive for Efficient Behavior — 27
- B. The Negligence Standard — 35
- C. Efficiency of Defenses to Liability Based on Negligence — 46
- D. Nuisance Law: Assigning and Exchanging Rights — 71
- E. Trespass and Nuisance: Transaction Costs and Impediments to Bargaining — 88
- F. Strict Liability — 108
- G. Efficient Defenses to Strict Liability — 131
- H. Problems in Calculating Damages — 142

INDEX — 159

# Table of Contents

|  | Page |
|---|---|
| PREFACE | iii |
| ACKNOWLEDGMENTS | v |
| TABLE OF CASES | xiii |

**Chapter 1. Introduction** ........................................................ 1
A. Efficiency and Utility Maximization ............................... 1
    *Cidis v. White* ............................................................... 2
    Notes and Questions .................................................... 3
B. Efficiency and Wealth Maximization .............................. 6
    *Ross v. Wilson* .............................................................. 6
    Notes and Questions .................................................... 8
C. Comparing Utility and Wealth Maximization: The Pareto Criteria and the Role of Compensation .......... 11
    *United States v. Causby* .............................................. 13
    Notes and Questions .................................................... 14
D. Efficiency and Equity ....................................................... 17
    *Pitsenberger v. Pitsenberger* ...................................... 18
    Notes and Questions .................................................... 19
E. Externalities and Inefficiency ......................................... 20
    1. Internalizing Externalities Through Damage Awards .... 21
        *Orchard View Farms, Inc. v. Martin Marietta Aluminum, Inc.* .................................................................. 21
        Notes and Questions ................................................ 22
    2. Internalizing Externalities Through Regulation .......... 24
        *United States v. The City of Niagara Falls* ............. 24
        Notes and Questions ................................................ 25

**Chapter 2. The Economic Analysis of Tort Law** ................ 27
A. Liability as an Incentive for Efficient Behavior .............. 27
    *Winn Dixie Stores, Inc. v. Benton* .............................. 27
    Notes and Questions .................................................... 28
    *Drake v. Lerner Shops of Colorado, Inc.* ................... 30
    Notes and Questions .................................................... 31
    *Schomaker v. Havey* .................................................... 33
    Notes and Questions .................................................... 34
B. The Negligence Standard ................................................. 35
    1. The Cost-Benefit Approach to Liability ..................... 35
        *United States v. Carroll Towing Co.* ....................... 35
        Notes and Questions ................................................ 37
    2. Modern Applications of the Learned Hand Formula .... 39
        *McCarty v. Pheasant Run, Inc.* ............................... 39
        Notes and Questions ................................................ 41

|   |   |   | Page |
|---|---|---|---|
| B. | The Negligence Standard—Continued | | |
| | *Davis v. Consolidated Rail Corporation* | | 42 |
| | *Notes and Questions* | | 45 |
| C. | Efficiency of Defenses to Liability Based on Negligence | | 46 |
| | 1. | Contributory Negligence | 48 |
| | | *Butterfield v. Forrester* | 48 |
| | | *Notes and Questions* | 49 |
| | | *Haeg v. Sprague, Warner & Co., Inc.* | 49 |
| | | *Notes and Questions* | 51 |
| | | *Levi v. Southwest Louisiana Electric Membership Cooperative* | 53 |
| | | *Notes and Questions* | 55 |
| | 2. | Last Clear Chance | 57 |
| | | *Perin v. Nelson & Sloan* | 57 |
| | | *Notes and Questions* | 58 |
| | 3. | Apportioned Comparative Negligence | 60 |
| | | *Scott v. Alpha Beta Company* | 60 |
| | | *Notes and Questions* | 61 |
| | | *Golden v. McCurry* | 62 |
| | | *Notes and Questions* | 63 |
| | 4. | Nonapportioned Comparative Negligence | 65 |
| | | *Galena and Chicago Union Railroad Company v. Jacobs* | 65 |
| | | *Notes and Questions* | 66 |
| | 5. | Assumption of Risk | 67 |
| | | *Ordway v. Superior Court* | 67 |
| | | *Notes and Questions* | 68 |
| | | *Kelly v. Checker White Cab* | 69 |
| | | *Notes and Questions* | 71 |
| D. | Nuisance Law: Assigning and Exchanging Rights | | 71 |
| | 1. | Competing Uses and the Coexistence of Property Rights | 71 |
| | | *Bryant v. Lefever* | 72 |
| | | Coase, The Problem of Social Cost | 73 |
| | | *Notes and Questions* | 74 |
| | | *Sturges v. Bridgman* | 76 |
| | | *Notes and Questions* | 77 |
| | 2. | The Coase Theorem and the Efficient Exchange of Rights | 78 |
| | | *Fontainebleau Hotel Corp. v. Forty-Five Twenty-Five, Inc.* | 79 |
| | | *Notes and Questions* | 80 |
| | | *Prah v. Maretti* | 81 |
| | | *Notes and Questions* | 83 |
| E. | Trespass and Nuisance: Transaction Costs and Impediments to Bargaining | | 88 |
| | 1. | Trespass, the Coase Theorem, and Transaction Costs | 88 |
| | | *Ploof v. Putnam* | 88 |
| | | *Notes and Questions* | 89 |
| | | Calabresi and Melamed, Property Rules, Liability Rules, and Inalienability: One View of the Cathedral | 91 |

|   |   |   | Page |
|---|---|---|---|
| E. | Trespass and Nuisance: Transaction Costs and Impediments to Bargaining—Continued | | |
| | | *Vincent v. Lake Erie Transport Co.* | 92 |
| | | *Notes and Questions* | 94 |
| | 2. | Nuisance, Impediments to Bargaining, and the Choice of Remedies | 95 |
| | | *Boomer v. Atlantic Cement Company* | 96 |
| | | *Notes and Questions* | 98 |
| | | *Spur Industries, Inc. v. Del E. Webb Development Co.* | 100 |
| | | *Notes and Questions* | 102 |
| | | *Carpenter v. Double R Cattle Company, Inc.* | 103 |
| | | *Notes and Questions* | 107 |
| F. | Strict Liability | | 108 |
| | 1. | Strict Liability and the Best Cost Avoider | 108 |
| | | *Spano v. Perini Corporation* | 108 |
| | | *Notes and Questions* | 110 |
| | | Shavell, Strict Liability Versus Negligence | 111 |
| | | *Notes and Questions* | 112 |
| | | *Greenman v. Yuba Power Products, Inc.* | 114 |
| | | *Notes and Questions* | 115 |
| | 2. | Strict Liability and Allocative Efficiency | 116 |
| | | *Doe v. Miles Laboratories, Inc.* | 116 |
| | | *Notes and Questions* | 118 |
| | 3. | Risk–Aversion and Loss Spreading | 121 |
| | | *Escola v. Coca Cola Bottling Co.* | 121 |
| | | *Notes and Questions* | 122 |
| | | *Shepard v. Superior Court* | 125 |
| | | *Notes and Questions* | 127 |
| | 4. | Strict Liability and Duty to Rescue | 128 |
| | | *Osterlind v. Hill* | 128 |
| | | *Notes and Questions* | 129 |
| G. | Efficient Defenses to Strict Liability | | 131 |
| | 1. | Unforeseeable Misuse | 131 |
| | | *Daniell v. Ford Motor Co.* | 131 |
| | | *Notes and Questions* | 132 |
| | | *Cryts v. Ford Motor Company* | 132 |
| | | *Notes and Questions* | 134 |
| | 2. | Unreasonable Assumption of Risk | 135 |
| | | *Williams v. Brown Manufacturing Company* | 135 |
| | | *Notes and Questions* | 138 |
| | 3. | Comparative Negligence | 138 |
| | | *Murray v. Fairbanks Morse* | 138 |
| | | *Notes and Questions* | 141 |
| H. | Problems in Calculating Damages | | 142 |
| | 1. | The Collateral Source Rule | 142 |
| | | *Anheuser-Busch, Inc. v. Starley* | 142 |
| | | *Notes and Questions* | 143 |

## TABLE OF CONTENTS

Page

H. Problems in Calculating Damages—Continued
    2. Measuring Future Losses ............................................. 144
       *Kaczkowski v. Bolubasz* ............................................. 144
       *Notes and Questions* ................................................. 148
    3. Valuing Human Life .................................................... 149
       *Sherrod v. Berry* ....................................................... 150
       *Notes and Questions* ................................................. 152
    4. Punitive Damages and Overdeterrence ....................... 154
       *Sturm, Ruger & Co., Inc. v. Day* ........................... 154
       *Notes and Questions* ................................................. 156

INDEX .............................................................................................. 159

# Table of Cases

The principal cases are in bold type. Cases cited or discussed in the text are roman type. References are to pages. Cases cited in principal cases and within other quoted materials are not included.

American Airlines v. Ulen, 29
**Anheuser-Busch v. Starley, 142,** 143

**Boomer v. Atlantic Cement Co., 96,** 98, 100, 102, 103
**Booth v. Rome, W. & O. T. R. Co., 110,** 111, 120
**Bryant v. Lefever, 72,** 74, 81, 87
**Butterfield v. Forrester, 48,** 49

**Carpenter v. Double R Cattle Co., Inc., 103,** 108
**Carroll Towing Co., United States v., 35,** 37
**Causby, United States v., 12,** 13, 14, 15, 16, 20, 23
**Cidis v. White, 2,** 3, 4, 9, 15
City of (see name of city)
Conway v. O'Brien, 38
Cryts v. Ford Motor Co., 132, 134

**Daniell v. Ford Motor Co., Inc., 131,** 132, 134
Davies v. Mann, 59
**Davis v. Consolidated Rail Corp., 41,** 42, 45, 46
**Doe v. Miles Laboratories, Inc., 116,** 118, 120
**Drake v. Lerner Shops of Colorado, Inc., 30,** 31, 32, 33

**Escola v. Coca Cola Bottling Co. of Fresno, 121,** 122

**Fontainebleau Hotel Corp. v. Forty-Five Twenty-Five, Inc., 79,** 80, 81, 83

**Galena and Chicago Union Railroad Company v. Jacobs, 65,** 66, 67
**Golden v. McCurry, 62,** 64, 141
**Greenman v. Yuba Power Products, Inc., 114,** 115, 116, 119

**Haeg v. Sprague, Warner & Co., 49,** 51, 52, 53, 55, 56, 58
Heeg v. Licht, 110, 113
Hentschel v. Baby Bathinette Corp., 38

**Kaczkowski v. Bolubasz, 144,** 148, 149
**Kelly v. Checker White Cab, 69,** 71
Koseris v. J. R. Simplot Co., 99

Larsen v. General Motors Corp., 134
**Levi v. Southwest Louisiana Elec. Membership Co-op. (SLEMCO), 53,** 55, 56, 58, 67

Madden v. C & K Barbecue Carryout, Inc., 41, 45
**McCarty v. Pheasant Run, Inc., 39,** 41, 42, 52
**Murray v. Fairbanks Morse, 138,** 141, 142

Nelson v. Hall, 69
**Niagara Falls, City of, United States v., 24**

**Orchard View Farms, Inc. v. Martin Marietta Aluminum, Inc., 21,** 22, 23, 118
**Ordway v. Superior Court (Casella), 67,** 68, 69, 71, 112, 113
**Osterlind v. Hill, 128,** 130

**Perin v. Nelson & Sloan, 57,** 58
**Pitsenberger v. Pitsenberger, 18,** 19
**Ploof v. Putnam, 88,** 89, 90, 94, 95, 99
Pomer v. Schoolman, 52
**Prah v. Maretti, 81,** 83, 86

Reynolds Metals Co. v. Lampert, 157
Rhode Island Hosp. Trust Nat. Bank v. Zapata Corp., 32
**Richman v. Charter Arms Corp., 120,** 124, 125
**Ross v. Wilson, 6,** 8, 9, 15, 20

**Schomaker v. Havey, 33,** 34, 35
**Scott v. Alpha Beta Co., 51,** 60, 61
**Shepard v. Superior Court, 125,** 127
**Sherrod v. Berry, 150,** 152
**Spano v. Perini Corp., 108,** 110, 113, 114, 116, 120
**Spur Industries, Inc. v. Del E. Webb Development Co., 100,** 102, 103
**Sturges v. Bridgman, 76,** 77, 78, 81, 87, 90

Sturm, Ruger & Co., Inc. v. Day, 154, 156, 157

United States v. ____(see opposing party)

Vincent v. Lake Erie Transp. Co., 90, 92, 94, 95

Williams v. Brown Mfg. Co., 135, 138
Winn Dixie Stores, Inc. v. Benton, 27, 28, 29, 31, 32

York v. Stallings, 99

# THE ECONOMIC ANALYSIS OF TORT LAW

*

# Chapter 1

# INTRODUCTION

The law is designed to resolve the conflicting claims that arise when people interact in society. Benefits from the use and ownership of property, from promises based on contracts, and from engaging in activities that present risks to others are accompanied by corresponding burdens: the burden of being excluded from another's property, the obligation to perform one's own promises, and the risk of injury caused by another's activity. Legal rules allocate the benefits and burdens of social interaction, following complex, everchanging, and sometimes unfathomable doctrines.

Economics also is concerned with how to resolve competing claims. While there are economists evaluating law from all political perspectives, many take the traditional or neo-classical perspective that allocates the benefits and burdens of a legal rule according to a single principle, *economic efficiency*. Given the appeal of a single principle on which to base judgments regarding the propriety of legal rules and the fact that both law and economics are concerned fundamentally with the same questions, it is not surprising that lawyers and legal scholars have looked to economics for guidance in evaluating the wisdom and likely effects of legal rules.

This casebook introduces the basic concepts of economics and applies them to legal problems. Economic analysis can shed light on the consequences of the law's murky operations by focusing on the incentives created by the law. Applying economic principles to legal problems brings a better understanding of the implications of legal rules.

## A. EFFICIENCY AND UTILITY MAXIMIZATION

Economics studies rational choice in a world of scarcity. The fundamental goal of economic analysis is getting the most from the scarce resources available to satisfy society's needs and wants by allocating them efficiently among competing uses. The meaning of these terms—rational choice, scarcity, and efficiency—are explored in the following cases.

## CIDIS v. WHITE

District Court, Nassau County, Fourth District, 1972.
71 Misc.2d 481, 336 N.Y.S.2d 362.

GITELMAN, JUDGE.

In this action, plaintiff, a duly licensed optometrist, was requested by defendant, Carol Ann White, an infant, 19 years of age, to furnish her with contact lenses. She advised plaintiff that she urgently desired them as soon as possible. She agreed to pay $225.00 for the lenses and gave the doctor her personal check for $100.00. Plaintiff, accordingly, after examining infant defendant's eyes immediately ordered the lenses from his laboratory and incurred an indebtedness of $110.00. The examination was held on Thursday evening, the lenses were ordered on Friday, and received by the doctor on Saturday. On Monday morning the infant called and disaffirmed her contract on advice and insistence of her father, and stopped payment on her check. The infant was 19 years of age, working, and although living at home with her parents, paid for her room and board.

The plaintiff established that the contact lenses could be used by no one but the infant and have no market value at all, thus resulting in an absolute loss to the plaintiff of $110.00.

The question presents itself as to whether or not the contact lenses were "necessaries." The term "necessaries" as used in the law relating to the liability of infants therefor is a relative term, somewhat flexible, except when applied to such things as are obviously requisite for the maintenance of existence, and also depends on the social position and situation in life of the infant.

An analogy may be drawn between the instant case and the situation that existed in the case of Vichnes v. Transcontinental & Western Air, Inc. and in Bach v. Long Island Jewish Hospital. In the *Vichnes* case an infant purchased a round trip ticket to California and after using it tried to disaffirm and recover the money he paid. The Appellate Term reversed the Municipal Court and dismissed his claim. In the *Bach* case, an emancipated infant attempted to disaffirm her consent to a cosmetic operation performed on her. The Supreme Court, Nassau County, refused to permit her to do so. In both of these cases, the infant had received full benefit and could not place the defendant in status quo. So also in this case, since the contact lenses are of no value to anyone except the infant defendant, the plaintiff has suffered a loss and cannot be put back in status quo except by payment of a reasonable sum.

The Court has in mind the case of International Text Book Co. v. Connelly, which holds that an infant is not liable for a sum in excess of the fair value of the necessaries furnished even though he has contracted to pay more.

Accordingly, and for the purpose of doing substantial justice between the parties, judgment is granted in favor of the plaintiff and against the defendant, Carol Ann White, in the sum of $150.00. Since the defendant, Carol Ann White, is emancipated, no judgment may be granted against her father, the defendant, Richard A. White, and accordingly the complaint is dismissed as to him. During the trial the father urged that his daughter should not be penalized for obeying her father. The Court suggests that there is nothing to prevent the father from paying the judgment for his daughter, if he is so minded.

## *Notes and Questions*

1. The study of economics begins with assumptions about what motivates people to act. In *Cidis,* both White and Cidis apparently entered the contract voluntarily and deliberately—neither was forced to deal with the other. Given such facts, it seems likely that each entered the contract out of self-interest. Each expected to be happier, better-off, and more satisfied after the exchange.

Economists usually do not bother with why people desire certain things or whether they should desire those things at all. Recognizing and accepting that people find happiness in different ways, economists are more interested in *how* individuals pursue happiness, satisfaction, and fulfillment—what economists refer to as *utility.*

*Question:* Is it reasonable to suppose that both Cidis and White thought they were improving their own levels of utility when they struck their bargain, even though it is quite unlikely they actually thought of it in those terms?

2. Economists assume that people generally prefer more utility to less utility. Rational individuals therefore attempt to *maximize* their utility and extract the highest possible level of happiness from the limited resources available to them. Rational maximization requires more of people than simply striking bargains that leave them better off. To maximize her utility, Carol Ann White must use her presumably limited monetary resources to buy those items that bring her the *most* utility. It would be irrational for her to spend $225 on contact lenses if another use of the money—say, to purchase a stereo—would bring her even more happiness.

While White may have thought that she would gain the most utility by using her $225 to buy contact lenses, her father obviously had different ideas. Perhaps he thought his daughter's interests would be better served by using the money for school books or college tuition. In making such a decision, White's father implicitly recognized that the world is a place of *scarcity.* Valuable resources—including food, energy, land, time, and labor, not to mention Carol Ann's bankroll—are finite in amount. Allocating resources to one purpose often sacrifices the opportunity to use those resources for something else. Using clean air as a dumping ground for airborne pollutants interferes with using the air for healthy breathing. A government on a balanced budget must choose between spending money on nuclear weapons or social programs.

Economists refer to the opportunities foregone by choosing to use limited resources for another purpose as the *opportunity cost* of using the resources. By spending her $225 on contact lenses, White incurred the opportunity cost of not being able to spend that money on school books or college tuition. From an opportunity cost perspective, she gave up school books and tuition payments for the lenses. She rationally maximized her utility (was a *rational maximizer*) only if she valued the lenses more than the other opportunities she sacrificed.

*Questions:* What opportunity cost did Cidis incur when he spent his time providing contact lenses for White? Would Cidis be a rational maximizer if he could have used the same time to sell lenses to someone willing to pay more than White?

3. Scarcity and rationality provide the basis for understanding the concept of *efficiency*. Scarcity does not mean that every item desired is as hard to find as a flawless diamond. Scarcity in an economic sense means that the item's supply is sufficiently limited that not enough exists to satisfy all desires. The item must be allocated among competing uses. Rationality is more controversial, primarily because it is often misunderstood. Economists do not believe that everyone always acts rationally. People sometimes behave in an apparently self-destructive fashion. People sometimes make mistakes and are sometimes too tired or uninformed to choose wisely among alternatives. Economists do assume, however, that people *generally* attempt to make themselves as well-off as possible. Economists also recognize that sometimes people gain utility by making others better off as well.

When resources are scarce, rational maximizers want to use their resources to the best possible advantage—to "get the most" out of them. If people seek happiness or utility, allocating scarce resources efficiently means allocating them in a fashion that maximizes the happiness or utility people derive from them.

The exchange Cidis and White contemplated provides an example of an efficient reallocation that may increase the level of utility derived from scarce resources. No rational maximizer would give up one resource in exchange for another unless she valued the second resource more. If Cidis and White were rational maximizers, then at the time of the contract White valued the lenses more than the $225, and Cidis valued the money more than the lenses and the time needed to fit them. The exchange would not increase the total amount of resources available, but it would increase the total amount of utility those resources provided by making both Cidis and White feel better off. Thus, if Cidis and White were rational maximizers, it would have been efficient to allow them to reallocate their resources through exchange.

4. As the preceding note suggests, voluntary exchange can be an important means of efficiently redistributing resources so as to maximize utility. In most cases, the law respects and enforces voluntary contractual exchanges. In Cidis v. White, however, the court refused to require White

to perform the terms of her contractual obligation because, under New York State law, she was still a minor. The contracts of minors are generally regarded as voidable or unenforceable against the minor, although an adult who contracts with a minor will be bound. Even if the contract is for necessaries, a minor is liable only if she has actually used the necessaries or is for some other reason unable to return them so as to restore the merchant to the status quo. If Cidis had sought to enforce his contract with White before the lenses had been ordered from the laboratory, the contract would have been unenforceable.

*Questions:* Does the legal rule that minors lack capacity to enter binding contracts imply that utility maximization is unimportant, at least for minors? Might there be another explanation for the rule?

5. Denying minors the capacity to enter into binding contracts yet holding adult sellers to their promises might discourage adults from providing goods and services to minors. An exception to the incapacity rule is made for the provision of "necessaries," "such things as are obviously requisite for the maintenance of existence."

*Question:* Is this exception based simply on a desire to provide essential services to minors or on a conclusion that minors are more likely to be rational when it comes to necessities? Keep in mind the limitation on enforcement of a minor's contract that requires return of the "necessaries" or limits the amount the minor must pay to the "fair value" of the goods received.

6. When setting the fair value the minor must pay, the court is substituting its own judgment regarding an item's value for the voluntary bargaining of the parties.

*Question:* Under what circumstances could a court determination of the exchange price lead to an inefficient allocation of resources?

7. It is difficult for a decisionmaker (other than the parties to an exchange) to estimate how much utility other persons gain or lose as a result of an exchange. Of course, the decisionmaker can always ask the parties involved. But there may be reason to doubt the accuracy of a party's response when he is not required to "put his money where his mouth is." Consider Carol Ann White's incentives had the Court, after ruling that she was not bound by the contract, asked her what the "fair value" of the lenses was.

Because of the difficulty of estimating how much utility someone else derives from a particular good or service, economists prefer whenever possible to rely on the individual's behavior as the best measure of the value she attaches to that good or service. If individuals are rational maximizers, their behavior in choosing how to allocate their resources will be a reliable reflection of their values. If Carol Ann chooses to buy contact lenses rather than school books, that indicates Carol Ann gets more utility from the lenses. The economist's assumption that individuals' actual choices reflect their preferences and values is described as the *theory of revealed preferences.*

## B. EFFICIENCY AND WEALTH MAXIMIZATION

Allocative efficiency means using scarce resources to the greatest possible advantage, "getting the most" out of them. Whether a particular use is efficient will depend, by definition, on what exactly one wants to gain or accomplish. One might wish to allocate resources so as to maximize the utility people derive from them in order to achieve the greatest overall level of happiness. While a laudable goal in theory, in practice utility maximization can be difficult to implement. No direct means of measuring utility exists. If Carol Ann White chooses to purchase contact lenses, presumably she derives utility from the lenses. Unfortunately, it is impossible to know how *much* utility she derives. There is no ready way to measure how many "utils" Carol Ann gleans from contact lenses as opposed to textbooks, much less compare the value of one person's utils to another person's.

One can measure, however, the amount of money Carol Ann is willing to pay for her lenses. If Carol Ann decides to spend $225 on contact lenses but would only pay $100 for school books, one can determine not only that Carol Ann values the lenses more than the books, but also that she values the lenses at least $125 more. Individuals' willingness to pay money for particular goods can serve as a rough indicator of the value they attach to those goods. The more money a person is willing to pay for something, the more utility she expects to derive from it and the more she values it. Perhaps it is sensible to pursue a policy of maximizing wealth (the dollar value of scarce resources as measured by individuals' willingness and ability to pay for them) instead of maximizing utility.

### ROSS v. WILSON
Court of Appeals of New York, 1955.
308 N.Y. 605, 127 N.E.2d 697.

VAN VOORHIS, JUDGE.

The controversy in this proceeding concerns the sale of the schoolhouse which served common school district No. 1 of the Towns of Ellicott and Gerry, in Chautauqua County, before it was superseded by a central school district. This district had been known as the Ross Mills District. In February, 1953, the board of education of the recently formed central school district called a special meeting of the qualified voters of the former common school district to vote upon whether to close the school and sell the school property. Such procedure is required by subdivision 6 of section 1804 of the Education Law, which also provides that if the common school district schoolhouse is sold, the net proceeds be apportioned among the taxpayers of the common school district.

At the special meeting of the common school district called by the board of education in 1953, four propositions were submitted: (1)

Should the school of the former common school district be closed? (2) Should the school property be sold to Ross Mills Church of God for $2,000? (3) Should the property be sold to Ross Grange No. 305 for $3,000? (4) Should the property be sold by public auction to the highest bidder? The notice stated that proposition number 1 would be voted upon, "and as many of the succeeding propositions as is necessary to dispose of the property". At the meeting, the proposal to close the school was carried. A motion was then made but declared out of order that the meeting should next ballot upon whether to sell the school property at public auction to the highest bidder. Then proposition number 2 was presented to the meeting to sell the school property to Ross Mills Church of God for $2,000. It was carried by a vote of 32 to 24. That ended the meeting.

* * * [S]ubdivision 6 of section 1804 of the Education Law, pursuant to which this schoolhouse was sold, does not expressly state that it must be sold to the highest bidder upon the organization of a central school district. * * *

* * *

* * * But if the Legislature does not require a schoolhouse to be sold at public auction, it by no means follows from that circumstance that the Legislature intended to authorize the public officials charged with the administration of school property, or even the majority of qualified electors voting at a school district meeting, to sell the property for a smaller amount than has been offered with due formality by a proper purchaser for a lawful use. * * * Whichever procedure is prescribed by the Legislature for selling this publicly owned property, it was the duty of the board of trustees and of the district meeting to obtain the best price obtainable in their judgment for any lawful use of the premises. In this respect, their powers and duties are similar to those of trustees. * * *

* * *

The amount of money involved is small, but the principle is important; the offer which was rejected was to pay 50% more for this schoolhouse than the one which was accepted. Bogert, writing on Trusts and Trustees, says (§ 745): "Whether the trustee should endeavor to sell by negotiation with possible buyers, or should put the property up at auction, depends upon the circumstances of the individual case. He should use the method which will, considering the place of sale and the type of property for sale, be apt to bring the best price." In the present situation, the Legislature has determined that it was not necessary to sell this property at auction, although that procedure would have been permissible, but the latitude allowed in the method of sale was designed to enable these public fiduciaries to adopt the method which in their judgment would bring the best price, and it was their duty to sell at the best price which it brought, not deliberately to select and to favor a buyer at a lower price than was otherwise obtainable. * * *

\* \* \*

\* \* \* The direct result of what occurred is, in effect, to approve a contribution of $1,000 by the school district to the church. \* \* \*

This contribution by a common school district to a particular church is not made in aid of any educational activity conducted by the church, but operates as an outright gift of public funds to a church for its general church purposes. Even if the facts of the case did not present the special situation of the use of public money for the support of a religious establishment, neither a common school district meeting, nor the district trustees, are empowered to expend the resources of the school district for other than educational objects. \* \* \*

\* \* \*

For the reasons mentioned, we think that there was a total lack of power in the school district to accept an offer of $2,000 from the Church of God of Ross Mills and at the same time to reject an equally bona fide offer of $3,000 from the grange. \* \* \* The order appealed from should be reversed and the determinations of the Commissioner of Education and of the board of education approving the sale to the Church of God of Ross Mills should be annulled, with costs to appellants in this court and in the Appellate Division.

\* \* \*

## *Notes and Questions*

1. The resource to be allocated in *Ross* was a schoolhouse no longer required for educational purposes. Buildings are scarce and the schoolhouse potentially could serve various other needs. Wealth maximizing would require the schoolhouse to be allocated to the group or individual who valued it most highly, as measured by willingness to pay money for it.

Between a willing buyer and seller, it is easily determined who values the schoolhouse more. If the buyer is willing and able to pay enough to induce the seller to part with the building, the buyer must attach a higher dollar value to the building than the seller does. Thus, the school district's sale of the schoolhouse to the Ross Mills Church of God for $2,000 would increase the monetary value of the schoolhouse. In *Ross,* the bargain between the School District and the Church of God did not mean the schoolhouse would go it its *most* valuable use, only that it would go to a *more* valuable use. Another potential buyer may be willing and able to pay even more; in this case, the Grange had offered $3,000. Negotiations among all parties interested in purchasing the schoolhouse—including the Ross Mills Church of God, the Grange, and any other bidders—would reveal who was willing to pay the highest price, and so valued the schoolhouse the most.

*Questions:* How did the school district's decision to ignore the Grange's offer and sell the schoolhouse to the Church of God for $2,000 interfere with maximizing wealth—i.e., the value of resources as measured by people's willingness to pay for them? Did the school district's decision to sell to the Church of God for $2,000 really amount to a "contribution" to the Church of $1,000? Would the Church of God have been better or worse off if the Grange had only bid $1,999?

2. The notes following *Cidis* examined how voluntary exchange can efficiently redistribute resources in a fashion that increases overall utility. As *Ross* illustrates, voluntary exchange can also increase wealth. Indeed, voluntary negotiations among all interested parties can *maximize* wealth by ensuring that a particular resource is allocated to the highest bidder who, by definition, values the resource the most as measured by willingness to pay.

To appreciate wealth maximization, it may be useful to envision society's wealth as a pie. Other things being equal, a larger pie is preferable to a smaller one because there is more wealth to divide among society's members. Among economists, the Gross Domestic Product (GDP) is a familiar measure of the total value (wealth) of the goods and services produced in the United States during a given time period. It measures the quantity of goods and services produced and the values actually placed upon them, in terms of the prices paid for them. If in a given year the total goods and services produced yields a higher value, then the GDP increases, and society has more wealth.

The GDP may be too narrow a measure of social well-being because many scarce resources allocated by society are not included in the "goods and services" category. Goods such as clean air, privacy, and leisure time are rarely traded in the marketplace but are desirable and scarce commodities that people would be willing to bargain for and exchange if markets existed. A more comprehensive measure of the size of the social "pie" would reflect all the items people value, not just goods and services traded on organized markets. Thus, the goal of wealth maximization should perhaps be the greatest possible "gross domestic valuation" or "GDV." GDV is maximized and society is best off when every resource—tangible and intangible, market and non-market—goes to its highest-valued use.

*Ross* typifies most cases in which the court exhibits no conscious concern for wealth maximization as a social goal and no explicit recognition of the social implications of arrangements that interfere with the parties' ability to bargain freely over the purchase and sale of scarce resources. Rather, the court seems concerned only with the taxpayers' rights and the apparent unfairness of depriving them of the ability to obtain the best price for their property.

*Questions:* Suppose that in open bidding the prosperous farmers who belong to the Ross Grange were willing to offer $3,000 for the schoolhouse, while the impoverished members of the Ross Mills Church were only willing to pay $2000. Would that necessarily mean that the Grange's members would derive more utility from the schoolhouse? Would the auction system maximize utility?

3. If some allocations might be wealth maximizing but not utility maximizing (and vice versa), one should be careful in choosing what to maximize. This Chapter has already explored some of the difficulties of adopting utility maximization as a goal. In particular, it is impossible to gauge even one person's level of utility or satisfaction. Even if it were possible, one cannot compare the value of one person's utils to another

person's utils. In addition to the problems of measuring and making interpersonal comparisons of utility, utility maximization also has undesirable distributional implications. Some people may have a greater capacity to enjoy life and derive satisfaction from scarce resources. Following the principle of utility maximization, resources would be allocated to those happy-go-lucky individuals who have a greater capacity for enjoyment while dour and impossible-to-satisfy law or economics professors would go without any resources.

Wealth maximization avoids some of the measurement problems associated with utility maximization. Although one may not trust what people always *say* about how highly they value a particular good or service, one can usually trust their behavior when they express their willingness (and ability) to pay through the actual purchase or sale of resources. Moreover, while the utils of two people are not comparable, one person's dollar is as valuable as another's. Money thus provides a common measuring rod for comparing the relative values that different persons attach to particular resources.

Because wealth is much easier to quantify than utility, economists customarily use individuals' relative willingness and ability to pay money to judge the propriety of a particular reallocation of resources. But defining the value of a resource according to peoples' willingness and ability to pay for it also has distributional implications. Wealth maximizing inevitably requires that a greater share of resources go to wealthier people. Even if the poor congregation of the Ross Mills Church of God coveted the schoolhouse while the prosperous farmers of the Grange only mildly preferred it, the Grange's greater wealth might enable the farmers to outbid the Church.

> *Questions:* If the New York Court of Appeals had upheld the school district's decision to sell the schoolhouse to the Ross Mills Church of God for $2,000, can one be certain that that decision would interfere with wealth maximization, i.e., prevent the schoolhouse from going to its most valuable use? Might a subsequent *reallocation* correct the inefficiency resulting from the school district's decision?

4. In an earlier appeal before the New York Commissioner of Education, the Commissioner had upheld the district's discretion to sell to a lower bidder on the ground that "[t]he type and character of the purchaser * * * is often a matter of vital import to the rural communities of this State. * * * If the sale were mandated to be to the highest bidder, it may well be that a 'saloon', filling station or other enterprise undesirable to a specific community might be forced upon it." 127 N.E.2d at 699.

Suppose that the Grange would derive more utility from the schoolhouse than the Church, and the Grange was willing and able to pay more than the Church. Does this mean that the Grange's use of the schoolhouse is the most valuable use? Others in the community might be affected by the sale of the schoolhouse to the Grange, as they might be affected by the sale to a saloon. Those adversely (or positively) affected by the sale to a particular party might even be willing and able to express their desires by paying to ensure that the schoolhouse went to a particular party.

*Question:* If the preferences of parties adversely (or positively) affected by a sale are not taken into account, does a decision to sell the schoolhouse to the highest bidder necessarily maximize utility? Wealth?

## C. COMPARING UTILITY AND WEALTH MAXIMIZATION: THE PARETO CRITERIA AND THE ROLE OF COMPENSATION

Both utility and wealth maximization share a common feature—judgments as to the desirability of allocations depend on the initial distribution of certain characteristics among society's members. For utility maximization, the characteristic is the capacity to derive happiness, pleasure, or satisfaction; in the case of wealth maximization, the characteristic is wealth. Many find the implications of relying for policy purposes on initial distributions of capacity to derive pleasure or of wealth troubling. A classification scheme designed by Vilfredo Pareto in the early 1900's provides one solution to this problem and also to the analytical difficulties presented by the impossibility of interpersonal utility comparisons. A neutral, nonjudgmental method for identifying desirable allocations and changes in the allocation of goods, Pareto's system still enjoys wide-spread use because of its appealing and generally accepted criteria for judgment.

The first application of the Pareto criteria is to evaluate the desirability of *changes* in the distribution of goods. Pareto's system allows that evaluation without regard to the desirability of the *initial* distribution among individuals of either their abilities to pay or enjoy and without the need for interpersonal utility comparisons. Imagine a society in which all resources have already been allocated to particular individuals. Now imagine a change in allocations that left at least one person better off and no one worse off. Surely that change is desirable from any perspective. Economists refer to such a change in the allocation of resources as a *Pareto superior* change.

The voluntary exchange of goods or services for money or other goods or services is a simple example of a Pareto superior reallocation of rights. The optometrist, Cidis, only agreed to sell the contact lenses to Carol Ann White because he valued the $225 more than the lenses and the labor required to fit them. White agreed to buy the lenses because she thought she would be better off with them than with the $225. At least one party is better off, probably both. If the parties are acting rationally and no one else is adversely affected by the sale, only a misanthrope would prefer the original allocation of resources to the reallocation.

Any reallocation of resources that leaves at least one person worse off is described as *Pareto inferior.* If Cidis is forced to give the lenses to White without charge, then she is better off but he is worse off. From a utility maximizing perspective, one cannot say that her gain in utility is greater than his loss in utility. Because one person is worse off, economists conclude that the change is Pareto inferior to the prior allocation.

Pareto superiority and inferiority are ways of evaluating changes in allocations; a reallocation is Pareto superior if at least one party is made better off and no one is made worse off, but Pareto inferior if at least one party is made worse off. A second common use of Pareto's system is to evaluate allocations themselves rather than changes in allocations. *Pareto optimal* describes a characteristic of an allocation rather than a reallocation.

An allocation of resources is Pareto optimal if there is no possible reallocation that could make at least one person better off without making someone worse off. Suppose that society has allocated its resources so that Cidis has the contact lenses (along with the skill to fit them) and White has $225. If Cidis is willing to fit and sell the lenses for $225 and White is willing and able to pay that price, this original allocation is *not* Pareto optimal because a later exchange (reallocation) could make someone person better off without making anyone worse off. Now suppose that White buys the lenses for $225. Now no reallocation could make anyone better off without making someone worse off. If the contact lenses are with the person who values them most, then no one will be willing and able to pay her enough to make her give them up. That is Pareto optimal; optimal since all resources are going to their highest valued use; "Pareto" optimal because no further Pareto superior reallocations are possible.

Given a limited amount of resources, it is possible for more than one Pareto optimal allocation to exist. Suppose Cidis owns the contact lenses and has the skills required to fit them, while White strongly desires the lenses but does not have $225. The allocation of the lenses to Cidis is Pareto optimal because White cannot be made better off (by giving her the lenses) without making Cidis worse off. Yet, if the lenses are initially allocated to White, that allocation may also be Pareto optimal, since White cannot give Cidis the lenses without making herself worse off and White may be unwilling to sell them to Cidis for any price he would be willing to pay.

Although Pareto's system of evaluating allocations and reallocations of resources is widely accepted, its practical value is limited. The Pareto criteria for evaluating changes in allocations are quite strict: if a million people benefit and one is harmed, the reallocation is still Pareto inferior. If many different allocations of resources pass the test of Pareto optimality, how can one determine which allocation is best? United States v. Causby examines one possible method of expanding the usefulness of Pareto's classifications: compensation for forced reallocations.

## UNITED STATES v. CAUSBY

Supreme Court of the United States, 1946.
328 U.S. 256, 66 S.Ct. 1062, 90 L.Ed. 1206.

DOUGLAS, JUSTICE.

* * *

Respondents own 2.8 acres near an airport outside of Greensboro, North Carolina. It has on it a dwelling house, and also various outbuildings which were mainly used for raising chickens. The end of the airport's northwest-southeast runway is 2,220 feet from respondents' barn and 2,275 feet from their house. The path of glide to this runway passes directly over the property—which is 100 feet wide and 1,200 feet long. The 30 to 1 safe glide angle approved by the Civil Aeronautics Authority passes over this property at 83 feet, which is 67 feet above the house, 63 feet above the barn and 18 feet above the highest tree. * * *

* * * Since the United States began operations in May, 1942, its four-motored heavy bombers, other planes of the heavier type, and its fighter planes have frequently passed over respondents' land buildings in considerable numbers and rather close together. They come close enough at times to appear barely to miss the tops of the trees and at times so close to the tops of the trees as to blow the old leaves off. The noise is startling. And at night the glare from the planes brightly lights up the place. As a result of the noise, respondents had to give up their chicken business. As many as six to ten of their chickens were killed in one day by flying into the walls from fright. The total chickens lost in that manner was about 150. Production [of eggs] also fell off. The result was the destruction of the use of the property as a commercial chicken farm. Respondents are frequently deprived of their sleep and the family has become nervous and frightened. Although there have been no airplane accidents on respondents' property, there have been several accidents near the airport and close to respondents' place. These are the essential facts found by the Court of Claims. On the basis of these facts, it found that respondents' property had depreciated in value. It held that the United States had taken an easement over the property on June 1, 1942, and that the value of the property destroyed and the easement taken was $2,000.

* * *

* * * [T]he United States conceded on oral argument that if the flights over respondents' property rendered it uninhabitable, there would be a taking compensable under the Fifth Amendment. It is the owner's loss, not the taker's gain, which is the measure of the value of the property taken. Market value fairly determined is the normal measure of the recovery. And that value may reflect the use to which the land could readily be converted, as well as the existing use. If, by reason of the frequency and altitude of the flights, respondents could

not use this land for any purpose, their loss would be complete. It would be as complete as if the United States had entered upon the surface of the land and taken exclusive possession of it.

We agree that in those circumstances there would be a taking. Though it would be only an easement of flight which was taken, that easement, if permanent and not merely temporary, normally would be the equivalent of a fee interest. It would be a definite exercise of complete dominion and control over the surface of the land. The fact that the planes never touched the surface would be as irrelevant as the absence in this day of the feudal livery of seisin on the transfer of real estate. * * * In the supposed case the line of flight is over the land. And the land is appropriated as directly and completely as if it were used for the runways themselves.

There is no material difference between the supposed case and the present one, except that here enjoyment and use of the land are not completely destroyed. But that does not seem to us to be controlling. The path of glide for airplanes might reduce a valuable factory site to grazing land, an orchard to a vegetable patch, a residential section to a wheat field. Some value would remain. But the use of the airspace immediately above the land would limit the utility of the land and cause a diminution in its value. * * *

* * * The airplane is part of the modern environment of life, and the inconveniences which it causes are normally not compensable under the Fifth Amendment. The airspace, apart from the immediate reaches above the land, is part of the public domain. We need not determine at this time what those precise limits are. Flights over private land are not a taking, unless they are so low and so frequent as to be a direct and immediate interference with the enjoyment and use of the land. We need not speculate on that phase of the present case. For the findings of the Court of Claims plainly establish that there was a diminution in value of the property and that the frequent, low-level flights were the direct and immediate cause. We agree with the Court of Claims that a servitude has been imposed upon the land.

### *Notes and Questions*

1. The reallocation of rights in *Causby* seems wealth maximizing since the government probably would have been willing to pay more for the use of the Causbys' airspace than the Causbys would have been willing to pay to keep it. The reallocation may even have been utility maximizing, though an informed guess is harder to make, because there is no easy way to compare (or even talk about) the pleasure or satisfaction lost by the chicken farmers and gained by the government. For a reallocation to be Pareto superior, however, neither party can be left worse off as a result. Without sufficient compensation to return the harmed party to her earlier position, the Pareto criteria for superiority will not be met. Full compensation ensures that the reallocation of airspace rights from the Causbys to the military was Pareto superior.

If a reallocation is Pareto superior, it increases both social utility and wealth. Consider the position of one party (the government in *Causby*) who is entitled to take another's property only after fully compensating the other. In *Causby*, the compensation awarded was $2,000. If that figure was properly calculated, the Causbys would suffer neither decreased utility nor reduced wealth from the taking. If either loss occurred, compensation was not truly "full." At this point, a rational government would only take the Causbys' property if the benefits exceeded $2,000. Should the government proceed with the taking, it must value the airspace more (get more utility from the airspace) than the $2,000. The efficient result is that government has more wealth and utility and the Causbys have no less.

*Questions:* Is the government more or less likely to take private property if compensation is not required? Are such uncompensated reallocations (takings) utility maximizing? Wealth maximizing?

2. The government in the taking context does not consciously consider the utility and wealth maximizing consequences of a reallocation any more than do private parties to an exchange. It is extremely unlikely that either the optometrist or the contact lens purchaser in *Cidis* actually considered the social implications of their exchange of resources or that the school district in *Ross* considered whether the sale to the Church affected the aggregate level of society's wealth. The beauty of the compensation requirement is that utility and wealth are maximized by people concerned only with their own well-being.

3. While full compensation is sufficient to guarantee that utility and wealth are maximized, it is not always necessary. A reallocation without compensation may also maximize utility and wealth. If a decisionmaker (such as a court or legislature) knows for certain which resource use generates the most utility or is valued most highly then compensation is unnecessary. Thus, in *Causby,* the court could have simply allowed the government to invade the Causby's airspace without paying any compensation.

Without compensation, however, it is difficult to ascertain which allocations are utility and wealth maximizing. The reallocation in *Causby* was almost certainly wealth maximizing. The loss of the Causby's chicken farm was a necessary sacrifice if the runway was to be used for military operations. During World War II, military operations were extremely important and valuable in promoting national interests of the United States. As measured by willingness and ability to pay, the value of the airspace for defense purposes would seem to be much greater than its value to the Causbys for quietly raising chickens. To ensure wealth maximization, it seems unnecessary to put this reallocation to the compensation test.

Because of the difficulties inherent in systematically comparing the Causbys' loss in utility to the nation's gain, however, it is harder to conclude that the reallocation is utility maximizing without compensation. It is easily said that all Americans should be pleased by the liberation of Europe from the Nazis. But one cannot rigorously compare the government's gain from using that runway to the Causby's loss when the government destroyed their livelihood and the peace and quiet of their family farm. The difficulty in comparing utility gains and losses among different people makes the compensation test more necessary to ensure that a reallocation maximizes utility.

4. The analytical difficulties inherent in utility maximization have led many scholars in law and economics to focus on wealth maximization. Since it is easier to measure, some find wealth a useful surrogate for utility. For others, wealth maximization's appeal rests on its own merits. Because maximizing wealth does not always maximize utility, however, several schools of thought in economics have emerged.

Under one school, the Pareto criteria are appropriate for judging whether a reallocation is efficient. This view implies that full compensation must be paid whenever a reallocation of resources would otherwise leave someone worse off. Without compensation, there is no way to be certain that the benefits enjoyed by the winning party outweigh the harm suffered by the loser.

Since many changes in policy involve making some people better off and some worse off, economists Kaldor and Hicks studied alternatives to the compensation requirement. Under the *Kaldor–Hicks* position, compensation need not be paid for a reallocation to be efficient. A reallocation is efficient if there is sufficient gain to create the *potential* for full compensation. As long as the winner gains more than the loser loses, the loser does not actually have to be paid.

Like Pareto's approach, the Kaldor–Hicks approach requires compensation that is "full," that is, enough compensation that the loser would be no worse off after the reallocation. If the winner would be willing and able to pay such "full compensation," then the reallocation meets the Kaldor–Hicks test and the compensation need not actually be paid. From the Kaldor–Hicks perspective, it is not necessary, or even desirable, that the compensation be paid; compensating everyone who suffers as a result of state action is complicated and expensive, and interferes with the government's everyday operation.

In *Causby*, the Paretian perspective would require that full compensation actually be paid in order to be certain that the benefit to the government from using the airspace over the chicken farm outweighed the Causbys' losses. Under the Kaldor–Hicks position, since it was obvious that the value of the airspace to a wartime military was greater than its value to the Causbys in raising chickens, compensation was unnecessary for the taking to be efficient.

A policy designed to ensure that the loser is "no worse off" inevitably requires a measure of the appropriate level of compensation. To be "no worse off," the loser must receive enough compensation to obtain the same level of utility as before the reallocation.

*Questions:* If the government would be willing and able to pay "full compensation" in *Causby*, does the Kaldor–Hicks approach maximize both utility and wealth? If the potential compensation for a taking is calculated by the property's fair market value, can a policy maker be assured that the Kaldor-Hicks criterion maximizes both utility and wealth?

5. The preceding note focused on the Pareto and Kaldor–Hicks criteria for evaluating reallocations of resources. To test your understanding of the utility and wealth maximization characteristics of these alternative tests, consider the following policy analysis. Suppose that the decisionmaker could establish the maximum each party was willing and able to pay for the airspace and found that the Government was willing and able to pay more. Following the Kaldor–Hicks requirement, the decisionmaker would then award the airspace to the Government, figuring that, since the Government was willing and able to pay more, it could potentially compensate the Causbys.

*Questions:* Would the decisionmaker's approach guarantee that both utility and wealth were maximized? Does the reallocation from the Causbys to the Government meet the Pareto and Kaldor–Hicks criteria for superior reallocations?

6. In this book, an efficient allocation of resources is one that cannot be improved in either the Paretian or Kaldor–Hicks sense. If an allocation is efficient, a reallocation that benefits one person more than it harms another is impossible and compensation is unavailable. When describing a change in the law as efficient, the Kaldor–Hicks convention is usually followed, although Pareto's approach is not abandoned. Pareto's approach is appealing for reasons unrelated to wealth or utility maximization. While economics typically has little to say about what is fair or just, Pareto's criteria are appealing from a fairness perspective; justice seems to require compensation of people who, like the Causbys, suffer from a governmental policy.

## D. EFFICIENCY AND EQUITY

Economists usually resist identifying particular individuals or classes of people as the proper recipients of rights to use or consume certain resources. To seem more scientific and to increase the acceptability of their conclusions among people with diverse social and political perspectives, they work hard to preserve the appearance of neutrality in their analysis. Economic analysis typically focuses on determining which allocation of scarce resources maximizes wealth. Economics is generally concerned with efficiency, not fairness.

Focusing on efficiency rather than fairness does not make economics a neutral and unbiased exercise. Directing resources to their most valuable uses and measuring value according to willingness and ability to pay biases allocations towards those with the greatest ability to pay. Among individuals with equally strong desires to own a certain house, the individual with the greater willingness and ability to express that desire by giving up money or other resources is judged the highest-valuing user; allocating the resource to his use is, by definition, allocatively efficient. Because efficiency analysis proceeds from a preexisting set of endowments of wealth, it does not question whether the initial distribution of "abilities to pay" is proper.

## PITSENBERGER v. PITSENBERGER
Court of Appeals of Maryland, 1980.
287 Md. 20, 410 A.2d 1052.

MURPHY, CHIEF JUDGE.

This is the first case in which we consider the constitutionality of Maryland's new legislation on property disposition in divorce and annulment * * *

* * *

John and Mary Pitsenberger were married on June 30, 1962, in Alexandria, Virginia. Five children were born as a result of the marriage. In August of 1978, Mary left the family home in Rockville, Maryland, taking two of the parties' five minor children and $10,000 from the parties' joint savings account. About one month later, the other three children went to live with Mary in a small three bedroom townhouse in Derwood, Maryland. Mary rented the house on a month-to-month lease, but she was informed that the lease would not be renewed after May of 1979. While living with Mary, the children remained enrolled in the neighborhood schools near the family home. Mary drove them to school each day.

On January 2, 1979, Mary filed a bill of complaint for a divorce *a mensa et thoro* on the grounds of constructive desertion in the Circuit Court for Montgomery County. She sought pendente lite custody of the children, child support, alimony and, pursuant to § 3–6A–06(d), an exclusive use and possession order for the family home and family use personal property (furniture, appliances, household furnishings and a 1973 Dodge Dart). On February 9, 1979, John filed his answer and a cross-bill of complaint for divorce *a mensa et thoro* on the grounds of desertion.

On February 16, 1979, a hearing was held before a domestic relations master to determine pendente lite the issues of child custody and support, alimony, and the need of the parties and the children to remain in the family home. Mary testified that she was on welfare and lacked funds to rent another house or apartment. Despite John's yearly salary of approximately $47,000, she said she had received no child support since August, 1978. With respect to alternative living arrangements, Mary explained that her mother's residence, a small three bedroom house in Alexandria, Virginia, provided insufficient living room for her family. The only other alternative was to stay at the three bedroom house of her brother-in-law and his wife and two children. Even if they could reside there on an emergency basis, she would have to drive each day from Bowie, Maryland, to the children's schools. * * *

The master recommended that Mary be awarded pendente lite custody of the minor children and that John pay $1,000 per month child support, as well as pay the mortgage, taxes and insurance for the family home. The master also recommended that Mary be awarded pendente lite use of the family home, the family personal property located in the home and the Dodge Dart * * *. These recommendations were adopted by the circuit court on May 23, 1979, and its order specified that Mary was awarded the *exclusive* use of the family home.

* * *

John * * * argues that § 3–6A–06 permits the unlawful taking of private property without just compensation in violation of the Fifth and Fourteenth Amendments of the United States Constitution, Article 24 of the Maryland Declaration of Rights, and Article III, section 40 of the Maryland Constitution. John contends that the use and possession order signed by the court on May 23, 1979, effectively takes his property by awarding Mary the exclusive use of the family home and family use personal property. John asserts that he is entitled to compensation in the amount of the fair market value of his possessory interest in the family home and for relocation expenses.

To constitute a taking in the constitutional sense, so that the State must pay compensation, the state action must deprive the owner of all beneficial use of the property * * * [I]t is not enough for the property owner to show that the state action causes substantial loss or hardship. John, as guardian of his minor children, is charged with their support, care and welfare. Because his children have the use of the family home and family use personal property, John is in fact using his property to properly house his children. John therefore has not been deprived of all beneficial use of his property. In sum, the use and possession order does not amount to a "taking" of private property in violation of the federal or state constitutions.

We thus conclude that Mary was properly awarded pendente lite use and possession of the family and family use personal property.

### Notes and Questions

1. The Maryland statute applied in *Pitsenberger* required a divorce court to divide a couple's property "fairly and equitably." In *Pitsenberger*, fairness and equity apparently required that Mary keep the family home and car, while John be ordered to leave the home. Three possible approaches to the equity and fairness issue are discussed below.

a. *Just Desserts*. The property should be assigned to the most deserving spouse. This approach requires a definition of "deserving." Perhaps the home and car should be awarded to the person who wants to remain married. If, hypothetically, John wanted to remain married but Mary insisted on a divorce after beginning an adulterous liaison, Mary should get nothing. Alternatively, perhaps the spouse who needs the property most deserves it. In that case, the lion's share should go to unemployed Mary while salaried John gets little or nothing.

b. *Equality of Treatment*. After selling the home and car, the decisionmaker divides the proceeds evenly between the parties. Under this rule, the Pitsenbergers should share the market value of these possessions.

c. *Ratified Consent.* The court should award the property to the individual in whose name the property is held and enforce any reallocation to which the parties consented. Thus, the court should enter an order that the property in John's and Mary's names belonged to John and Mary respectively, but should approve any swaps the two might agree to make.

*Questions:* Which view of fairness most closely approaches wealth maximization? Which views most closely reflect or offend our sense of fairness or equity?

2. An efficiency perspective on this distributional question might suggest that the property should be awarded to the person willing and able to pay more for it.

*Questions:* If the court awarded the home and car to the person who valued the property more, to whom would the property probably be awarded? Would this be a wealth maximizing allocation of resources?

3. People's willingness and ability to pay to influence the allocation of resources such as the Pitsenberger's house naturally depends on their wealth. The allocation of John's income between Mary and John is quite likely to influence the value they place on the house. Because the distribution of wealth among people influences the allocations that result from bargaining, changes in the distribution of wealth may change the allocation of resources. Alternative allocations of John's salary will affect who gets the house.

Compare two allocations of John's salary. In the first, Mary is awarded none of his salary and, in the second, Mary is awarded 70% of his salary. Imagine that after these distributions of John's salary are made, the house is allocated to the person willing and able to pay the most for it. Under the first allocation, it is quite probable that John will get the house. Under the second, it is more likely that Mary will get the house.

*Question:* Do the alternative allocations of John's salary affect the efficiency of the allocation of the house?

4. Returning to the principle of ratified consent, suppose that, after much discussion, the parties agreed that Mary would be allowed to rent the house, car and other property for $200 per month from her welfare check.

*Questions:* Would enforcing such a solution be wealth maximizing? Would it be utility maximizing? Does the fact that both parties consent to this arrangement make it seem fairer?

## E. EXTERNALITIES AND INEFFICIENCY

Previous cases in this chapter have considered the efficiency implications of allocating resources among economic actors. The cases also reveal that the activities of one actor may impose costs on another. The military use of the airport in United States v. Causby, for instance, imposed costs on the chicken farmers. The use of the abandoned schoolhouse in Ross v. Wilson as a saloon might impose costs on residents of the surrounding neighborhood. The activities of one person frequently affect others, occasionally creating benefits and sometimes imposing burdens on them.

The economic analysis of tort law is concerned with allocating the benefits and burdens of activities among members of society. Most tort claims arise as the result of the damage imposed on the plaintiff by the activity of the defendant. The following introductory cases consider how the burdens of engaging in activities may be minimized and how they might be allocated.

## 1. INTERNALIZING EXTERNALITIES THROUGH DAMAGE AWARDS

### ORCHARD VIEW FARMS, INC. v. MARTIN MARIETTA ALUMINUM, INC.

United States District Court Oregon, 1980.
500 F.Supp. 984.

BURNS, CHIEF JUDGE:

This diversity case is before the court on remand from the Ninth Circuit Court of Appeals for a retrial on the issue of punitive damages.

On March 31, 1971, Orchard View Farms, Inc. (Orchard View) filed this trespass action, seeking compensatory and punitive damages for injuries to its orchards between March 31, 1965 and the filing date. These injuries were alleged to have been caused by fluoride emitted from the aluminum reduction plant operated by Martin Marietta Aluminum, Inc. (the company or Martin Marietta). In April and May, 1973, the case was tried to a jury, which awarded Orchard View $103,655 compensatory damages and $250,000 punitive damages.

\* \* \*

In essence, any business is socially obliged to carry on an enterprise that is a net benefit, or at least not a net loss, to society. \* \* \*

In a world where all costs of production were borne by the enterprise, determining whether a firm produced a net benefit, or at least not a net detriment, to society would be as simple as examining the company's balance sheet of income and expenses. In the real world the task is more complex, because enterprises can sometimes shift a portion of their costs of production onto others. In the case of an industrial plant emitting pollution, those harmed by the emissions are, in effect, involuntarily bearing some of the firm's production costs.

Our society has not demanded that such externalized costs of production be completely eliminated. Instead, we tolerate externalities such as pollution as long as the enterprise remains productive: that is, producing greater value than the total of its internalized and externalized costs of production. A business that does not achieve net productivity is harmful to society, detracting from the standard of living it is designed to enhance. Because firms can sometimes impose a portion of their production costs upon others, the mere fact that a company continues to operate at a profit is not in itself conclusive evidence that it produces a net benefit to society.

Our system of law attempts to ensure that businesses are, on balance, socially beneficial by requiring that each enterprise bear its total production costs, as accurately as those costs can be ascertained. A fundamental means to this end is the institution of tort liability, which requires that persons harmed by business or other activity be compensated by the perpetrator of the damage. * * *

* * *

A business enterprise has a societal obligation to determine whether its emissions will result in harm to others. Because the damage from pollution can be difficult to perceive due to its subtle or incremental nature, and because it can be difficult to trace to its cause, the obligation of the enterprise extends not only to observation of property in the surrounding region but also to initiation and completion of unbiased scientific studies designed to detect the potential adverse effects of the substances emitted.

I find that the company failed to fulfill this obligation before or during the 1965–71 claim period by taking less than full cognizance of the damage inflicted upon the orchards and by generally shirking its responsibility to undertake competent scientific inquiry into the adverse effects of its emissions.

### Notes and Questions

1. The court characterized the pollution in *Orchard View Farms* as an "externalized cost" of Martin Marietta's aluminum-making activities. A cost is "external to" or "outside of" an economic actor's decisionmaking if he is not required to account for it when maximizing his well-being. If it does not have to pay for the damage to Orchard View Farms, Martin Marietta does not need to consider that damage when deciding how to maximize profits from its aluminum production. Industrial pollution is a classic example of an external cost.

*Externalities* are costs imposed or benefits conferred on others as a result of an individual's activities that he is not required to (in the case of costs) or able to (in the case of benefits) take into account in his decisionmaking.

> *Questions:* What is an example of an external benefit one landowner might confer on another? How do externalities affect the extent to which people impose costs and confer benefits on others?

2. Using their current technologies, the plaintiff cannot grow trees and the defendant cannot produce aluminum solely within their own parcels' boundaries without affecting their neighbors. The air the farm uses to nourish its trees is the same air Martin Marietta uses to carry away its airborne fluoride particles. Neither party is interested in possessing the other's land, so the allocation of the land is not at issue. The issue involves uses of land and the allocation of a second resource, the stream of air. It is not possible for both parties to use that stream of air compatibly using their current technologies. While the farm may be able to grow its trees under a dome with filtered air or the plant may be able to wash all of the

fluoride particles out of its emissions, neither possibility is presented in this case. The issue is who gets the right to use the stream of air.

*Questions:* The plaintiff was awarded damages to compensate it for the harm to its trees from the fluoride particles. Does that mean that the use of the stream of air was been allocated to the farm? Does it mean that the farm's use of the air was the more highly-valued use?

3. Consider how the court in *Orchard View Farms* viewed its role in the process of achieving allocative efficiency: "Our system of law attempts to ensure that businesses are, on balance, socially beneficial by requiring that each enterprise bear its total production costs."

*Questions:* Is the court's task finding which use is more valuable? Or does the court merely enable other parties to determine which use is more valuable? Note how this compares to the court's role in United States v. Causby in Chapter 1. Did either court decide which use is the most valuable or did it merely facilitate the determination? If the court did not decide how resources were allocated, who did?

4. Imagine a transaction between a buyer and seller of one ton of aluminum ingot. The seller is willing to sell aluminum for no less than $4 a ton and the buyer is willing and able to pay as much as $4.50 a ton. An exchange appears to be Pareto superior. The difference between the values the buyer and setter attach to the aluminum appears to ensure that the costs of producing a ton of aluminum (the bauxite ore, the electricity, the labor) are outweighed by the benefit the ton provides to the buyer.

From *Orchard View Farms,* however, one of the costs of producing aluminum is damage to the neighboring farm. If forced to pay damages resulting from his pollution, the manufacturer might be unable to sell that ton of ingot at a price high enough to ensure a profit. Once all the costs are considered, the buyer may be unwilling to pay the full cost of a ton of aluminum. Without internalizing costs, an inefficiently large amount of aluminum may be produced.

*Question:* What damages should be awarded to ensure that the allocatively efficient amount of resources are devoted to aluminum production?

5. The court's main concern in *Orchard View Farm* was that the defendant pay for his external costs. The external costs need not be eliminated; as much pollution as is efficient may continue. An allocatively efficient level of output of aluminum will occur even if the plaintiff is not compensated, as long as the defendant gives up an amount equal to the external costs imposed. The determination of the amount of plaintiff's injury is critical to calculating the optimal level of payment the firm must internalize, however, and it seems only fair that the payment should go to the person who suffers. Damages give plaintiffs an incentive to provide evidence on the magnitude of the external costs.

*Question:* If the damages were calculated, paid, and then dumped into the ocean (after taking out the attorneys' fee, of course!), would the defendant still take the amount of its liability for damages into account in deciding how much to produce?

6. In some cases, particularly class actions for environmental harms, damages are paid into a fund dedicated to a public use. To create proper incentives for the polluter, however, it must be assured that the polluter does not benefit from such a fund.

Questions: If, instead of dumping the damages into the ocean or paying them to the plaintiff, the damages were paid into a drug rehabilitation program or the school budget in the town where the factory was located, would the payment of damages still provide the proper incentives to the polluter?

## 2. INTERNALIZING EXTERNALITIES THROUGH REGULATION

### UNITED STATES v. CITY OF NIAGARA FALLS

U.S. District Court, Western District of New York, 1989.
706 F.Supp. 1053.

CURTIN, DISTRICT JUDGE.

\* \* \*

\* \* \* Defendant City of Niagara Falls [City] owns and operates a municipal sewerage system consisting of the WWTP [Niagara Falls Wastewater Treatment Plant] and a related ancillary wastewater and stormwater collection system, which includes the FST [Falls Street Tunnel]. The FST is a large, rock-hewn tunnel under the streets of Niagara Falls, New York, that for many years collected sewage, industrial waste, stormwater and groundwater and sent the combined flow to the WWTP for treatment prior to discharge into the Niagara River.
\* \* \*

During the early 1970s, it became evident that the WWTP was discharging an unacceptably high amount of toxic pollutants into the river. On January 9, 1974, pursuant to Section 402(a) of the Clean Water Act, the Regional Administrator of the Environmental Protection Agency [EPA] issued defendant NPDES Permit No. NY0026336, effective January 30, 1975, which established the terms and conditions under which the City may discharge pollutants. Pursuant to that permit, a new system was constructed at the WWTP to allow for chemical-physical treatment of sewage, followed by carbon adsorption. Completed in early 1978 at an approximate cost of $61 million (75% of which was derived from federal grants, and 12.5% from state grants), the carbon treatment system failed in July, 1978. [While that system was being repaired, the City discharged untreated water through the FST directly into the river. After repairs, the City failed to redivert the water back through the Wastewater Treatment Plant. Plaintiffs brought suit for a permanent injunction ordering the City to redivert the water.]

\* \* \*

\* \* \* [T]he discharge is a violation of that part of the Clean Water Act fundamental to furthering the Act's major underlying purpose of "establish[ing] a comprehensive long-range policy for the elimination of water pollution," as well as the stated objectives "to restore and maintain the chemical, physical, and biological integrity of the Nation's waters," and to "preserv[e] ... the environment and ... [protect] ... mankind and wildlife from harmful chemicals." The untreated FST discharge, therefore, continues not merely in derogation of "the integrity of the permit process" \* \* \*, but is a violation which undermines the substantive policies, purposes, and objectives of the Clean Water Act, a violation for which this court has already determined plaintiffs are entitled to relief. The instant case is thus one in which injunctive relief, if warranted on balancing the equities, is proper as a means of furthering those policies, purposes and objectives.

\* \* \*

\* \* \* The essential balance that must be struck is whether the harm to the environment caused by the FST discharge is outweighed by the engineering difficulties which the City would face, and the economic burden which the users of the City's sewer system would bear, should all or part of that discharge be ordered to be re-diverted through the WWTP for treatment.

\* \* \*

\* \* \* I am convinced that injunctive relief is appropriate in this case \* \* \*. Accordingly, I find that the most prudent exercise of discretion under all of the circumstances presented would be to grant plaintiff's request for a permanent injunction ordering immediate re-diversion of the maximum portion of the FST flow that can now be accomplished [to the WWTP].

\* \* \*

## *Notes and Questions*

1. The Clean Water Act addresses the external costs of water pollution by limiting the pollutants that can be added to navigable waters by any source, a regulation comparable to limiting the amount of fluoride Martin Marietta can emit from its aluminum plant. Rather than relying on a liability system to internalize costs and thereby reduce externalities to an allocatively efficient level, the Clean Water Act simply prohibits undesirable pollution. It attempts to control the total by estimating the limitations that must be imposed on each pollution source in order to reach its goal. This solution substitutes the government's judgment for the private parties' in calculating the optimal amount of pollution. Economists usually assume that individuals can determine better than government bureaucrats the value individuals place on resources.

*Question:* What are the risks of using government directives to control external costs like pollution?

2. The Clean Water Act established a federal system of control over water quality in navigable waters. Without federal regulation of water

pollution, states and municipalities could allow or prohibit pollution as they chose. To attract industry and development from neighboring areas, jurisdictions could compete by providing more lenient pollution laws.

*Questions:* In the context of the Clean Water Act, how does this competition lead to the inefficient allocation of resources? What are the states' incentives without federal intervention and how might they lead to inefficient overpollution?

3. The regulatory approach of the Clean Water Act supplements the common law rights of owners of property on waterways. Sections 850 and 850A of the Restatement (Second) of Torts detail the waterfront property owners' rights. Section 850 states:

A riparian proprietor is subject to liability for making an unreasonable use of the water or a watercourse or lake that causes harm to another riparian proprietor's reasonable use of water or his land.

Section 850A (h) makes clear that one factor relevant when determining the reasonableness of a use is "the protection of existing values of water uses, land, investments and enterprises." Comment (a) to § 850A concludes that "It is usually unreasonable * * * for a new user to destroy existing values created by a use that was reasonable in its inception."

*Question:* Translated into its application to waterways, does this Restatement rule lead to an efficient use of the common waterway?

# Chapter 2

# THE ECONOMIC ANALYSIS OF TORT LAW

## A. LIABILITY AS AN INCENTIVE FOR EFFICIENT BEHAVIOR

People's daily activities inevitably consume scarce resources, at a minimum, human energy or time. It is easy to appreciate that many activities result in the unintentional destruction of property or injury to persons. The economic analysis of tort law focuses on the allocation of the risks of loss due to the destruction of property or injury to persons created by those activities. Tort law may be viewed as a system of rules designed to maximize wealth by allocating risks so as to minimize the costs associated with engaging in daily activities. The materials in this chapter explore how tort law allocates the costs of accidents to those in the best position to minimize those costs. The economic analysis of tort law begins by examining how the law encourages people to allocate resources to accident prevention.

### WINN DIXIE STORES, INC. v. BENTON
District Court of Appeal of Florida, Fourth District, 1991.
576 So.2d 359.

STONE, JUDGE.

The appellee was injured in a slip and fall in appellant's market. We affirm a final judgment, entered following a jury verdict for the plaintiff, and find no error in the trial court's denial of Winn Dixie's motions for directed verdict and for judgment notwithstanding the verdict.

At the point of the fall there was a puddle of milk, five to eight inches long and three to four inches wide. There were also milk drops on the floor in a thirty foot trail from the milk container case to the puddle and for another fifty feet from the puddle to the checkout lines.

The drops were in an even pattern, one to one and a half feet apart. A leaky half gallon or gallon milk carton, one quarter empty, was found at the checkout area immediately after the fall. The appellant asserts that the store is normally busy at the time of the accident but appellee argues that this is refuted by the evidence that there were no other customers in the dairy aisle. The floor had not been swept for more than one-half hour prior to the incident. There was evidence that the store manager did not conduct his customary floor inspection that afternoon, and the manager's testimony that he had "inspected" that particular aisle fifteen minutes before the accident was questioned by plaintiff's challenges to the credibility of the witness.

The evidence, any conflicts in the evidence, and all reasonable conclusions which may be drawn from the evidence, must be resolved in favor of the appellee.

It was plaintiff's burden to prove that the milk was on the floor sufficiently long to charge Winn Dixie with notice. Notice may be proved by circumstantial evidence. It has frequently been recognized that the condition of the floor, the nature of the substance on the floor, and the surrounding circumstances, may be sufficient to support an inference by the jury that a dangerous condition existed long enough for the store employees to know, or that they should have known, of the condition. Under such circumstances the issue is for the jury to resolve even where the evidence may be susceptible of more than one reasonable inference.

Resolving whether the store should have discovered the danger in this case did not require the jury to build an inference on an inference. Nor do we consider resolution of the notice issue here to require pure speculation, deemed unacceptable in *Winn Dixie Stores, Inc. v. Gaines Publix Super* and *Markets, Inc. v. Schmidt*.

It was within the province of the jury to decide whether the milk had been dripping for a sufficiently long period to be discovered in the exercise of reasonable care.

WARNER, JUDGE, dissenting.

In my view the evidence shows that a *maximum* of five to ten minutes passed between the last time a store employee walked down the aisle and the injury to appellee occurred. The milk puddle was fresh and there were no tire tracks through it. The evidence is insufficient to show that the management knew or should have known that the dripping milk was on the floor for a sufficient time to be discovered.

## *Notes and Questions*

1. The activities of operating a grocery store and shopping for groceries consume resources and create risks. One of the risks created materialized in *Winn Dixie* when Dorothea Benton slipped and fell on spilt milk. Being made liable for Benton's injury gives Winn Dixie an incentive to think about how to operate this store in the future. Closing down the store

is one way to ensure that no similar accidents occur in the future. If the store is to remain open, however, the owners must choose whether to find other ways to avoid such accidents or accept the financial consequences of letting accidents occur occasionally.

Almost every activity presents the risk of accidents. While the risks in flying airplanes, keeping pet bears, and racing automobiles are obvious, many seemingly harmless activities pose risks as well. Smelling a flower presents the risk of inhaling a bumble bee; serving spaghetti poses the risk of choking to death on a meatball. Accidents impose costs on victims and society would be better off, in both utility and wealth terms, if accidents did not occur.

The risk of accidents can be reduced by investing in precautionary measures. Accident avoidance techniques other than closing down the store in *Winn Dixie* included stationing an employee in every aisle with a mop to clean up immediately or inspecting the floors more frequently to make sure that they are clean and dry. These alternatives vary from relatively inexpensive ways of avoiding injury to customers (regular inspections) to extremely costly ways (closing down). Society would certainly be better off if both the cost of having accidents occur and the cost of safety precautions could be avoided. In his 1970 book, The Costs of Accidents: A Legal and Economic Analysis, Guido Calabresi described the harms resulting from accidents when they occur and the costs of preventing accidents as *primary accident costs*. From a wealth maximizing perspective, one goal of tort law is minimizing primary accident costs, the sum of the cost of having and the cost of avoiding accidents.

2. The possibility of accidents presents a policy dilemma, whether to bear the costs of having accidents or the costs of avoiding accidents. By imposing liability on the grocery store in *Winn Dixie,* the court informed the defendant and owners of other groceries that when they fail to use reasonable care to discover hazards in their stores, they will be required to pay for harm that results. This rule of law internalizes to the stores costs that otherwise would be external to their decisionmaking. This liability rule forces grocery store owners to choose between bearing the costs of such accidents in the future and bearing the costs of taking precautions.

*Question:* How does the imposition of liability align the profit-making incentives of the grocery store owner with the societal goal of wealth maximization?

3. In American Airlines v. Ulen, 186 F.2d 529 (D.C. Cir., 1949), an airplane flying from Washington D.C. to Mexico City, Mexico crashed into the top of Glade Mountain in southwest Virginia killing both the pilot and co-pilot and seriously injuring Violet Ulen. While Glade Mountain is 4080 feet high, the pilot's flight plan called for flying at an altitude of 4000 feet on that leg of the flight. The court found that the pilot was negligent as a matter of law.

*Questions:* What purpose is served by making American Airlines liable in *Ulen?* Is it likely that the imposition of liability will induce pilots to take more care in planning their routes?

## DRAKE v. LERNER SHOPS OF COLORADO, INC.

Supreme Court of Colorado, 1960.
145 Colo. 1, 357 P.2d 624.

DOYLE, JUSTICE.

\* \* \* Plaintiff instituted the action seeking damages resulting from a fall suffered as she emerged from the defendant's store. Plaintiff fell to the sidewalk and suffered a fractured hip and other injuries. Trial was had to a jury and at the close of the plaintiff's evidence dismissal was ordered. She seeks review of the judgment.

The defendant operates a clothing store at the corner of 16th and Champa streets in Denver. One entrance is on 16th Street and the other is on Champa. The injury occurred as plaintiff was leaving the store from the Champa Street entrance where there are two sets of heavy glass doors leading to the outside. The inside set of doors were opened inward, and the outside set were closed and had to be pushed open by one making an exit. Beyond the outer set of doors is an area three feet in length leading to the sidewalk and which is some five inches above the sidewalk. This area is terrazzo and is on the floor level of the store. As one exits from the store there are decals on either side of the doors at about eye level. These have the words "Step Down" an them. The opposite side of the decals read "Pull".

Plaintiff testified that as she walked out the sun was shining and its reflection against a white building across the street was such that she could not see well and that she did not observe the "Step Down" signs, and was not aware of the five inch drop-off to the sidewalk. As a consequence she fell and was injured.

The injury occurred on August 6, 1957, and on that day the sun was shining brightly. Photographs introduced in evidence tended to show that the warning signs were difficult to read up close. Another photo introduced by defendant established that the sign was clear from a few feet distance.

In granting the defendant's motion the trial court found the occurrence to have been an accident; that the defendant was free of negligence. In his remarks the judge concluded:

> "The Court further finds from the evidence in this case that there was no breach of any duty by the defendant. I believe the evidence unequivocally shows, and the Court so finds, that there is no dangerous condition existing in the Lerner Shops at the entrance on Champa Street; further, that nowhere in the evidence can the Court find that there is any defective condition. Now, the law is pretty well settled on the question that all the duty the defendant has is ordinary care for safe conditions.

\* \* \*

> "The Court feels from the evidence in this case that the plaintiff has relied solely on a mere accident and not upon any negligence on the part of the defendant."

In urging that the court erred in holding that the evidence was insufficient as a matter of law, plaintiff argues that the evidence gave rise to conflicting inferences and that the court pronounced its own view—that the facts presented justify a contrary finding that a condition of danger foreseeable to defendant existed, and that defendant failed in its duty to give adequate warning or in any other manner to protect the plaintiff.

The question for determination is whether the maintaining of a step under the circumstances described constitutes sufficient negligence to require submission of the case to a jury. We conclude that it does not.

* * *

In order to establish a prima facie case of negligence, plaintiff's evidence must establish the existence on the premises of an unreasonable risk of harm to her as an invitee. The mere existence of risk is not sufficient. Some degree of risk is present in our every activity and if existence of hazard alone were the standard, it would mean that the happening of an accident would be sufficient to raise a presumption of negligence and the landowner would be an insurer of the safety of his patrons. Such is not the law. The condition created by the conduct or activity of the landowner must pose an *appreciable* risk of harm. The defendant's conduct must threaten harm.

Considering the evidence in a light most favorable to plaintiff, it cannot be said that the condition about which she complains was such as to create an appreciable risk of harm. A step down of five inches is not a hazard which of itself suggests likelihood of harm, and consequently defendant was not required to eliminate it or to provide safeguards other than those which it did provide in order to satisfy the standard required by law. The photographs here indicate that defendant gave a reasonable warning; that the step was plainly visible, and it cannot be said that defendant's failure to provide against the reflection of the sun on the building opposite his own constituted negligence. * * * Here no actionable threat of harm is apparent.

The judgment is affirmed.

## Notes and Questions

1. Unlike *Winn Dixie*, where the court required the defendant to pay damages to the injured customer, the court in *Drake* denied compensation to the customer. If the imposition of liability is designed to give store owners an incentive to avoid accidents, the holding in *Drake* suggests that there must be some accidents that defendants need not avoid. The incentives created by the imposition of liability only result in precautions by the rational maximizer if the cost of those precautions is less than the expected liability from future accidents. Since both having and avoiding accidents impose costs and the wealth of society is maximized by minimizing those costs, the allocative efficiency goal in tort law is described as minimizing primary accident costs. Since primary accident costs include both the costs

of having and the costs of avoiding accidents, the efficiency goal explicitly recognizes that, from a societal perspective, some accidents are not worth avoiding. A tort law designed to minimize accident costs is actually encouraging accidents, a heartless perspective that places wealth maximization above safety. Some accidents will be avoided and some will not.

Courts recognize that some precautions are not worth taking. As Judge Breyer said in Rhode Island Hospital Trust National Bank v. Zapata Corp., 848 F.2d 291, 295 (1st Cir. 1988), "One does not, for example, coat the base of the Grand Canyon with soft plastic nets to catch those who might fall in, or build cars like armored tanks to reduce injuries in accidents even though the technology exists."

If Lerner Shops is not going to be liable, then the choice between accident avoidance and accident liability is easy for them. The cost of having accidents is external to their decisionmaking since Grace Drake and any future victims will have to pay their own medical bills. Remember that the court found that there was "no appreciable risk of harm," that the step down was "not a hazard which of itself suggests likelihood of harm." Remember that the sun shining off a bright, white building across the street may make it quite difficult to take precautions against accidents like this one.

> *Questions:* If society's goal is to minimize primary accident costs, does the rule in *Drake* create efficient incentives? Which is the lower of the two sources of primary accident costs, avoidance or the expected losses if the accident occurs?

2. Oliver Wendell Holmes, in The Common Law 77 (1881, Howe ed. 1963), argued that it makes no sense to incur the administrative costs of inserting the government into private disputes unless there is something to be gained: "[T]he prevailing view is that [the state's] cumbrous and expensive machinery ought not to be set in motion unless some clear benefit is to be derived from disturbing the *status quo*. State interference is an evil where it cannot be shown to be a good." The possibility of a more efficient allocation of resources provides an argument that state interference is a "good" in cases where imposing liability gives defendants incentives to minimize primary accident costs. Where liability will not affect primary accident costs, the justification is not present.

The prevailing view described in Holmes's writing reflected a basic distaste for government intervention ("State intervention is an evil where it cannot be shown to be a good."). Calabresi suggests an economic rationale for finding no liability in cases where the accident cannot be avoided at reasonable cost. *Tertiary accident costs* are those costs associated with administering the torts system, including the "cumbrous and expensive machinery" of the courts.

> *Question:* How does denying recovery to Grace Drake minimize tertiary costs?

3. When economists compare accident avoidance cost and accident liability cost, they typically speak of the latter in terms of *expected* costs. If people incur expenditures for avoidance, it is certain that the resources devoted to precaution will be consumed. Once the store manager in *Winn*

*Dixie* pays people to inspect the aisles more frequently, that expenditure of money and time cannot be recaptured. If he decides to risk the accident and bear the cost of liability if the accident occurs, however, he may get lucky and never have another accident. The sun may never blind another customer leaving the Lerner Shops as in *Drake* and no one will ever have to pay for personal injuries resulting. In fact, the court in *Drake* believed that the possibility of a recurrence was so remote that it was not worth considering.

If a rational cost minimizer considers both the likelihood that an accident will occur and the severity of the harm if it occurs, his position is not unlike that of any gambler, who considers the size of the pot and the likelihood he will win it, or a highway speeder, who considers the penalties from being caught and the likelihood of apprehension. State lotteries advertise the probability of winning, either in terms of the probability of winning (about 1 in 3.5 for some instant lotteries) or the percentage of revenues returned in winnings (around 56 cents of each dollar). It is not too farfetched to believe that a rational person betting on accidents (or investing in accident avoidance) will similarly consider the *expected* return from his investment or *expected* cost of liability. Economists sometimes refer to the expected accident liability as the *discounted* cost of letting accidents occur. The cost of an accident occurring is discounted (reduced) by the probability that it will occur. Thus if there is a 25% chance of an accident occurring and the harm if it occurs is valued at $200,000, then the expected or discounted accident liability is only $50,000 (.25 x $200,000). The expected cost of letting accidents occur is the *risk* associated with an activity.

*Question:* If medical expenses and compensation for pain, suffering, and inconvenience in *Drake* were valued at $25,000 and the probability of one recurrence of this accident in the next year were 1 in 10,000, would it be efficient for a store owner to invest $5.00 a year in avoiding this accident?

## SCHOMAKER v. HAVEY
Supreme Court of Pennsylvania, 1927.
291 Pa. 30, 139 A. 495.

PER CURIUM.

\* \* \*

On the night of October 18, 1925, while defendant was driving his coupe automobile along a road in Allegheny county, he was hailed by plaintiff's husband, and, at the latter's request, defendant agreed to give him a lift in his car. The coupe had one other occupant beside defendant, and the deceased elected to stand on the running board, with his head, shoulders, arms, and part of his body inside the window on the side opposite the driver. As the car approached an intersecting road, defendant increased the speed of his car from between 20 and 25 miles to 40 or 45 miles an hour, and, upon reaching the intersection, suddenly swerved his automobile to the left, then to the right, and upset. Schomaker was thrown to the ground sustaining injuries which resulted in his death.

We have held, as a matter of law, that it is contributory negligence to stand on the platform of railroad trains, also to stand on the running boards of street railway cars, and we recently intimated that riding on a running board of a moving motor car constituted contributory negligence.

In Harding v. Philadelphia R. T. Co., we said:

"It is * * * clear that one who takes a position of manifest and imminent danger assumes the risk of his position."

Certainly, standing on the running board of a moving automobile is as dangerous as standing on a similar place on a street car, if not more so, and a person who takes such a position on an automobile is guilty of plain contributory negligence.

In Smith v. Ozark Water Mills Co., the Supreme Court of Missouri properly said:

"The action of the deceased in standing on the running board of an automobile * * * is an act of negligence concerning which reasonable men could not have a difference of opinion. The law is well settled that where a person voluntarily assumes a position of imminent danger when there is at hand and accessible to him a place of comparative safety, and by reason of having taken the dangerous position he is injured, he can have no recovery against another who is also negligent because such person's negligence in taking the dangerous position is one of the direct and proximate causes of the injury and contributes thereto."

As stated by us in Thane v. Scranton Traction Co.:

"Whether [the injured person, had he occupied a different position on the car], would have received some other injury, equal or greater, is conjectural and irrelevant; [since] if he is to recover at all it must be for the injuries received, not for what he might have received under different circumstances."

The order of the court below [denying recovery to the plaintiff] is affirmed.

## *Notes and Questions*

1. Analyzing the efficiency implications of barring recovery when the plaintiff is contributorily negligent, as in *Schomaker,* starts the same way as the analysis of the implications of holding the defendant liable. If the defendant is not legally liable for the medical bills and other damages, the plaintiff must bear those costs. One or the other will pay; one party will be given the incentive to minimize the costs that the possibility of another similar accident presents. It is unreasonable to expect Schomaker to respond to any incentives; he died from injuries received when he was thrown to the ground. The court in *Schomaker,* by finding that the plaintiff was contributorily negligent, gave other people who find themselves in the same position as Schomaker the incentive to choose between

potential medical expenses or the inconvenience of riding *inside* the car. It is the *prospective* application of the incentives that provides the efficiency-enhancing benefit of imposing liability.

2. The defendant in *Schomaker* could also have avoided the accident, of course, by insisting that the plaintiff not ride on the running board. Making the defendant liable would have given him, and other drivers similarly situated, incentive to avoid such accidents in the future.

*Question:* What efficiency reason might there be for making the plaintiff/passenger pay rather than making the driver pay?

## B. THE NEGLIGENCE STANDARD

### 1. THE COST–BENEFIT APPROACH TO LIABILITY

One way to structure incentives to minimize primary accident costs is through the definition of reasonable care. In the 1940's, Judge Learned Hand described the negligence standard as a balancing between the two sources of primary accident costs: accident avoidance and accident liability. In United States v. Carroll Towing Co., he defined reasonable care in algebraic terms.

### UNITED STATES v. CARROLL TOWING CO.
Circuit Court of Appeals, Second Circuit, 1947.
159 F.2d 169.

L. HAND, CIRCUIT JUDGE.

These appeals concern the sinking of the barge, "Anna C," on January 4, 1944, off Pier 51, North River. [The barge, "Anna C" was owned by Conners Company. On the day in question, it was tied up to a pier along with a flotilla of other barges. The "Carroll," a tug owned by the Carroll Towing Company and chartered by the Grace Lines, attempted to move one of the other barges. In the process, the "Anna C" broke away from the pier and floated down the North River where she collided with a tanker whose propeller broke a hole in her bottom. Because there was no watchman or "bargee" aboard the "Anna C", no one informed the "Carroll" and another nearby tug, the "Grace," that the "Anna C" was leaking. As a result, the "Anna C" sank and her cargo was lost. While there were a number of parties to this suit, including the United States government (for whom the flour was being shipped), the relevant part of this decision relates to the attempt by Conners Company to recover damages from Carroll Towing for the sinking of the "Anna C." Under the admiralty law, the applicable law governing torts on navigable waterways, if defendants Carroll Towing and Grace Lines could demonstrate that the plaintiff Conners' negligence also contributed to the loss, they would be excused from paying a portion of the damage. The opinion addresses whether Conners' failure to have a bargee protecting the barge amounted to negligence.]

We cannot * * * excuse the Conners Company for the bargee's failure to care for the barge, and we think that this prevents full recovery. * * * We do not * * * attribute it as in any degree a fault of the "Anna C" that the flotilla broke adrift. Hence she may recover in full against the Carroll Company and the Grace Line for any injury she suffered from the contact with the tanker's propeller, which we shall speak of as the "collision damages." On the other hand, if the bargee had been on board, and had done his duty to his employer, he would have gone below at once, examined the injury, and called for help from the "Carroll" and the Grace Line tug. Moreover, it is clear that these tugs could have kept the barge afloat, until they had safely beached her, and saved her cargo. This would have avoided what we shall call the "sinking damages." Thus, if it was a failure in the Conner Company's proper care of its own barge, for the bargee to be absent, the company can recover only one third of the "sinking" damages from the Carroll Company and one third from the Grace Line. For this reason the question arises whether a barge owner is slack in the care of his barge if the bargee is absent.

* * * Since there are occasions when every vessel will break from her moorings, and since, if she does, she becomes a menace to those about her; the owner's duty, as in other similar situations, to provide against resulting injuries is a function of three variables: (1) The probability that she will break away; (2) the gravity of the resulting injury, if she does; (3) the burden of adequate precautions. Possibly it serves to bring this notion into relief to state it in algebraic terms: if the probability be called P; the injury, L; and the burden, B; liability depends upon whether B is less than L multiplied by P: i.e., whether $B < PL$. Applied to the situation at bar, the likelihood that a barge will break from her fasts and the damage she will do, vary with the place and time; for example, if a storm threatens, the danger is greater; so it is, if she is in a crowded harbor where moored barges are constantly being shifted about. On the other hand, the barge must not be the bargee's prison, even though he lives aboard; he must go ashore at times. We need not say whether, even in such crowded waters as New York Harbor a bargee must be aboard at night at all; it may be that the custom is otherwise and that, if so, the situation is one where custom should control. We leave that question open; but we hold that it is not in all cases a sufficient answer to a bargee's absence without excuse, during working hours, that he has properly made fast his barge to a pier, when he leaves her. In the case at bar the bargee left at five o'clock in the afternoon of January 3rd, and the flotilla broke away at about two o'clock in the afternoon of the following day, twenty-one hours afterwards. The bargee had been away all the time, and we hold that his fabricated story was affirmative evidence that he had no excuse for his absence. At the locus in quo—especially during the short January days and in the full tide of war activity—barges were being constantly "drilled" in and out. Certainly it was not beyond reasonable expectation that, with the inevitable haste and bustle, the work might

not be done with adequate care. In such circumstances we hold—and it is all that we do hold—that it was a fair requirement that the Conners Company should have a bargee aboard (unless he had some excuse for his absence), during the working hours of daylight.

[Accordingly, while recovery of collision damages is not diminished at all, the Conners Company must bear a share of liability for the sinking damages.]

## *Notes and Questions*

1. Under the Learned Hand rule, a party is found negligent and therefor liable for (at least part of) the damages resulting from his actions if $B < PL$. "B," the burden of adequate precautions, is the accident avoidance cost. "P" is the probability that an accident will occur. "L" is the cost of the resulting losses, if the accident does occur. "PL" (the probability of the accident multiplied by the gravity of the resulting injury) is the risk associated with the activity, the expected liability or the discounted accident cost.

Learned Hand suggested that when the costs of preventing an accident are less than the expected loss (properly discounted by the probability of an accident occurring), it is negligent not to take precautionary measures. A corollary of this view is that when the costs of precautions are greater than the expected loss, it is *not* negligent to decline to avoid the accident. In such circumstances, it is not efficient to take precautionary measures. The Learned Hand formula has had great influence on the development of the negligence standard.

2. Learned Hand referred to "P" as the probability that the barge would break away from the dock. Consider what "P" represented in the factual context in *Carroll Towing*.

*Question:* Is the probability that the barge would break away from the dock the same as the probability that an accident will result?

3. Both the probability of an accident occurring and gravity of harm if an accident does occur vary at different times of the day and night. The decrease in activity in the harbor at night is likely to decrease the likelihood of an injury (fewer barges moving about) and the severity of the harm (fewer other boats to collide with a drifting barge; the barge might run aground instead). The burden of taking precautions may even change from day to night if night bargees cost less. This all makes the calculations quite complicated. It might be impossible for a statistician to calculate even the probability of the accident that actually occurred. And the probability of that precise sequence occurring is likely to have been rather small. Other likely accidents include the barge colliding into the side of another boat or running aground.

*Questions:* Must the owner or bargee take all of these possible accidents into account in deciding whether to take precautions? Does an efficient balancing of costs require that the factfinder take all of these possibilities into account in deciding whether the parties were negligent?

4. One goal of the liability system is internalizing the external costs that accidents impose on others. The defendant who fails to take precautions that cost less than the expected loss from an accident is liable for damages if the accident occurs.

*Questions:* If people are liable for damages whenever they are found to be negligent, why are people ever negligent? Is it because people are not rational?

5. The distributional implications of the right to impose risks on others is clear; victims suffer so that actors may prosper. Whether the distributional implications are troublesome may depend on whether those who are actors are systematically different from those who are victims or whether we all take our turns playing different roles. In automobile accident cases with negligent drivers, for instance, the distributional implications may be slight since almost everyone drives. The implications may be different, however, if the injuries result from use of defective products.

In Hentschel v. Baby Bathinette Corp., 215 F.2d 102, 112 (2d Cir. 1954), the court held that a manufacturer was not negligent for using magnesium strips in constructing a baby bath. The bathinette caught fire for reasons unrelated to its construction. Yet, because of the materials used, it burned intensely and caused bursts of bluish flame to shoot across the hallway from the bathroom in which it was located into a nearby bedroom, burning the plaintiff. Citing another opinion by Judge Learned Hand, Conway v. O'Brien, 111 F.2d 611 (2d Cir. 1940), as an example of how courts take "social welfare" into account, Judge Frank dissented from a finding that the bathinette was reasonably fit for its intended use:

> Today, in this legal province of negligence, considerations of social welfare, or "social value," do (and should) affect the decisions as to a defendant's liability or the duty he owes to a plaintiff. Can anyone really believe * * * that it will promote an important "social value" to protect, from liability to purchasers, the makers and sellers of an article which, in case of fire, will create a hazard far greater than would otherwise exist, a hazard of which they are (or should be) aware but of which the purchasing householders are kept ignorant? What sound social policy inheres in such a rule? * * * My colleagues' ruling will tend to encourage the vending of such commodities perilous to human lives. The social interest in the free trade of goods, the need to avoid legal rules tending unduly to paralyze business initiative, and the fostering of a legitimate profit motive, do not extend that far.

Compare Learned Hand's definition of negligence to the explanation of reasonable care provided by the Restatement (Second) of Torts § 283 comment f: "Where a defendant's negligence is to be determined, the 'reasonable man' is a man who is reasonably 'considerate' of the safety of others and does not look primarily to his own advantage."

*Question:* Is the Restatement explanation of reasonable care consistent with Learned Hand's definition of negligence?

## 2. MODERN APPLICATIONS OF THE LEARNED HAND FORMULA

### McCARTY v. PHEASANT RUN, INC.
United States Court of Appeals, Seventh Circuit, 1987.
826 F.2d 1554.

POSNER, CIRCUIT JUDGE. .

\* \* \* Dula McCarty, a guest at the Pheasant Run Lodge in St. Charles, Illinois, was assaulted by an intruder in her room, and brought suit against the owner of the resort. The suit charges negligence, and bases federal jurisdiction on diversity of citizenship. The parties agree that Illinois law governs the substantive issues. The jury brought in a verdict for the defendant, and Mrs. McCarty appeals on a variety of grounds.

In 1981 Mrs. McCarty, then 58 years old and a merchandise manager for Sears Roebuck, checked into Pheasant Run—a large resort hotel on 160 acres outside Chicago—to attend a Sears business meeting. In one wall of her second-floor room was a sliding glass door equipped with a lock and a safety chain. The door opens onto a walkway that has stairs leading to a lighted courtyard to which there is public access. The drapes were drawn and the door covered by them. Mrs. McCarty left the room for dinner and a meeting. When she returned, she undressed and got ready for bed. As she was coming out of the bathroom, she was attacked by a man with a stocking mask. He beat and threatened to rape her. She fought him off, and he fled. He has never been caught. Although Mrs. McCarty's physical injuries were not serious, she claims that the incident caused prolonged emotional distress which, among other things, led her to take early retirement from Sears.

Investigation of the incident by the police revealed that the sliding glass door had been closed but not locked, that it had been pried open from the outside, and that the security chain had been broken. The intruder must have entered Mrs. McCarty's room by opening the door to the extent permitted by the chain, breaking the chain, and sliding the door open the rest of the way. Then he concealed himself somewhere in the room until she returned and entered the bathroom.

\* \* \* Her theories of negligence are that the defendant should have made sure the door was locked when she was first shown to her room; should have warned her to keep the sliding glass door locked; should have equipped the door with a better lock; should have had more security guards (only two were on duty, and the hotel has more than 500 rooms), should have made the walkway on which the door opened inaccessible from ground level; should have adopted better procedures for preventing unauthorized persons from getting hold of keys to guests' rooms; or should have done some combination of these things. The suggestion that the defendant should have had better procedures for keeping keys away from unauthorized persons is irrelevant, for it is extremely unlikely that the intruder entered the room through the front door. The other theories were for the jury to accept or reject, and its rejection of them was not unreasonable.

There are various ways in which courts formulate the negligence standard. The analytically (not necessarily the operationally) most precise is that it involves determining whether the burden of precaution is less than the magnitude of the accident, if it occurs, multiplied by the probability of occurrence. (The product of this multiplication, or "discounting," is what economists call an expected accident cost.) If the burden is less, the precaution should be taken. This is the famous "Hand Formula" announced in United States v. Carroll Towing Co., an admiralty case, and since applied in a variety of cases not limited to admiralty.

We are not authorized to change the common law of Illinois, however, and Illinois courts do not cite the Hand Formula but instead define negligence as failure to use reasonable care, a term left undefined. But as this is a distinction without a substantive difference, we have not hesitated to use the Hand Formula in cases governed by Illinois law. The formula translates into economic terms the conventional legal test for negligence. This can be seen by considering the factors that the Illinois courts take into account in negligence cases: the same factors, and in the same relation, as in the Hand Formula. Unreasonable conduct is merely the failure to take precautions that would generate greater benefits in avoiding accidents than the precautions would cost.

Ordinarily, and here, the parties do not give the jury the information required to quantify the variables that the Hand Formula picks out as relevant. That is why the formula has greater analytic than operational significance. Conceptual as well as practical difficulties in monetizing personal injuries may continue to frustrate efforts to measure expected accident costs with the precision that is possible, in principle at least, in measuring the other side of the equation—the cost or burden of precaution. For many years to come juries may be forced to make rough judgments of reasonableness, intuiting rather than measuring the factors in the Hand Formula; and so long as their judgment is reasonable, the trial judge has no right to set it aside, let alone substitute his own judgment.

Having failed to make much effort to show that the mishap could have been prevented by precautions of reasonable cost and efficacy, Mrs. McCarty is in a weak position to complain about the jury verdict. No effort was made to inform the jury what it would have cost to equip every room in the Pheasant Run Lodge with a new lock, and whether the lock would have been jimmy-proof. * * * And since the door to Mrs. McCarty's room was unlocked, what good would a better lock have done? No effort was made, either, to specify an optimal security force for a resort the size of Pheasant Run. No one considered the fire or other hazards that a second-floor walkway not accessible from ground level would create. A notice in every room telling guests to lock all doors would be cheap, but since most people know better than to leave the door to a hotel room unlocked when they leave the room—and the sliding glass door gave on a walkway, not a balcony—the jury might have thought that the incremental benefits from the notice would be slight. Mrs. McCarty testified that she didn't know there was a door behind the closed drapes but the jury wasn't required to believe this. Most people on checking into a hotel room, especially at a resort, are curious about the view; and it was still light when Mrs. McCarty checked in at 6:00 p.m. on an October evening.

* * *

[The jury verdict for the defendant is] Affirmed.

## *Notes and Questions*

1. Thinking about the negligence rule in BPL terms draws attention to the quantitative elements of proof lacking in Dula McCarty's case. While recognizing that many elements of the parties' cases are nonquantifiable, Judge Posner faults the plaintiff for not presenting such evidence as the dollar cost of locks on the hotel room doors or the optimal size of a security force for the hotel grounds. Thinking explicitly about these expenditures as accident avoidance costs rather than trying to judge whether the defendant's behavior was "reasonable" in the abstract requires the factfinder to focus on whether these expenditures really would have prevented the accident. Judge Posner's demand for evidence that these expenditures would have prevented the accident at reasonable cost might be interpreted either as imposing an extra burden on the plaintiff to be specific or as an aid in helping the plaintiff frame her argument. Judge Posner clearly subscribes to the latter interpretation. In Davis v. Consolidated Rail Corp., which follows, the plaintiff has offered satisfactory evidence of the feasibility of accident avoidance measures and the burden shifted to the defendant to use precision in demonstrating the infeasibility of the measures.

2. In *McCarty,* Judge Posner explicitly recognized the social cost-benefit analysis implicit in the Learned Hand test: "Unreasonable conduct is merely the failure to take precautions that would generate greater benefits in avoiding accidents than the precautions would cost." Notice how the formulaic approach enables Posner to take an objective view of the situation without succumbing to the emotional appeal of the plaintiff's case. In another case using the BPL approach, Judge Robertson of the Missouri Supreme Court, Madden v. C & K Barbecue Carryout, Inc., 758 S.W.2d 59, 64 (Mo.1988), praised the advantages of this perspective:

> This method of analysis (which is certainly more complex than is set out here) has been dubbed "law and economics". To its credit, law and economics has been criticized both by those who argue that the tort system favors plaintiffs and those who believe it tilts toward defendants. While I harbor no illusions that law and economics is the holy grail of tort law, it is nonetheless helpful in analyzing cases such as this one which present particularly troubling choices. It is helpful

because it allows us to consider cases from a neutral perspective and ex ante, with a view toward determining appropriate rules of law which generate cost-effective behaviors within society. By focusing on these neutral considerations we are freed, to some extent, from the condemnation leveled by those who argue that we now compensate injury without regard to fault. In my credo, the tort system serves responsibly only when it requires a finding of fault as a necessary predicate to any award of compensation.

*Questions:* Does employing the Learned Hand formula help the jury ignore the distributional implications of the negligence rule? If it helps the jury divorce itself from its passions, does the Learned Hand rule promote the minimization of primary accident costs?

3. The jury in *McCarty* found that the defendant was not negligent and therefore did not reach the question of whether the plaintiff was contributorily negligent.

*Question:* If neither the Pheasant Run Lodge nor Dula McCarty could have avoided the risk of attack by using reasonable care, are primary and tertiary accident costs minimized by making the defendant or the plaintiff bear the loss?

4. Assume that when she checked into her room at Pheasant Run, Dula McCarty correctly calculated that the probability of being attacked by an intruder was sufficiently low that it did not make economic sense to check to see whether the sliding glass door was locked, even though the costs of being attacked are high. If the resort was similarly not negligent, then one would predict that neither these parties nor similarly situated parties would take precautions to avoid similar accidents in the future.

*Questions:* Do you suppose that Ms. McCarty checked the lock on the door the next time she checked into a hotel? Do you suppose the resort took any precautions to avoid similar attacks despite winning this case? Would either of these acts be irrational?

## DAVIS v. CONSOLIDATED RAIL CORPORATION

United States Court of Appeals, Seventh Circuit, 1986.
788 F.2d 1260.

POSNER, CIRCUIT JUDGE.

\* \* \* The suit arises from an accident that occurred in 1983. The plaintiff, Davis, was 33 years old at the time, an experienced railroad worker who for the past six years had been employed as an inspector of cars by the Trailer Train Company, a lessor of piggyback cars to railroads. He made the inspections in railroad yards, among them Conrail's marshaling yard in East St. Louis. On the day of the accident, Davis, driving an unmarked van that was the same color as the Conrail vans used in the yard but that lacked the identifying "C" painted on each Conrail van, arrived at the yard and saw a train coming in from east to west. He noticed that several of the cars in the train were Trailer Train cars that he was required to inspect. The train halted, and was decoupled near the front; the locomotive, followed by several cars, pulled away to the west. The remainder of the train was stretched out for three-quarters of a mile to the east; and because it lay on a curved section of the track, its rear end was not visible from the point of decoupling. An employee of Conrail named Lundy saw Davis sitting in his van, didn't know who he was, thought it was queer he was there, but did nothing.

Shortly afterward Davis began to conduct the inspections. This required him to crawl underneath the cars to look for cracks. One of the cars was the third from the end (that is, from the point where the train had been decoupled). Unbeknownst to Davis, a locomotive had just coupled with the other (eastern) end of the train. It had a crew of four. Two were in the cab of the locomotive. The other two, one of whom was designated as the rear brakeman, were somewhere alongside the train; the record does not show just where, but neither was at the western end of the train, where Davis was. The crew was ordered to move the train several car lengths to the east because it was blocking a switch. The crew made the movement, but without blowing the train's horn or ringing its bell. The only warning Davis had of the impending movement was the sudden rush of air as the air brakes were activated. He tried to scramble to safety before the train started up but his legs were caught beneath the wheels of the car as he crawled out from under it. One leg was severed just below the knee; most of the foot on the other leg was also sliced off. * * *

Davis brought this suit against Conrail, charging negligence. * * * A jury found for Davis [and] assessed damages at $3 million[.] * * *

* * *

On the question of Conrail's negligence, Davis presented three theories to the jury. The first was that Conrail's employee Lundy, whose auto was equipped with a two-way radio, should have notified the crew of the train that an unknown person was sitting in a van parked near the tracks. We consider this a rather absurd suggestion. Lundy had no reason to think that the man in the van would climb out and crawl under a railroad car. If he had called the crew and told them there was a man in a van by the tracks, they undoubtedly would have replied, so what? * * *

In the famous negligence formula of Judge Learned Hand, which is recognized to encapsulate the more conventional verbal formulations of the negligence standard, a defendant is negligent only if $B < PL$, meaning, only if the burden of precautions is less than the magnitude of the loss if an accident that the precautions would have prevented occurs discounted (multiplied) by the probability of the accident. If P is very low, elaborate precautions are unlikely to be required even if L is large and here the necessary precautions would have been elaborate.

Davis's second theory of Conrail's negligence is even more fantastic. It is that before the train was moved a member of the crew should have walked its length, looking under the cars. The probability that someone was under a car was too slight, as it reasonably would have appeared to the crew, to warrant the considerable delay in moving the train that would have been caused by having a crew member walk its entire length and then walk back, a total distance of a mile and a half. It might have taken an hour, since the crew member would have had to look under each one of the train's 50 cars, and since the cars were only 12 inches off the ground, so that he would have had to get down on all fours to see under them.

Davis's third theory is more plausible. He argues that it was negligent for the crew to move the train without first blowing its horn (also referred to as the whistle) or ringing its bell. Since no member of the crew was in a position where he could see the train's western end, which was now its rear end, a reasonable jury could find—we do not say we would have found if we had been the triers of fact—that it was imprudent to move the train without a signal in advance. Although the crew had no reason to think that Davis was under a car, someone— whether an employee of Conrail or some other business invitee to the yard (such as Davis)—might have been standing in or on a car or between cars, for purposes of making repairs or conducting an inspection; and any such person could be severely, even fatally, injured if the train pulled away without any warning or even just moved a few feet. Regarding the application of the Hand formula to such a theory of negligence, not only was B vanishingly small—for what would it cost to blow the train's horn?—but P was significant, though not large, once all the possible accidents that blowing the horn would have averted are added together. For in determining the benefits of a precaution—and PL, the expected accident costs that the precaution would avert, is a measure of the benefits of the precaution—the trier of fact must consider not only the expected cost of this accident but also the expected cost of any other, similar accidents that the precaution would have prevented. Blowing the horn would have saved not only an inspector who had crawled under the car (low P), but also an inspector leaning on a car, a railroad employee doing repairs on the top of a car, a brakeman straddling two cars, and anyone else who might have business in or on (as well as under) a car. The train was three-quarters of a mile long. It was not so unlikely that somewhere in that stretch a person was in a position of potential peril to excuse the crew from taking the inexpensive precaution of blowing the train's horn. Or so at least the jury could conclude without taking leave of its senses.

Against this conclusion Conrail and Trailer Train hurl a number of arguments. One is that precautions would not have been effective; Davis himself testified that he would not have heard the train's bell. But we do not consider this so damaging a concession as the defendants do. Davis would not have heard the bell, no, but it does not mean that he would not have heard the horn. The horn is deafening, and Conrail's assertion (for which no evidence was offered) that the horn would have been inaudible at three-quarters of a mile is as implausible as it is unsubstantiated.

A better point is that there is so much traffic in a marshaling yard that sounding the horn every time a train is moved would cause a cacophony that would deprive the horn of its efficacy as a warning. If horns were blowing all the time, Davis would not know, when the horn sounded, whether it was the horn for this train or some other train. Either he would ignore it or he would be spending all his time scrambling out from under and then back under the cars he was inspecting. The problem with this argument is that Conrail put in no evidence on how busy the marshaling yard was either at the time of the accident or at any other time. We know it is a large (four square miles) and busy yard, but we do not know how frequently trains are actually moved in a large and busy yard. Every 15 minutes? Every hour? Conrail could easily have put in evidence on this point, but did not. Moreover, Davis is not contending that due care requires that the horn be blown before every move. Maybe this move was special, because of the length of the train in combination with the curvature of the track and the fact that all of the crew members were at or near the front of the train. Even if the yard is very busy, if the horn were sounded only in the unusual case where there was more than average danger from a sudden movement the danger of cacophony would be diminished.

* * *

Although the evidence of the defendants' negligence is thin, * * * we can find no reversible error.

Affirmed.

## *Notes and Questions*

1. It is easy to say, after the fact, that precautions should have been taken but, as Judge Robertson, in Madden v. C & K Barbecue Carryout, Inc., 758 S.W.2d 59, 66 (Mo. 1988), insists, "foreseeability must never be measured after the fact; when an injury has occurred, whatever precautions were taken were (obviously) inadequate to prevent that injury." The factfinder in *Davis* must imagine himself in the position of the railroad prior to the accident. If he has any compassion at all, the engineer will regret not having blown the whistle to warn the inspector, but was it unreasonable not to have blown it? Since it was so easy to do, the railroad must provide a specific explanation of why the whistle was not blown. The requirement of specificity has shifted to the defendant in this case, who failed to show either that the precaution would be ineffective or too expensive.

2. In his analysis of the plaintiff's theories of negligence, Judge Posner applied the Learned Hand formula to determine whether Conrail was negligent. The second and third theories offered two accident avoidance measures available to Conrail—having a crew member walk the length of the train checking to see that there was no one under the cars or, alternatively, having the crew blow the train's horn or ring its bell before moving the train to warn people working under the cars.

*Question:* What differences in the balancing of burdens and risks in the Learned Hand formula support rejection of the second and acceptance of the third theories?

3. The excerpt from *Davis* illustrates a case where only one party, the defendant, is negligent. Cases might also arise where the plaintiff rather than the defendant is negligent. Under traditional rules of tort law, if the only negligent party is the defendant, the plaintiff recovers full damages. If the only negligent party is the plaintiff, the plaintiff recovers no damages.

*Question:* Are primary and tertiary accident costs minimized by these traditional negligence rules in cases where only one of the parties is negligent?

## C. EFFICIENCY OF DEFENSES TO LIABILITY BASED ON NEGLIGENCE

The principal issue throughout this chapter is whether tort law minimizes accident costs. The assignment of liability leads to the minimization of accident costs only if people respond to the incentives created by the law. To provide incentives for parties to minimize primary accident costs, it will be desirable to place liability on the party that is in the best position to evaluate the risks and take cost-justified precautions to avoid them. Deterrence in tort law relies on the notion that placing liability on a particular type of actor for past acts will deter similarly situated actors in the future.

The cases thus far have focused on how the cost-benefit approach to liability is applied. It may be easier to appreciate the efficiency of tort law in differing factual contexts if those cases can are classified according to which party could have avoided the accident at reasonable cost, that is, which party was negligent. In simple, two-party accident cases, there are three categories of accidents: (I) Neither party was negligent, (II) Only one party was negligent, and (III) Both parties were negligent.

Within the first category of accident cases, there are two types of factual circumstances; either the injurer was in the best position to avoid the accident or the victim was. Because neither was negligent, neither of them had a cost of avoidance that was less than the expected accident cost, but there still may have been a difference in their relative ability to avoid the accident. It may be that the injurer was the best cost avoider, in which case similarly situated potential injurers in the future also are likely to be the best cost avoiders. Alternatively, the victim may have been the best cost avoider, in which case similarly situated potential victims in the future also are likely to be the best cost avoiders. Any factual circumstances in this Category falls into one of the two situations.

CATEGORY I: NO NEGLIGENCE
    A. INJURER IS BEST COST AVOIDER

### B. VICTIM IS BEST COST AVOIDER

For Category IA and IB cases, neither party, if paying strict attention to the costs involved and responding rationally, would avoid the accident, even if he had to pay the costs if the accident occurred. As discussed in the notes and questions following *Drake*, above, the assignment of liability will not affect primary accident costs as long as the parties rationally evaluate their options according to the Learned Hand formula.

In circumstances where only one party is negligent (has available cost-justified precautions), the factual circumstances fall into Category II. Category IIA describes situations where only the injurer is negligent and Category IIB describes situations where only the victim is negligent.

## CATEGORY II: ONLY ONE PARTY NEGLIGENT
### A. INJURER IS BEST COST AVOIDER
### B. VICTIM IS BEST COST AVOIDER

If only one party is negligent, the best cost avoider in Category II must be the negligent party; for the best cost avoider B is less than PL. Since the other party is not negligent, his cost of avoidance, B, must be greater than the risk presented, PL.

In Category IIA, the injurer, but not the victim, could avoid the accident by taking cost-justified precautions. Holding the injurer (defendant) liable in Category IIA gives him and similarly situated others an incentive to avoid accidents in the future, since he and similarly situated defendants know that they will have to bear the higher expected accident cost if they do not.

In Category IIB cases, the defendant would not be liable under a negligence theory, because he had no cost-justified precautions available. In Category IIB cases the denial of recovery to the victim gives him and similarly situated others an incentive to avoid the accident in the future. Since the victim (plaintiff) is the lower cost avoider of accidents, it is efficient to give him the incentive. The task of the factfinder faced with Category II situations is determining which party has cost-justified precautions available and making him bear the costs of the accident.

In this section, the analysis is about to become more complicated. The cases in this section present situations in which both parties have reasonable precautionary measures available to them. In order to minimize primary accident costs, it makes sense in such cases to encourage the person with the least costly method of avoiding the accident to do so. Where both parties are negligent, the cases fall into Category III.

## CATEGORY III: BOTH PARTIES ARE NEGLIGENT
### A. INJURER IS BEST COST AVOIDER

## B. VICTIM IS BEST COST AVOIDER

Category IIIA describes those situations in which both parties are negligent, but the injurer can avoid the accident at lower cost. Category IIIB describes those situations in which both parties are negligent, but the victim is the best cost avoider. The economic analysis of defenses in tort law focuses on whether the law provides incentives that lead to the minimization of accident costs.

### 1. CONTRIBUTORY NEGLIGENCE

#### BUTTERFIELD v. FORRESTER

Court of King's Bench, 1809.
11 East's Reports 59, 103 Eng.Rep. 926.

This was an action on the case for obstructing a highway, by means of which obstruction the plaintiff, who was riding along the road, was thrown down with his horse, and injured. At the trial * * *, it appeared that the defendant, for the purpose of making some repairs to his house, which was close by the road side at one end of the town, had put up a pole across this part of the road, a free passage being left by another branch or street in the same direction. That the plaintiff left a public house not far distant from the place in question at 8 o'clock in the evening in August, when they were just beginning to light candles, but while there was light enough left to discern the obstruction at 100 yards distance: and the witness, who proved this, said that if the plaintiff had not been riding very hard he might have observed and avoided it: the plaintiff however, who was riding violently, did not observe it, but rode against it, and fell with his horse and was much hurt in consequence of the accident; and there was no evidence of his being intoxicated at the time. On this evidence Bayley J. directed the jury, that if a person riding with reasonable and ordinary care could have seen and avoided the obstruction; and if they were satisfied that the plaintiff was riding along the street extremely hard, and without ordinary care, they should find a verdict for the defendant: which they accordingly did.

* * *

Lord Ellenborough C.J.

A party is not to cast himself upon an obstruction which has been made by the fault of another, and avail himself of it, if he do not himself use common and ordinary caution to be in the right. In cases of persons riding upon what is considered to be the wrong side of the road, that would not authorize another purposely to ride up against them. One person being in fault will not dispense with another's using ordinary care for himself. Two things must concur to support this action, an obstruction in the road by the fault of the defendant, and no want of ordinary care to avoid it on the part of the plaintiff.

[Judgment for the defendant was affirmed.]

## Notes and Questions

1. *Butterfield* is generally accepted as the case in which the English courts adopted the doctrine of contributory negligence, which relieves a negligent defendant of any liability if he can prove that the plaintiff was also negligent.

*Questions:* For which party in *Butterfield* was B<PL? Following the court's decision, are potential injurers or potential victims given an incentive to avoid such accidents in the future?

2. Contributory negligence cases necessarily involve situations in which both the plaintiff and the defendant could avoid the accident at reasonable cost.

*Questions:* If cost-justified precautionary measures are available to two or more parties, which should be given the incentive to avoid the accident if primary accident cost minimization is our goal? Is there any way to tell from the facts of *Butterfield* which party can avoid the accident at least cost?

3. The opinion in *Butterfield* clearly indicates that both parties were at fault. Factual circumstances like this fall into Category III of tort cases, for which there are two subcategories reflecting which party could have avoided the accident at least cost. For primary accident costs to be minimized, the least cost avoider of accidents must be given an incentive to take precautionary measures whenever they are less costly than the risks presented by the activity. The law must be structured so that the incentive is given to potential injurers in Category IIIA cases and to potential victims in Category IIIB cases. The following cases and notes illustrate alternative interpretations of reasonable care that create different incentives for injurers and victims.

## HAEG v. SPRAGUE, WARNER & CO., INC.

Supreme Court of Minnesota, 1938.
202 Minn. 425, 281 N.W. 261.

HOLT, JUSTICE.

Plaintiff got the verdict in this automobile collision case. Defendant appeals from the order denying its motion in the alternative for judgment notwithstanding the verdict or a new trial.

The impact occurred in daylight at the right-angle intersection, three miles south of the southern limits of the City of Minneapolis, of County Highway No. 52, also known as Nicollet Avenue, and rural Hennepin County Road, known as Eighty-Sixth Street South. The former lies north and south; the latter east and west. Plaintiff approached from the west, on Eighty-Sixth Street, in his ton and one-half Chevrolet truck; Harry Thompson, employee of defendant, and owner of a Chevrolet sedan, came from the south on Highway No. 52. Eighty-Sixth Street is a rough gravel road from 9 to 14 feet wide. Highway No. 52 has a smooth, bituminous-treated surface. Its "black top" is about 27 feet wide. From shoulder to shoulder its width is 36 to

37 feet. The country is flat. There is a clear view in all directions. There were no distracting circumstances on either road at the time of the collision.

We adopt defendant's argument that plaintiff was guilty of contributory negligence as a matter of law. So we must and do put the evidence in the light most favorable to plaintiff. Plaintiff testified to having seen Thompson's car at least four times at various distances south of the point of collision, and that it was traveling from 50 to 60 miles per hour until the collision. The first time plaintiff was about 200 feet west and going at about 30 miles an hour. Then Thompson was 400 to 500 feet to the south. When plaintiff was 30 feet from the intersection he saw Thompson's car 150 to 175 feet away. At that point plaintiff released his accelerator and let his truck coast at the rate, as he says, of about 20 miles an hour into the intersection.

Plaintiff's testimony is that as he entered the intersection Thompson's automobile was still about 100 to 125 feet south of it and apparently not slackening its speed. He testified that "I entered the intersection first, and I expected him to slack up and let me through." The next view plaintiff had of the oncoming car took place when the former was in the center of the intersection, halfway across, and the latter about 50 to 60 feet south. It does not appear at what speed Thompson's car was then going. The impact occurred about 13 feet east of the center line of the highway, on its eastern edge. * * *

* * *

It is important that, coming as it was, from plaintiff's right, Thompson's car had the statutory right of way unless the latter had forfeited such right by reason of excessive speed. The latter, as to both right of way and the forfeiture of it, were given to the jury by the charge. Thompson admits a speed of about 45 miles per hour until the moment when he saw plaintiff was not going to yield him the right of way. Then, so he testified, he applied the brakes until he got the machine down to "half speed" at the time and place of the collision. The jury must have chosen not to believe Mr. Thompson's testimony on that point. But this much is clear—plaintiff never entertained the thought of yielding the right of way, his intention all along being to get across Nicollet Avenue ahead of Thompson's car.

Plaintiff's case, all through, stresses reliance upon plaintiff's supposed right to assume that Mr. Thompson would have exercised ordinary care to avoid a collision. The latter's negligence must be taken as established by the verdict. Plaintiff's supposed reliance upon Mr. Thompson's exercise of due care is of no moment for the simple reason that this is a case, if ever there can be one, where such reliance was itself negligence. We stress again the obvious truth of fact and law that it is not due care to depend upon the exercise of care by another when such dependence is itself accompanied by obvious danger. Without binding plaintiff by his own testimonial estimate of speed, or by that of any other witness, we are not yet able to ignore this alternative.

Either Thompson's car had the right of way or it was being driven in excess of 45 miles per hour. So when plaintiff entered Nicollet Avenue, Thompson's car was so close and going at such rate of speed that it was the clearest kind of negligence for plaintiff not to stop. If Thompson was driving at 50 miles per hour, he was traveling 73 1/2 feet a second. He could not have stopped his car within 125 feet with instantaneous application of the brakes. And that stopping distance would be increased in proportion to the so-called reaction time needed by Mr. Thompson to apply the brakes after discovering the emergency. We do not hold plaintiff chargeable as with knowledge of such exact figures, or with consciousness, at the moment, of their import. But it is clear that the circumstances were such as to make a collision inescapable if he persisted, as he did, in his attempt to cross Nicollet Avenue ahead of Thompson.

* * *

No one can appreciate more than we the hardship of depriving plaintiff of his verdict and of all right to collect damages from defendant; but the rule of contributory negligence, through no fault of ours, remains in our law and gives us no alternative other than to hold that defendant is entitled to judgment notwithstanding the verdict. It would be hard to imagine a case more illustrative of the truth, that in operation, the rule of comparative negligence would serve justice more faithfully than that of contributory negligence. We but blind our eyes to obvious reality to the extent that we ignore the fact that in many cases juries apply it in spite of us. But as long as the legislature refuses to substitute the rule of comparative for that of contributory negligence we have no option but to enforce the law in a proper case. We cannot escape the conclusion that this case compels its application.

The order must be reversed with directions to enter judgment for defendant notwithstanding the verdict.

So ordered.

### Notes and Questions

1. In *Haeg* it was clear that both parties were negligent. The jury found that the defendant's employee, Thompson, was negligent, when it awarded the verdict to the plaintiff. Thompson had apparently been driving too fast for the prevailing conditions. The court found that the plaintiff, Haeg, was contributorily negligent. Haeg had failed to adjust his behavior to take into account the negligence of Thompson, incorrectly relying on a "supposed right to assume that Mr. Thompson would have exercised ordinary care to avoid a collision." The court held that relying on the other's exercise of due care "was itself negligence." As a result, the court reversed the jury's verdict for the plaintiff and entered judgment for the defendant. The comparative negligence rule to which the court referred would have apportioned liability between the two parties rather than assigned all the liability to the plaintiff. (Comparative negligence is discussed further in the materials following Scott v. Alpha Beta Company, below.)

2. Apparently either party, acting alone, could have avoided the accident in *Haeg* by slowing down. Either could have *unilaterally* prevented the collision. Consistent with minimizing primary accident costs, it would be efficient to have that party who could avoid the accident most easily be the one to take precautions. It would be duplicative and wasteful for both to take precautions if one party alone could avoid the accident. Following the accident discussed in *Haeg,* Thompson may very well want to sue Haeg for damages to his Chevrolet. But whichever party is the plaintiff will lose in this contributory negligence state, whether he is the best cost avoider of the accident or not.

> *Questions:* Under the contributory negligence rule as applied in Minnesota when *Haeg* was decided, would the incentives lead to primary accident cost minimization if the plaintiff was the least cost avoider of the accident? If the defendant was the least cost avoider?

3. The rule in *Haeg,* no absolute right to assume that other people are being careful, is clearly the dominant rule. See, *e.g.,* Prosser and Keeton on the Law of Torts (Keeton gen. ed. 5th ed. 1984) 198–199 ("[A] person is required to realize that there will be a certain amount of negligence in the world." "The duty to take precautions against the negligence of others thus involves merely the usual process of multiplying the probability that such negligence will occur by the magnitude of the harm likely to result if it does, and weighing the result against the burden upon the defendant of exercising such care."). The Restatement (Second) of Torts, § 466, says, "The plaintiff's contributory negligence may be * * * (a) an intentional and unreasonable exposure of himself to danger created by the defendant's negligence, of which danger the plaintiff knows or has reason to know." Section 302A is generally in accord, though it is addressed to the duty to protect others: "An act or an omission may be negligent if the actor realizes or should realize that it involves an unreasonable risk of harm to another through the negligent or reckless conduct of the other or a third person."

At least one judge appears to have a different interpretation of how the reasonable person is expected to behave. While the reasonable person will still avoid accidents only if the cost of avoidance is less than the risk presented, people are entitled to assume that other people are acting reasonably. Interpreting Illinois law in Pomer v. Schoolman, 875 F.2d 1262, 1268 (7th Cir. 1989), Judge Posner said, "A person cannot be deemed negligent for failing to take precautions against an accident that potential victims could avoid by the exercise of elementary care; negligence is failing to take the care necessary and proper to prevent injury to reasonably careful persons." And in a portion omitted from the excerpt of McCarty v. Pheasant Run, Inc., above, Posner said, "It is a bedrock principle of negligence law that due care is that care which is optimal given that the potential victim is himself reasonably careful; a careless person cannot by his carelessness raise the standard of care of those he encounters." While the first quote and beginning of the second may be interpreted as allowing injurers to assume that potential victims are acting reasonably, the latter part of the quote from *McCarty* makes it clear that potential victims are also entitled to assume that potential injurers will act reasonably. In his treatise, Economic Analysis of Law 155 (3d ed. 1986), Posner says that the law defines due care as "the care that is optimal if the other party is exercising due care."

*Questions:* If Haeg were entitled to assume that Thompson would act reasonably, how would that affect the legal outcome in *Haeg*? Would this entitlement affect the efficiency of the incentives provided in negligence cases fitting into Categories I (no negligence) and II (one person negligent)? Would including this entitlement in the definition of reasonable care affect the efficiency of incentives provided in contributory negligence cases, subcategories IIIA and IIIB?

4. The facts in *Haeg* are a bit unusual, in that the plaintiff actually observed the defendant acting carelessly. The rule in the Restatement (Second) of Torts § 466 is that plaintiffs have a duty to protect themselves from the negligence of others about which they know or *have reason to know*. The Restatement (Second) of Torts § 302A holds defendants to a stricter standard. A potential injurer is negligent if he realizes or *should* realize that his act involves an unreasonable risk of harm to another because of the other's negligent or reckless conduct. Levi v. Southwest Louisiana Electric Membership Cooperative illustrates the application of such a rule.

### LEVI v. SOUTHWEST LOUISIANA ELECTRIC MEMBERSHIP COOPERATIVE

Supreme Court of Louisiana, 1989.
542 So.2d 1081.

DENNIS, JUSTICE.

\* \* \*

The plaintiff, Giovanni Levi, an oil field roustabout-pumper for Amoco Oil Company, sustained near fatal permanently disabling injuries when the erected mast of a paraffin removal truck rig upon which he was working came in contact or close proximity with an uninsulated 14,400 volt electric distribution line being operated by Southwest Louisiana Electric Membership Cooperative (Slemco). The accident occurred on February 16, 1982 at the E.C. Stuart # 2 Well in the Section 28 Dome Field, in St. Martin Parish, an oil field owned by Amoco Oil Company. In the 1960's Slemco had constructed an uninsulated electrical distribution line to serve most of the 22 wells producing in the field. The power company routed the line so as to avoid crossing a well driveway or coming in close proximity to the well by placing the line either across the main road from the well or behind the well, with the exception of the E.C. Stuart # 2 Well where the line crossed the access road leading to the well 40.5 feet from the well head and 25.7 feet overhead. Slemco failed to avoid a driveway traversal or a close encounter between its line and the E.C. Stuart # 2 Well because that well was omitted from the power company's original construction plan due to oversight or to the fact that no electricity was supplied to this well or both.

\* \* \*

On the day of the accident Levi and another Amoco employee, while servicing wells in the field, found it necessary to dismantle the lubricator to make a repair. After borrowing some tools they looked for a dry place to work on the device. They did not intend to service the E.C. Stuart # 2 Well that day but in order to get off the main road and find a dry place to repair the rig they drove the truck into that well site and parked. The truck was headed toward the well with its front end approximately 3–4 feet from the well and its rear end approximately 15–16 feet from the point at which the high power line crossed the access road. It was necessary for the workers to raise the mast off the truck and lower the lubricator to the ground to make the repairs. Using control levers on the side of the truck, Levi raised the mast tip up, over the truck and back toward the power line. Levi had noticed the distribution line at this location on previous occasions but failed to pay attention to it on the day of the accident. Levi recalled only that he last saw the mast when it was at a 45 degree angle in front of the truck. Shortly thereafter, the mast either touched the power line or came close enough for electrical arcing to occur. 14,400 volts of electricity escaped from the power line and coursed through the mast, the truck and Levi's body.

As a result of the accident, Levi suffered the amputation of both legs just below the knees and severe burns over 25% of his body. At the time of the trial, he had been hospitalized 10 times for 11 different surgical procedures.

Levi filed suit against Slemco and its insurer. The case was tried before a jury. In response to written interrogatories, the jury found that Slemco's conduct did not fall below the reasonable standard of care. The trial court denied plaintiff's motions for a judgment notwithstanding the verdict and for a new trial. Levi appealed, and the court of appeal affirmed. This court granted writs to determine whether the principles of law had been applied correctly below * * *.

* * *

In the present case there is no dispute as to the fact that the power company had actual knowledge of the oil company's regular use of trucks with erectable high masts around its wells. Because this activity had continued on a regular basis over a long period of time the power company should have been aware of the physical characteristics of this equipment and any electrical hazard it might create. * * * Since the power company knew that its uninsulated 14,400 volt electric line passed near the oil wells at a level of only 25 to 26 feet above ground, the company should have known that electrical hazards would be created if masts were raised near the line.

* * *

We do not think reasonable minds can disagree with the conclusion that the power company, particularly with its superior knowledge, skill and experience in electrical safety, should have recognized that its conduct under these circumstances involved a risk of harm to oil field workers. Aside from the obvious serious possibility that an inattentive worker might raise the mast while parked on the access road too near the power line, there were similar chances that a falling mast could pass dangerously close to the line or that a careless roustabout might attempt to drive under the line on his way to another well without fully lowering his mast. The power company complains that it should not be charged with recognition of any risk that takes effect through a victim's negligence. But the ordinary reasonable person, and even more so the power company, is required to realize that there will be a certain amount of negligence in the world. When the risk becomes serious, either because the threatened harm is great, or because there is an especial likelihood that it will occur, reasonable care may demand precautions against "that occasional negligence which is one of the ordinary incidents of human life and therefore to be anticipated." It is not due care to depend on the exercise of care by another when such reliance is accompanied by obvious danger.

Moreover, the power company had actual knowledge of previous instances of oil field workers' negligence or inattentiveness in moving erect masts under or near the uninsulated power lines. Its own employee testified that he had warned other roustabout crews of danger on two previous occasions when they drove under the uninsulated electric line on a board road with their masts partially or fully erect.

\* \* \*

When the components of the evidence are brought into relief and weighed in the light of their interrelationships, reasonable minds must agree that the minimal burden of adequate precautions was clearly outweighed by the product of the chance and the gravity of the harm. Accordingly, the power company was guilty of negligence that was a legal cause of plaintiff's injuries, or, in other words, the company breached its duty to take precautions against the risk that took effect as those injuries, and the lower courts committed manifest error in not reaching this conclusion.

\* \* \*

Reversed and Remanded to the Court of Appeal.

### *Notes and Questions*

1. *Levi* is a Category III case where the court viewed both parties as negligent. The court did not consider the legal implications of that conclusion because it focused on the jury's finding that Slemco had acted reasonably. Louisiana is a comparative negligence state where a finding that both parties were negligent would permit Mr. Levi to recover at least some of his damages. The court held that Slemco had a duty to reduce risks to even a careless employee and that duty applied even when the probability of carelessness was less than certain, as it was in *Haeg*. The court's interpretation of due care required Slemco to take precautions to

avoid harm to Mr. Levi despite his carelessness—in fact, because of his likely carelessness.

2. Either party in *Levi* could have unilaterally prevented the electrocution. Slemco could have insulated the overhead wire. Mr. Levi could have avoided the accident by carefully scrutinizing the site and perhaps choosing another location for the repair of his lubricator. Either of these *unilateral avoidance measures* would have avoided the accident. If Levi had been careless, the insulation would have protected him. If Levi had been careful, the insulation would have been unnecessary. If we could ensure that one party would avoid the accident, it would be wasteful for both to bear the burden of avoiding the accident. Duplicative avoidance would more than double the cost compared to the least cost avoider doing so alone.

> *Questions:* Where unilateral avoidance by one party is the least costly way to avoid accidents, does the contributory negligence rule ever provide incentives for both parties to avoid the accident? Does the possibility of duplication depend on whether the defendant or plaintiff can avoid the accident at least cost? Does the possibility of duplication depend on whether Judge Posner's interpretation or the *Haeg* and *Levi* interpretation of reasonable care is followed?

3. In the full opinion in *Levi,* the court identified another precautionary technique, putting a warning sign on the power pole and an orange ball warning on the power line. The court concluded that the warning sign and orange ball would have called Mr. Levi's attention to the warning at the E.C. Stuart well, causing him to be more attentive to danger. This precaution requires that both parties work together to avoid the harm. *Cooperative precautionary measures* may be less expensive than the unilateral measures described in the previous question. Instead of insulating the wire or driving to another lubricating location (the more costly unilateral avoidance measures), a warning combined with greater attentiveness could produce the same result. Levi could use the more convenient location for repairing the lubricator and avoid the overhead wire by noting the location of the bright orange ball.

> *Questions:* Do contributory negligence rules provide proper incentives for both parties to take cooperative precautionary measures when they are a less costly means of avoiding the accident than unilateral means? Does your conclusion depend on whether Judge Posner's interpretation or the *Haeg* and *Levi* interpretations of "due care" apply?

4. Studying the efficiency characteristics of the contributory negligence rules naturally raises the issue of whether negligence law would be more efficient if there were no contributory negligence defense.

> *Questions:* Would a pure negligence rule (defendant is liable whenever he is negligent) lead to efficient results in Category I, II, and III cases? Does your conclusion depend on which interpretation of "due care" is followed?

### 2. LAST CLEAR CHANCE

## PERIN v. NELSON & SLOAN

California District Court of Appeal, Fourth District, 1953.
119 Cal.App.2d 560, 259 P.2d 959.

MUSSELL, JUSTICE.

This is an action for damages for personal injuries sustained by the plaintiff when a truck operated by one of the defendants' employees was backed onto plaintiff's foot. At the time of the accident plaintiff, who was a cement finisher, was engaged in smoothing and finishing a slab of cement which had been poured from defendants' transit mix truck. The area being poured was about 20 feet square. Plaintiff was on his knees at the south edge of the square reaching out to the north as far as he could, his feet approximately 24 inches from the cement, when the driver backed the truck onto the plaintiff's foot, imbedding it in the ground and injuring it. Plaintiff heard the noise of the truck and an order to "back it up", but he was intent on his work and did not see the truck when it was being backed.

The driver testified that after he had poured the cement in the east side of the square, he was told to back up; that he then backed his truck slowly; that as he started backing, he saw the plaintiff smoothing off the cement and "figured he had plenty of room to back up;" that it appeared to him that plaintiff was out of range of the wheels; that during all the time he was backing, he was watching plaintiff; that plaintiff was then on his knees on the ground smoothing the cement and did not look up at him.

The cause was tried before a jury and a verdict was returned in favor of plaintiff. Defendants appeal from the judgment thereupon entered.

While defendants state in their brief that a reversal of the judgement is sought on the grounds that the evidence is insufficient to sustain the judgment and that plaintiff was guilty of contributory negligence as a matter of law, their argument is directed to the contention that the trial court committed prejudicial error in instructing the jury on the doctrine of last clear chance.

The elements of this doctrine are set forth in Daniels v. City & County of San Francisco, where it said:

"Whether or not the doctrine of last clear chance applies in a particular case depends entirely upon the existence or nonexistence of the elements necessary to bring it into play. Such question is controlled by factual circumstances and must ordinarily be resolved by the fact-finder. An instruction stating the doctrine is proper when there is evidence showing: '(1) That plaintiff has been negligent and, as a result thereof, is in a position of danger from which he cannot escape by the exercise of ordinary care; and this includes not only where it is physically impossible for him to escape, but also in cases where he is totally unaware of his danger, and for that reason unable to escape; (2) that defendant has knowledge that the plaintiff is in such a situation, and knows, or in the exercise of ordinary care should know, that plaintiff cannot escape from such situation, and (3) has the last clear chance to avoid the accident by exercising ordinary care, and fails to exercise the same, and the accident results thereby, and plaintiff is injured as the proximate result of such failure.'"

In the instant case the uncontradicted evidence shows that plaintiff was in a position of danger. There is also evidence to support an inference that he was totally unaware of his danger and for that reason unable to escape. Plaintiff was not required to show that his ability to escape from his threatened danger was a physical impossibility. The doctrine applies equally if he was wholly aware of his danger, and for that reason unable to escape.

* * *

There was also substantial evidence that the truck driver had the last clear chance to avoid the accident by the exercise of ordinary care. Under the circumstances and conditions described in the record before us, the jury was entitled to determine whether the driver was aware, or in the exercise of the ordinary care should have been aware, of plaintiff's danger and had the last clear chance to avoid the accident.* * *

Defendants contend that plaintiff was guilty of contributory negligence as a matter of law and that his negligence was continuing up to the time of the accident. However, where as here, all of the elements of the last clear chance doctrine are present, the continuous negligence rule does not operate to the exclusion of the last clear chance doctrine.

Judgment affirmed.

## Notes and Questions

1. In *Perin*, the temporal element presents a new analytical dimension to the contributory negligence defense. Perin may very well have been negligent for failing to look up from his cement finishing when he heard the order for the truck to back up in his direction. Although California, at the time, followed the contributory negligence rule, the court concluded that recovery by the plaintiff would not be barred. When the particular factual circumstances described in the case occur, the last clear chance doctrine gives the defendant an incentive to avoid accidents by making him liable for all damages. As in *Haeg* and *Levi*, the defendant must take reasonable precautions to avoid risks created by the (here, known) negligence of others.

2. While it is clear that defendant was negligent in these cases (and therefore the cases belong in either Category II or III), describing the plaintiff's situation is not as simple. When trying to categorize last clear

chance cases according to the classification scheme suggested in this chapter, it is critical to recognize that the cases are of two sorts. The plaintiff may be in danger either because he is aware of the danger and it has become extraordinarily difficult for him to escape (a very high avoidance cost) or because he is unaware of the danger and therefore cannot avoid it until it is too late. Once the plaintiff has negligently put himself in peril and is unable to extricate himself, the factual circumstances sound very much like a Category II situation. At the time of the accident, only the defendant has available reasonable means to avoid the accident. The second type of case sounds very much like a Category III case; the plaintiff could avoid the accident at reasonable cost if only he would look up and notice the danger.

*Questions:* If the case is of the Category II variety, which of the parties is likely to be the best cost avoider of the accident? If the case is of the Category III variety, which of the parties is likely to be the best cost avoider of the accident? Does the last clear chance rule provide efficient incentives in both of these cases to minimize primary accident costs?

3. The last clear chance doctrine originated in the 1842 English case of Davies v. Mann, 10 M. & W. 546, 152 Eng. Rep. 588. The defendant negligently ran into the plaintiff's donkey, which the plaintiff had (also negligently) left tethered in the road. The plaintiff's negligence was held not to bar recovery because the defendant had the "last clear chance" to avoid the accident.

The facts of *Davies* and the considerable confusion surrounding the precise factual requirements and doctrinal reasons for the last clear chance rule have resulted in the rule being referred to as the "jackass" doctrine. There is no widely accepted single explanation for this exception to the general rule barring recovery in contributory negligence cases. Some courts allow the exception on grounds that the temporal element makes the plaintiff's negligence more remote, less proximate, to the injury and that the defendant's negligence is therefore a more substantial factor in producing the injury. Others have justified the rule on the grounds that the defendant's conduct amounted to gross negligence compared to plaintiff's ordinary negligence and that therefore recovery would not be barred. Despite the doctrinal confusions, the motivation for the doctrine is clear. Courts found that denying recovery was unduly harsh to plaintiffs, who might have been only slightly careless, and inappropriately generous to defendants, who were totally excused from the consequences of their own negligence.

Eventually, courts and legislatures responded to the apparent inequities and perhaps the inefficiencies in the contributory negligence doctrine by replacing it with comparative negligence. All but a very few of the comparative jurisdictions have eliminated the last clear chance doctrine altogether.

## 3. APPORTIONED COMPARATIVE NEGLIGENCE

### SCOTT v. ALPHA BETA COMPANY

California Court of Appeal, Second District, 1980.
104 Cal.App.3d 305, 163 Cal.Rptr. 544.

ASHBY, ASSOCIATE JUSTICE.

Plaintiff Phameline Scott slipped and fell in a grocery store of defendant Alpha Beta Company. A jury found defendant 60 percent negligent and plaintiff 40 percent negligent and awarded plaintiff $120,000 damages after reduction on account of her negligence. The trial court denied defendant's motions for judgment notwithstanding the verdict and for new trial. Defendant appeals from the judgment and the denial of its motion for judgment notwithstanding the verdict, contending there is no substantial evidence of negligence on its part. Plaintiff also appeals from the judgment, contending there is no substantial evidence of contributory negligence on her part.

At about 7 p. m. on September 10, 1976, plaintiff walked into defendant's grocery store at 3581 Century Boulevard in Lynwood. It was raining "kind of heavy" at the time, and had been raining all day.

Defendant's employees had placed a 20-foot long rubber mat inside the entrance to the store, because defendant's terrazzo floor was known to become slippery when wet. Normally the store has about 2,000 customers per day.

When plaintiff stepped off the rubber mat, she slipped; her leg went out from underneath her and she fell down. Lying on the floor, plaintiff noticed that the floor was wet.

Plaintiff suffered injury to her left knee and had surgery shortly after the accident. Her knee will never be normal and she may require further surgery or an artificial knee in the future.

\* \* \*

Dr. Silver testified on behalf of defendant that based upon a review of plaintiff's medical records in his opinion plaintiff had a weakness of the left leg and a "trick knee" prior to the accident, and that such condition was compounded by plaintiff's obesity. In his opinion it was possible plaintiff's knee gave out on her to cause her fall. This evidence is relevant not only on the issue of proximate cause but also on the issue of contributory negligence, the theory being that persons with known handicaps may have to exercise a greater degree of care in particular circumstances than other persons.

It was raining rather heavily and according to the defense witnesses plaintiff was wearing pink furry house slippers. A person in plaintiff's position might reasonably be expected to know that the floor adjacent to the mat could be wet, even without negligence on defendant's part, or that her slippers might remain wet when she reached the end of the mat. In her testimony plaintiff made no claim to having taken any special cautions in stepping from the mat to the floor. The jury might have thought plaintiff should have seen water on the floor. Under all the circumstances, we think the jury might reasonably conclude that plaintiff failed to exercise due care for her own safety.

\* \* \*

The judgment is affirmed. The order denying defendant's motion for judgment notwithstanding the verdict is affirmed.

## Notes and Questions

1. The jury in *Scott* applied the comparative negligence doctrine, which has replaced contributory negligence in the vast majority of states. In California, the damages are divided or apportioned between the parties in proportion to fault; whichever party is more negligent bears a larger portion of the damage. In *Scott*, the jury apparently thought that the store was more negligent, attributing 60% of the negligence to it, though it may be that the jury simply wanted the store to pay the larger share of the damages.

*Questions:* Under the comparative negligence system, which party has incentive to make the cost-benefit analysis involved in deciding whether or avoid the accident? Under the contributory negligence system, who would have been given the incentive to make the cost-benefit analysis in *Scott?*

2. In *Scott*, the defendant's 60% share of liability amounted to $120,000; Phameline Scott's total damages were $200,000. Unlike a pure negligence rule or a contributory negligence rule, where all of the loss falls on one party, each party in a comparative negligence jurisdiction must compare the cost of avoidance to the expected *share* of liability he will bear. A party's share is 100% if he or she alone is negligent, less than 100% if both are negligent.

*Questions:* Assume that each fall by a customer would present the same damage and apportionment of damages as in *Scott*. If the probability of a customer slipping is .01 and the cost of providing a safe surface is 50 cents per customer, would comparative negligence give the Alpha Beta store an incentive to provide a safe surface? If Ms. Scott's accident avoidance cost (the inconvenience of owning a pair of rubber soled shoes and wearing them instead of the pink furry house slippers) was 75¢ per trip to the store and the shoes would eliminate her 1% chance of slipping, would Ms. Scott have an incentive to avoid such accidents in the future? Do these incentives lead to the minimization of primary accident costs?

3. Opponents of comparative negligence often argue that the switch from contributory negligence will increase tertiary accident costs, the costs of administering the torts system.

*Question:* How is comparative negligence likely to increase tertiary costs borne by the victim, the injurer, the courts, and juries?

4. In a comparative negligence jurisdiction, the jury must determine which party was more negligent and how much more. It seems reasonable

to conclude that of two parties facing the same risk and doing nothing to prevent it, the party that could avoid the risk at lower cost is more negligent. If a store could avoid an accident with an expected cost of (.01 x $200,000) $2000 for 50 cents per customer and a customer could avoid it for 75 cents, the store appears to be more negligent.

It is less obvious how the jury decides "how much more" negligent one party is than the other. Justice Faulkner, in his dissent in Golden v. McCurry, offers a model of jury decisionmaking that is as appealing as any.

## GOLDEN v. McCURRY

Supreme Court of Alabama, 1980.
392 So.2d 815.

PER CURIAM.

The significant issue presented by this appeal is whether this Court should abolish the common law rule of contributory negligence and replace it with the rule of comparative negligence.

The basic facts giving rise to the lawsuit are as follows: Plaintiff Correll Golden had ridden home from work in a truck. He alighted from the truck and was crossing Highway 164 to reach his home which was located across the highway. Golden was struck by defendant McCurry's automobile while he was still on the travelled portion of the highway. Golden claimed in his lawsuit that his injuries were proximately caused by McCurry's negligence or wantonness. McCurry claimed that Golden's own negligence contributed to his injuries. Golden asked the court to strike McCurry's contributory negligence defense and adopt the doctrine of comparative negligence. The trial court refused; Golden then stipulated that he was 1% negligent; McCurry stipulated that he would contend throughout the trial that Golden was contributorily negligent and that Golden's negligence proximately contributed to his injuries. Both parties conducted pre-trial discovery.

Claiming that he was entitled to a judgment as a matter of law based upon the pleadings and discovery of record, defendant McCurry filed a motion for summary judgment, which the trial court granted. Golden appeals.

\* \* \*

After due and deliberate consideration, we hold that, even though this Court has the inherent power to change the common law rule of contributory negligence, it should, as a matter of policy, leave any change of the doctrine of contributory negligence to the legislature.

\* \* \*

FAULKNER, JUSTICE, dissenting in part and concurring in part.

\* \* \*

The question of whether contributory or comparative negligence should be adopted in this state is riddled with economic considerations. Judge Learned Hand formulated an algebraic equation to determine negligence: The defendant is liable if the loss (injury) caused by the accident multiplied by the probability of its occurrence is greater than the cost of avoiding the accident. *United States v. Carroll Towing Co.* The economically efficient solution, therefore, is to require the smaller cost to be incurred if it will prevent the larger accident cost.

In application to contributory negligence, if the plaintiff can prevent a $1000 accident at a cost of $50 and the defendant's avoidance cost is $100, the economically efficient solution is to refuse the plaintiff any recovery for failure to avoid the total loss at the lesser cost. If the defendant is liable in all instances without regard to the precautionary measures the plaintiff could have taken, there is no economic incentive for the plaintiff to avert the accident.

On the other hand, if the defendant is able to avoid the $1000 loss at a cost of $50 and the plaintiff's cost is $100, the defense of contributory negligence (assuming it is applicable) still mandates that the plaintiff cannot recover at all. In essence, therefore, this defense sanctions the least economically efficient solution because it provides no incentive for the defendant to spend the lesser avoidance cost cognizant that, if the plaintiff contributed even a little bit, the defendant will incur no liability (expense) at all.

The doctrine of comparative negligence—where the plaintiff's damages are diminished by the percentage of his own negligence that contributed to the accident—is not the panacea either. This doctrine tacitly advocates that more than the economically efficient amount of precautionary measures be taken. Using the same figures immediately above, if the defendant would be two-thirds liable and the plaintiff one-third liable, incurring $666.67 and $333.33 of the $1000 loss respectively, then both parties would opt for the lesser avoidance cost at an aggregate prevention cost of $150. This results in economic *inefficiency* because either amount alone would have been sufficient to avoid the total loss.

Conversely, neither party may decide to opt for the lesser avoidance cost in reliance upon the fact that the other party has an economic incentive to take precautionary measures. This results in compensating a total loss of $1000 that could have been avoided at the lesser amount of $50 or $100, individually, or at a collective amount of $150. Even though the combined expense of $150 is over precautionary, economically speaking, it is at least more economically efficient than incurring the total or partial accident expense.

This economic analysis becomes more intricate as we approach an examination of the respective forms of comparative negligence. I feel that we do this area of the law—and the public—a great disservice by failing to recognize, work through and resolve the economic issues endemic to this dilemma.

### *Notes and Questions*

1. It is quite possible that this case was intended to provoke a change in the law. Presumably knowing that the contributory negligence rule

would completely bar him from recovering any damages, Golden, the plaintiff, agreed ahead of time that he was negligent. If the contributory negligence rule was upheld, as it was by the Supreme Court of Alabama, Golden would get no damages at all. The trial court, under the contributory negligence rule, had no choice but to rule for McCurry. If the court decided to opt for comparative negligence, Golden had limited his risk by agreeing that he was only slightly negligent, 1%, compared to the defendant. Had the Supreme Court abandoned the contributory negligence rule in favor of comparative negligence, his recovery would have been diminished by only 1%.

2. When a state abandons the contributory negligence defense and adopts some form of the comparative negligence defense, the plaintiff's damage award is reduced by some proportion determined by the factfinder. Since the amount of damages each party must pay affects their incentives to avoid accidents in the future, it is important to know how that proportion is determined. Justice Faulkner offered the basic idea that since both parties were at fault they should divide damages in proportion to their fault, with the most careless person paying the most. Justice Faulkner thought that if one party could avoid the accident at half the cost of another then his failure to avoid the accident made him twice as negligent and his liability should be twice as great.

Using Faulkner's approach, each party's share of liability is determined by a ratio of his cost or burden of avoidance ("B" in the Learned Hand formula) to the other's burden of avoidance. In one of Faulker's examples, the potential injurer's burden of avoidance, $B_{injurer}$ was $50 and the potential victim's burden of avoidance, $B_{victim}$, was $100. The ratio of the two burdens is $50/$100, which is 1/2 (1 to 2). If the person who can avoid the accident at half the price should pay twice as much damages, as Faulkner suggests, then the ratio indicates that the injurer should pay $2 for every $1 to be paid by the victim.

> *Questions:* If the total damages are $60,000, how much would each party pay, using Faulkner's approach and numbers? If the ratio of victim's burden of avoidance to the injurer's was only 1% (1/100), as Golden stipulated, and if Golden's damages were $15,000, what would be McCurry's liability?

3. Employing Judge Faulkner's model for allocating shares of liability between parties, one can compare the relative efficiency of contributory and comparative negligence in any particular case. Assume that the following facts describe the situation faced by the parties in *Golden*. Either party can avoid using unilateral avoidance measures. If the accident occurs the loss to the plaintiff will be $15,000. The probability of the accident occurring if no precautions are taken is .01. The respective costs of avoidance for the injurer and victim are $1 and $100.

> *Questions:* Which party in *Golden* has an incentive to avoid future accidents of this sort? Is the comparative negligence rule efficient in this case? Are primary accident costs likely to be higher if a contributory negligence rule or comparative negligence rule is applied in this case?

4. Judge Faulkner offers the example of an expected loss of $1000 that can be avoided by the plaintiff for $100 and by the defendant for $50. He calculated correctly that the defendant would have to pay $666.67 and the plaintiff would have to pay $333.33, because the defendant would be two-thirds liable and the plaintiff one-third liable, and then concluded that both parties would opt for the lesser avoidance cost at an aggregate prevention cost of $150. "This" he claimed "results in economic inefficiency because either amount alone would have been sufficient to avoid the total loss." To check his conclusion that both would take precautions to avoid the accident, we need to know not only the loss and the burdens for both parties, but also the probability that this accident will occur again, P.

*Questions:* Is Judge Faulkner's example correct if the probability of an accident occurring is 12%? Is his analysis correct if the probability of an accident occurring is 36%? Are primary accident costs minimized by a contributory or comparative negligence rule if the probability is 12%? What if the probability is 36%?

5. Following Judge Faulkner's model of jury decisionmaking, the efficiency of the incentives provided by the comparative negligence rule depends on the relationships between PL and the burdens for the parties. Notes 3 and 4 illustrated that changing the probability that the accident will occur changes the efficiency of the incentives provided by the comparative negligence rules, assuming that the loss remains constant. Similar changes can be seen by changing the magnitude of the loss if the accident occurs or changing the burdens of the parties. The following question offers one last illustration of this property of comparative negligence.

*Questions:* Would application of the comparative negligence rule be efficient if P equals .001, L equals $10,000, $B_{injurer}$ equals $9 and $B_{victim}$ equals $8? Would comparative or contributory negligence minimize primary accident costs in this case?

6. Repeated examples would demonstrate that if avoidance costs for both parties are high relative to the risk, PL, then, as long as the parties have no right to assume that others will act carefully, neither has an incentive to avoid the accident and an insufficient amount is spent on accident avoidance. When avoidance costs for both parties are low relative to the risk, then both have an incentive to avoid the accident and an excessive amount is spent on accident avoidance. In all cases in between, the comparative negligence rule provides efficient incentives.

*Question:* Given their relative strengths and weaknesses in minimizing primary accident costs, is contributory negligence or comparative negligence the preferred doctrine?

## 4. NONAPPORTIONED COMPARATIVE NEGLIGENCE

### GALENA AND CHICAGO UNION RAILROAD COMPANY v. JACOBS

Illinois Supreme Court, 1858.
20 Ill. 478.

[Frederick Jacobs, a four and one-half year old boy, was run over by a locomotive on the tracks running past his parents home. Jacobs, through his lawyers, claimed that the accident was the result of the carelessness of the employees of the railroad company. The railroad claimed that the contributory negligence of the plaintiff prevents his recovery of any damages. The court reviewed a variety of cases where the defendant had claimed that the plaintiff was careless and adopted its own version of the contributory negligence defense.]

BREESE, J.

* * *

It will be seen, from these cases, that the question of liability does not depend absolutely on the absence of all negligence on the part of the plaintiff, but upon the relative degree of care or want of care, as manifested by both parties, for all care or negligence is at best but relative, the absence of the highest possible degree of care showing the presence of some negligence, slight as it may be. The true doctrine, therefore, we think is, that in proportion to the negligence of the defendant, should be measured the degree of care required of the plaintiff, that is to say, the more gross the negligence manifested by the defendant, the less degree of care will be required of the plaintiff to enable him to recover. Although these cases do not distinctly avow this doctrine in terms, there is a vein of it very perceptible, running through many of them, as, where there are faults on both sides, the plaintiff shall recover, his fault being to be measured by the defendant's negligence, the plaintiff need not be wholly without fault.

We say then, that in this, as in all like cases, the degrees of negligence must be measured and considered; and wherever it shall appear that the plaintiff's negligence is comparatively slight, and that of the defendant gross, he shall not be deprived of his action.

## Notes and Questions

1. For thirty years during the mid–1800's, Illinois, Tennessee, and Kansas experimented with the *Galena* rule. Also characterized as a "nonapportioned comparative negligence" rule, the *Galena* rule allowed plaintiffs to recover whenever their negligence was slight compared to defendant's. The courts' inability to define "slight" negligence along with the rise of traditional contributory negligence and other factors led to the eventual demise of the rule. But the economic characteristics of the *Galena* rule make it a particularly interesting object of study. For the purpose of this study, the rule is interpreted to mean that the plaintiff will not be denied full recovery unless his negligence is greater than that of the defendant. Another way to explain this rule is to say that the defendant is liable if he is negligent and his negligence is greater than that of the plaintiff.

Consider the six types of factual circumstances that have been discussed above:

CATEGORY I: NO NEGLIGENCE

A. INJURER IS BEST COST AVOIDER

B. VICTIM IS BEST COST AVOIDER

CATEGORY II: ONLY ONE PARTY NEGLIGENT
   A. INJURER IS BEST COST AVOIDER
   B. VICTIM IS BEST COST AVOIDER

CATEGORY III: BOTH PARTIES ARE NEGLIGENT
   A. INJURER IS BEST COST AVOIDER
   B. VICTIM IS BEST COST AVOIDER

*Question:* In which categories does the *Galena* rule provide efficient incentives?

2. The discussion following *Levi* introduced the distinction between unilateral and cooperative precautionary measures. Imagine that the *Galena* rule was applied to the facts of *Levi* and that the least costly method of preventing the accident was the cooperative efforts of the company suspending an orange warning ball on the wire and the employee using extra care (and the guidance provided by the ball).

*Question:* Would the *Galena* rule give the incentive for the parties to use the cooperative precautionary measures rather than the unilateral measures?

3. The South Dakota Comparative Negligence Statute reads in part:

In all actions brought to recover damages for injuries to a person or to his property caused by the negligence of another, the fact that the plaintiff may have been guilty of contributory negligence shall not bar a recovery when the contributory negligence of the plaintiff was slight in comparison with the negligence of the defendant, but in such case, the damages shall be reduced in proportion to the amount of plaintiff's contributory negligence.

Under this rule, the plaintiff's recovery is barred if he is more than slightly careless; if he is only slightly careless, his recovery is diminished slightly. This statute was presumably written to modify the harshness of the traditional contributory negligence statute, which denied all recovery even if the plaintiff was only slightly negligent.

*Question:* What are the efficiency implications of the South Dakota rule?

5. **ASSUMPTION OF RISK**

### ORDWAY v. SUPERIOR COURT
Court of Appeal, Fourth District, Division 3, 1988.
198 Cal.App.3d 98, 243 Cal.Rptr. 536.

CROSBY, ASSOCIATE JUSTICE.

\* \* \*

Judy Casella, a veteran jockey who had ridden in 500 professional horse races without incident, was thrown from her mount and further injured when the equine fell and rolled over her during a quarterhorse race at Los Alamitos Race Course on January 3, 1983. The tragic chain of events began when Over Shadow, owned by petitioner Homer Ordway, tangled with another steed, Speedy Ball, who then stumbled in front of Casella's horse. The California Horse Racing Board determined the jockey riding Over Shadow violated a board rule by "crossing over without sufficient clearance, causing interference," and he was suspended for five racing days. Alleging "negligence, carelessness and unlawful conduct," Casella sued the riders, trainers, and owners of Over Shadow and Speedy Ball.

\* \* \*

\* \* \* The correct rule is this: If the defendant's actions, even those which might cause incidental physical damage in some sports, are within the ordinary expectations of the participants—such as blocking in football, checking in hockey, knock-out punches in boxing, and aggressive riding in horse racing—no cause of action can succeed based on a resulting injury. It is of no moment that the participants may be penalized for these actions by the officials. Routine rule violations, such as clipping in football, low blows in boxing, and fouls in horse races are common occurrences and within the parameters of the athletes' expectations.

Here defendant jockeys were attempting to win a horse race. There has never been any suggestion that they, much less the owners of their horses, were motivated by a desire to injure plaintiff. Defendants' conduct, while perhaps negligent, was within the range to be anticipated by the other riders, or should have been. As a professional rider, Casella reasonably assumed the risk of her tragic injury. As with other persons who reasonably assume similar risks, her remedy was to purchase insurance from her athletic income beforehand, not to pursue a lawsuit against her counterparts in the sport afterward. The action, accordingly, is barred as a matter of law. Defendants are entitled to summary judgment.

### Notes and Questions

1. In *Ordway,* the jockey, Judy Casella, was denied recovery because she had knowingly and voluntarily assumed the risks inherent in horse racing. The economic analysis of defenses to liability based on negligence requires a determination of whether the jockey was the best cost avoider of the accident. Denying liability would then give the best cost avoider the incentive to avoid the accident. The difficulty in *Ordway* is that the injured jockey had apparently been riding carefully, while Over Shadow's jockey was careless enough to be sanctioned by the California Horse Racing Board.

Not racing at all is one precaution an individual can take to avoid being injured in a professional horse race. This may be the only available precaution, which is why people say that the risks are "inherent" in the sport. If so, then the race organizers and the horse owners can only avoid all injuries by not racing (or so drastically changing the rules that sport is fundamentally changed).

*Questions:* If these are the only available precautions, to what category of factual circumstances do such tort cases belong? What rule of liability minimizes primary and tertiary accident costs for this category of cases? Is the assumption of risk doctrine, which completely bars recovery in cases like this, an efficient rule?

2. *Ordway* falls into a group of assumption of risk cases commonly denominated *primary assumption of risk*. In this group of cases, it is not necessary to discuss either actor's negligence. Rather, the fact that the injured party was aware of and voluntarily accepted the risks presented relieves the defendant of any obligation to protect her. A typical example of such acceptance of risk and relief from responsibility is the baseball stadium, where the spectators' knowledge of the possibility of balls being hit into the stands relieves the stadium owner from having to screen in the entire stadium. The defendant is, therefore, not negligent for failing to take precautions and there is no fault on his part to balance against the victim's behavior. The plaintiff simply cannot recover.

3. Aggressive sporting activities and dangerous occupations may involve risks the participants do not knowingly and voluntarily assume.

*Question:* If a football player, angry at an opponent for tackling him just shy of a touchdown, jerks his opponent's helmet off and kicks him in the head, is it efficient to apply the doctrine of primary assumption of risk to prevent the opponent from recovering damages?

4. Justice Crosby distinguishes two dog bite cases. In one situation, the actual facts in Nelson v. Hall, 165 Cal.App.3d 709, 211 Cal.Rptr. 668 (1985), a rabid dog bit a veterinary assistant in the course of her work. In the other, a victim was bitten while foolishly attempting to pet a rabid dog negligently allowed to remain in a veterinarian's waiting room. The law would give different results in the two cases, denying recovery to the veterinary assistant and merely reducing the recovery (under comparative negligence) of the victim in the waiting room.

*Question:* Is there any economic basis for the distinction between these two cases?

### KELLY v. CHECKER WHITE CAB

Supreme Court of Appeals of West Virginia, 1948.
131 W.Va. 816, 50 S.E.2d 888.

HAYMOND, JUDGE.

The plaintiff, Violet Kelly, instituted this action of trespass on the case in the Circuit Court of Kanawha County to recover from the defendants Checker White Cab, Inc., a corporation, and its employee, Don Withrow, damages for personal injuries sustained by her when a taxicab owned by the company, driven by Withrow and in which she was riding as his guest, skidded and ran off a public highway in that county in the early morning of January 1, 1946. At the time of the wreck the taxicab was returning from Spencer to Charleston.

* * *

The plaintiff and her companion testified that, on the trip from Charleston to Spencer, Withrow drove the taxicab at a speed of thirty five to forty miles per hour, that the taxicab skidded three or four times, and that each time the plaintiff protested the speed at which he was driving she told him that if he did not reduce the speed she would get out. They also testified that on the return trip, between Spencer and Clendenin, a distance of about thirty miles, he drove at a speed of from fifty to sixty five miles per hour, that the taxicab slipped and skidded on the slippery road, and that they told him eight or nine times in that distance that he was driving too fast, that they were "scared to death," and that unless he slowed down they would get out. Their version was that after each protest he would reduce the speed until he thought they had forgotten but that in a short time he would again resume his excessive speed. They said that despite their protests he was driving on an icy stretch of road at the rate of sixty to sixty five miles per hour when they saw the truck approaching in front of them and that at that time both vehicles were traveling in the center of the highway.

* * *

The conduct of the defendant Withrow, in driving the taxicab from Charleston to the place at which it skidded from the highway, and especially from Spencer to that point, constituted clear and almost continuous negligence * * *.

* * *

The testimony of the plaintiff is that she observed the careless and dangerous manner in which the driver of the taxicab operated it between Charleston and Spencer and between Spencer and the scene of the wreck and that she protested vigorously against the speed at which he was driving three or four times before they arrived at Spencer and eight or nine times between Spencer and Clendenin. At both of those places he stopped a sufficient length of time to enable her to leave the taxicab if she had wanted to do so. She told him that she was "scared to death" and threatened to get out unless he reduced the speed. She knew that he gave no effective heed to any of her protests, that they were uttered in vain, that he had resumed the excessive speed after only temporarily reducing it following each protest, and that he would and did continue to travel at a speed which caused her to believe that her safety was endangered. She had realized her danger when she actually got out of the taxicab at Spencer and at Clendenin and she must have known that the threat to her safety would continue, as it did, if she did not finally leave it at either place. Yet, despite the fear which she expressed for her own safety, she again voluntarily entered the taxicab at Spencer and at Clendenin and continued to ride in it until the accident which she feared, and in which she was injured, actually occurred. The inconvenience or the hardship of retiring from the taxicab at an unseasonable hour of the morning and of remaining in Spencer or in Clendenin was ignored or declined by her at the fully apprehended risk of her own personal safety. Her decision to reject the one and to accept the other was not a legal excuse for her willingness to continue to ride toward her destination in Charleston. Her failure to quit the taxicab and remain out of it at Spencer or at Clendenin, which she had the fair and reasonable opportunity to do, defeats her right of recovery against the driver of the taxicab and relieves him of liability for her injury.

### *Notes and Questions*

1. Like Judy Ordway's, Violet Kelly's recovery was barred because she knowingly confronted and (apparently) willingly accepted a risk. The cases are different from both a legal and economic perspective, however, because in *Kelly* the defendant's negligence was proved. In *Ordway,* the court found that the defendant had no duty to protect Judy Ordway from the risk. Cases like *Kelly* are placed in the category of *secondary assumption of risk* cases. In secondary assumption of risk cases, the attention shifts from whether the defendant had a duty to protect the plaintiff to the character of the plaintiff's behavior.

2. The court characterized Violet's behavior saying "The inconvenience or the hardship of retiring from the taxicab at an unseasonable hour of the morning and of remaining in Spencer or in Clendenin was ignored or declined by her at the fully apprehended risk of her own personal safety." It does not seem to matter whether her behavior was reasonable or not. In this case, whether the victim was reasonable in assuming the risk did not seem to matter; the fact that she knowingly and voluntarily accepted it was enough. Under the modern view, however, the plaintiff's secondary assumption of a risk is a complete bar to recovery (in contributory negligence states) or a factor to be balanced against the defendant's conduct (in comparative negligence states), only if it was unreasonable to have assumed the risk.

*Question:* Is the modern rule, requiring that a knowing and voluntary assumption of the risk be unreasonable, more efficient at reducing primary accident costs than a rule that reduces (or bars) recovery even if the assumption of the risk was reasonable?

## D. NUISANCE LAW: ASSIGNING AND EXCHANGING RIGHTS

### 1. COMPETING USES AND THE COEXISTENCE OF PROPERTY RIGHTS

Conflicting uses of land may give rise to a tort claim when one actor's use of her land causes damage to another. However the rights to possession of land are initially assigned, there remains the question of which one of the conflicting uses shall be permitted. Assigning rights to property thus involves more than determining real estate boundaries. Property is not a patch of ground but a collection of rights to the exclusive use of resources. For example, ownership of real property may involve the right to occupy the land; the right to occupy or control the use of the airspace above the land to a particular altitude or even infinitely; the right to receive the sunlight and rain that falls on the land; the right to erect structures on the land that block light and rain from others; the right to clean air passing over the land; and the right to use air passing over the land to carry away smoke and other pollutants. Interference with these rights may constitute a nuisance. The cases in this section explore the criteria courts use in deciding to whom such rights should be assigned. At stake in these cases is who should bear the primary accident costs associated with activities on the land.

## BRYANT v. LEFEVER

Court of Appeals, 1879.
4 C.P.Div. 172, 48 L.J. 380, C.P.

Bramwell, L.J.:

The plaintiff says that he is possessed of a house, that for more than twenty years this house and its occupants have had the wind blow to, over and from it, and that he has, as so possessed, the right that it should continue to do so. That the defendants have interfered with this right and prevented the free access and departure of the wind. He adds that they have committed a nuisance to him as so possessed. He has proved that he is possessed of a house more than twenty years old, that the wind had access to it and passage over it for twenty years without the hindrance recently caused by the defendants; that the defendants have caused a hindrance by putting on the roof of their house (which is as old as the plaintiff's), timber to a considerable height, thereby preventing the wind blowing to and over the plaintiff's house when in some directions, and passing away from it when in others; that this causes his chimneys to smoke as they did not before, to the extent of being a nuisance. The question is if this shews a cause of action. First, what is the right of the occupier of a house in relation to air, independently of length of enjoyment? It is the same as that which land and its owner or occupier have, it is not greater because a house has been built. That puts no greater burthen or disability on adjoining owners. What then is the right of land and its owner or occupier? It is to have all natural incidents and advantages as nature would produce them. There is a right to all the light and heat that would come, to all the rain that would fall, to all the wind that would blow; a right that the rain which would pass over the land should not be stopped and made to fall on it, a right that the heat from the sun should not be stopped and reflected on it, a right that the wind should not be checked, but should be able to escape freely; and if it were possible that these rights were interfered with by one having no right, no doubt an action would lie. But these natural rights are subject to the right of adjoining owners, who for the benefit of the community have and must have rights in relation to that use and enjoyment of their property that qualify and interfere with those of their neighbours; right to use their property in the various ways in which property is commonly and lawfully used. A hedge, a wall, a fruit tree, would each affect the land next to which it was planted or built. They would keep off some light, some air, some heat, some rain when coming from one direction, and prevent the escape of air, of heat, of wind, of rain when coming from the other. But nobody could doubt that in such case no action would lie. Nor will it in the case of a house being built and having such consequences. That is an ordinary and lawful use of property as much so as the building of a wall or planting of a fence, or an orchard. Of course the same reasoning applies to the putting of timber on the top of a house which, if not a common, is a perfectly lawful act, and it would be absurd to suppose that the defendants could lawfully put another storey to their house with the consequences to the plaintiff of which he complains, but cannot put an equal height of timber. These are elementary and obvious considerations, but if borne in mind will assist very materially in the decision of this case.

* * *

But it is said, and the jury have found, that the defendants have done that which has caused a nuisance to the plaintiff's house. We think there is no evidence of this. No doubt there is a nuisance, but it is not of the defendants' causing. They have done nothing in causing the nuisance. Their house and their timber are harmless enough. It is the plaintiff who causes the nuisance by lighting a coal fire in a place the chimney of which is placed so near the defendants' wall that the smoke does not escape, but comes into the house. Let the plaintiff cease to light his fire; let him move his chimney; let him carry it higher, and there would be no nuisance. Who, then, causes it? It would be very clear that the plaintiff did, if he had built the house or chimney after the defendants had put the timber on their roof; and it is really the same though he did so before the timber was there. But (what is in truth the same answer) if the defendants cause the nuisance, they have a right to do so. If the plaintiff has not the right to the passage of air, except subject to the defendants' right to build or put timber on their house, then his right is subject to their right, and though a nuisance follows from the exercise of their right, they are not liable. *Sic utere tuo ut alienum no laedas* is a good maxim. But, in our opinion, the defendants do not infringe it. The plaintiff would, if he succeeded. We are of opinion that judgment should be for the defendants on the cause of action the subject of this appeal.

## COASE, THE PROBLEM OF SOCIAL COST *
### 3 J. L. & Econ. 1, 2, 13 (1960).

This paper is concerned with those actions of business firms which have harmful effects on others. The standard example is that of a

---

* Copyright 1959 by the University of Chicago.

factory the smoke from which has harmful effects on those occupying neighbouring properties. The economic analysis of such a situation has usually proceeded in terms of a divergence between the private and social product of the factory * * *. The conclusions to which this kind of analysis seems to have led most economists is that it would be desirable to make the owner of the factory liable for the damage caused to those injured by the smoke, or alternatively, to place a tax on the factory owner varying with the amount of smoke produced and equivalent in money terms to the damage it would cause, or finally, to exclude the factory from residential districts (and presumably from other areas in which the emission of smoke would have harmful effects on others). It is my contention that the suggested courses of action are inappropriate * * *.

\* \* \*

The traditional approach has tended to obscure the nature of the choice that has to be made. The question is commonly thought of as one in which A inflicts harm on B and what has to be decided is: how should we restrain A? But this is wrong. We are dealing with a problem of a reciprocal nature. To avoid the harm to B would inflict harm on A. The real question that has to be decided is: should A be allowed to harm B or should B be allowed to harm A? The problem is to avoid the more serious harm. * * *

\* \* \*

* * * Who caused the smoke nuisance [in Bryant v. LeFever]? The answer seems fairly clear. The smoke nuisance was caused both by the man who built the wall *and* by the man who lit the fires. Given the fires, there would have been no smoke nuisance without the wall; given the wall, there would have been no smoke nuisance without the fires. Eliminate the wall *or* the fires and the smoke nuisance would disappear. [I]t is clear that *both* were responsible and *both* should be forced to include the loss of amenity due to the smoke as a cost in deciding whether to continue the activity which gives rise to the smoke. * * *

The judge's contention that it was the man who lit the fires who alone caused the smoke nuisance is true only if we assume that the wall is the given factor. This is what the judges did by deciding that the man who erected the higher wall had a legal right to do so. The case would have been even more interesting if the smoke from the chimneys had injured the timber. * * * [T]here can be little doubt that the man who lit the fires would have been liable for the ensuing damage to the timber, in spite of the fact that no damage had occurred until the high wall was built by the man who owned the timber.

### *Notes and Questions*

1. In *Bryant,* a pollution case with a novel twist, only the person emitting the smoke suffers the harm. The factual complexity giving rise to the lawsuit is that before the neighbors added another story to their house and piled lumber on top, the wind drew the smoke up the chimney just fine.

The argument that the neighbors were the *cause* of the smoke backing up in the chimney is quite appealing. If the neighbors were required to pay damages, then they would have an incentive to internalize the costs of their construction activities.

From Coase's perspective, however, both parties were engaged in activities which, when combined, resulted in damage. If there is no natural or obvious way to determine which party "causes" the harm in an incompatible uses case, the court's decision boils down to which party's use should be protected, the storage of lumber or the drafting of smoke. According to Coase, the problem is to "avoid the more serious harm"; that is, to protect the use with the greater value. Another way to phrase the question is to ask which party should internalize the costs of the activities, that is, be given an incentive to decide whether the activity should continue, cease, or be modified in some way.

Even though both the plaintiff and the defendant could take some action to minimize the cost, one party could avoid the detriment at less cost. Suppose that if the plaintiff must bear the cost of the smoking chimney, his only alternative is building his chimney higher, at a cost of £60. If the defendant must bear the cost, he might store his timber elsewhere, which would eliminate the plaintiff's harm but result in storage fees of £20 per year. Ignoring the distributional implications, eliminating the harm for £20 is preferred. The same benefit is achieved more inexpensively by making the person who can avoid the injury at the lowest cost liable for the costs.

Realizing that sometimes one party may be better able to avoid the harms of incompatible uses has led law and economics scholars to support rules placing liability on the party who can avoid the injury at the lowest cost, the *best cost avoider*. Ronald Coase's observation that every party to the injury "causes" the injury removes the moral overtones, the aura of blameworthiness, associated with conflicting land uses and allows analysts to focus on maximizing the value of land use. The "best cost avoider" approach supplies a substitute for the "causation" approach.

2. If the plaintiff could avoid the smoke only by building a new chimney for £40 and the defendant could avoid the injury only by renting storage space for £20, the defendant is the best cost avoider. But if the defendant does not have the £20, he will be unable to rent the storage space or pay the £40 for damages. Since neither choice is viable, his only alternative is to cease storing timber. Suppose that storing wood is the defendant's occupation. Putting the defendant out of work may seem to be a harsh result if the plaintiff is wealthy enough to build a higher chimney.

*Question:* Could such a result possibly be economically efficient?

3. Imagine that the plaintiff could avoid the injury by maintaining a higher chimney at a cost of £60 per year and the defendant could avoid the injury only by building a separate structure to hold his timber, at the cost of £50 per year. The plaintiff's damage, if neither of these precautions is taken, is £40 per year.

*Question:* If the injury can only be avoided by means that are more expensive than the cost of the accident, is making the best cost avoider liable still allocatively efficient?

## STURGES v. BRIDGMAN

Chancery Division, 1879.
XI C.D. 852.

THESIGER, L.J.:

The Defendant in this case is the occupier, for the purpose of his business as a confectioner, of a house in *Wigmore Street.* In the rear of the house is a kitchen, and in that kitchen there are now, and have been for over twenty years, two large mortars in which the meat and other materials of the confectionery are pounded. The Plaintiff, who is a physician, is the occupier of a house in *Wimpole Street,* which until recently had a garden at the rear, the wall of which garden was a party-wall between the Plaintiff's and the Defendant's premises, and formed the back wall of the Defendant's kitchen. The Plaintiff has, however, recently built upon the site of the garden a consulting-room, one of the side walls of which is the wall just described. It has been proved that in the case of the mortars, before and at the time of action brought, a noise was caused which seriously inconveniences the Plaintiff in the use of his consulting-room, and which, unless the Defendant had acquired a right to impose the inconvenience, would constitute an actionable nuisance. The Defendant contends that he had acquired the right * * * by uninterrupted [use] for more than twenty years.

* * * [T]he laws governing the acquisition of easements by [use] stands thus: Consent or acquiescence of the owner of the [affected land] lies at the root of prescription. * * * [A] man cannot, as a general rule, be said to consent to or acquiesce in the acquisition by his neighbour of an easement through an enjoyment of which he has no knowledge, actual or constructive, or which he contests and endeavours to interrupt, or which he temporarily licenses. It is a mere extension of the same notion, or rather it is a principle into which by strict analysis it may be resolved, to hold, that an enjoyment which a man cannot prevent raises no presumption of consent or acquiescence. * * *

It is said that if this principle is applied in cases like the present, and were carried out to its logical consequences, it would result in the most serious practical inconveniences, for a man might go—say into the midst of the tanneries of Bermondsey, or into any other locality devoted to a particular trade or manufacture of a noisy or unsavoury character, and, by building a private residence upon a vacant piece of land, put a stop to such trade or manufacture altogether. The case also is put of a blacksmith's forge built away from all habitations, but to which, in course of time, habitations approach. We do not think that either of these hypothetical cases presents any real difficulty. As regards the first, it may be answered that whether anything is a nuisance or not is a question to be determined, not merely by an abstract consideration of the thing itself, but in reference to its circumstances; what would be a nuisance in Belgrave Square would not necessarily be so in Bermondsey; and where a locality is devoted to a particular trade or manufacture carried on by the traders or manufacturers in a particular and established manner not constituting a public nuisance, Judges and juries would be justified in finding and may be trusted to find, that the trade or manufacture so carried on in that locality is not a private or actionable wrong. As regards the blacksmith's forge, that is really an *idem per item* case with the present. It would be on the one hand in a very high degree unreasonable and undesirable that there should be a right of action for acts which are not in the present condition of the adjoining land, and possibly never will be any annoyance or inconvenience to either its owner or occupier; and it would be on the other hand in an equally degree unjust, and from a public point of view, inexpedient that the use and value of the adjoining land should, for all time and under all circumstances, be restricted and diminished by reason of the continuance of acts incapable of physical interruption, and which the law gives no power to prevent. The smith in the case supposed might protect himself by taking a sufficient curtilage to ensure what he does from being at any time an annoyance to his neighbour, but the neighbour himself would be powerless in the matter. Individual cases of hardship may occur in the strict carrying out of the principle upon which we found our judgment, but the negation of the principle would lead even more to individual hardship, and would at the same time produce a prejudicial effect upon the development of land for residential purposes. The Master of the Rolls in the Court below took substantially the same view of the matter as ourselves and granted the relief which the Plaintiff prayed for, and we are of opinion that his order is right and should be affirmed * * *.

## *Notes and Questions*

1. The confectioner in *Sturges* argued that he had acquired a right to use his noisy mortars because he had used them without uninterruption for more than twenty years (the period traditionally held sufficient to acquire an "easement by prescription" in England). During those years, the plaintiff-doctor had no way to know about the defendant's mortars. Therefore, the doctor was in no position either to have objected or acquiesced to their use. Without the actual or constructive knowledge necessary to challenge the use, the court holds, the presumption of acquiescence (the foundation for an easement by prescription) is untenable and no easement is granted.

2. Having disposed of the issue of priority in time, Lord Justice Thesiger established that whether an activity is a nuisance depends on all the circumstances, in particular, where the activity is carried out and which party was in the best position to take precautions to avoid harming those whose land uses came later (a blacksmith could, at the time of setting up his shop, acquire sufficient surrounding land that what he does would be no annoyance to his neighbors).

*Question:* From the perspective of allocating resources to their most valuable uses, why are these factors relevant to whether a use is a nuisance?

3. Lord Justice Thesiger was explicitly promoting the development of cities and towns: "From a public point of view, [it would be] inexpedient that the use and value of the adjoining land should, for all time and under all circumstances be restricted and diminished by reason of the continuance of acts incapable of physical interruption." Yet he clearly was concerned with residential development even though the plaintiff in *Sturges* wanted to develop his residence to further his medical practice: "The negation of this principle would * * * produce a prejudicial effect upon the development of land for residential purposes."

From an efficiency perspective, there is no obvious reason to believe that land is generally valued more for residential than industrial or business purposes. The Lord Justice decided that residential use was more valuable but did not indicate what evidence supported his decision. Without evidence as to the value of competing uses, he relied on evidence about the neighborhood's characteristics and, inevitably, on his own values.

*Questions:* Is there a significant danger that the Lord Justice's closer identification with the doctor, a fellow professional, than with the confectioner, a tradesman, would affect his judgment about the relative value of their activities, about the significance of development of land for residential uses? Could class biases of this sort result in the inefficient allocation of land?

## 2. THE COASE THEOREM AND THE EFFICIENT EXCHANGE OF RIGHTS

In a free market with no obstacles to bargaining between the parties, voluntary exchange allocates goods to their most valuable uses. The previous section illustrated courts' attempts to wrestle with cases where the economic issue is the allocation of "costs" rather than goods. In his classic article, The Problem of Social Cost (which may have inspired the law and economics movement), Ronald Coase presented the fundamental insight that voluntary exchange not only allocates goods efficiently, but *costs* as well. Coase proposed that, as long as the parties can bargain freely, they will eventually come to an agreement that minimizes the costs or harms resulting from incompatible property uses. He noted, "It is always possible to modify by transactions in the market the initial legal delimitation of rights. And, of course, if such market transactions are costless, such a rearrangement of rights will always take place if it would lead to an increase in the value of production." That proposition, known as the *Coase Theorem,* is often stated as follows: As long as there are no obstacles to bargaining between the parties involved, resources will be allocated efficiently regardless of how property rights are initially assigned.

Coase's Theorem is a dramatic assertion because it means that, if there are no transaction costs, judges do not affect the allocative efficiency of resource use by assigning rights or liability to one party or the other. As Coase put it, "It is necessary to know whether the damaging business is liable or not for damage caused since without the establishment of this initial delimitation of rights there can be no market transactions to transfer and recombine them. But the ultimate result (which maximizes the value of production) is independent of the legal position if the pricing system is assumed to work without cost. * * * Judges have to decide on legal liability but this should not confuse economists about the nature of the economic problem involved." The excerpted opinions devote much attention to justifying their chosen assignments of rights. Coase's Theorem, however, implies that time could be saved by simply assigning rights randomly. If parties seeking conflicting land uses can bargain about which use should prevail, the party who values his use most highly will always prevail.

Consider the application of Coase's Theorem to *Fontainebleau Hotel*. Does it matter whether the law assigns a property right to cast a shadow to the Fontainebleau, or a right to sunlight to the Eden Roc?

## FONTAINEBLEAU HOTEL CORP. v. FORTY-FIVE TWENTY-FIVE, INC.

District Court of Appeals of Florida, 1959.
114 So.2d 357.

PER CURIAM.

This is an interlocutory appeal from an order temporarily enjoining the appellants from continuing with the construction of a fourteen-story addition to the Fontainebleau Hotel, owned and operated by the appellants. Appellee, plaintiff below, owns the Eden Roc Hotel, which was constructed in 1955, about a year after the Fontainebleau, and adjoins the Fontainebleau on the north. Both are luxury hotels, facing the Atlantic Ocean. The proposed addition to Fontainebleau is being constructed twenty feet from its north property line, 130 feet from the mean high water mark of the Atlantic Ocean, and 76 feet 8 inches from the ocean bulkhead line. The 14-story tower will extend 160 feet above grade in height and is 416 feet long from east to west. During the winter months, from around two o'clock in the afternoon for the remainder of the day, the shadow of the addition will extend over the cabana, swimming pool, and sunbathing areas of the Eden Roc, which are located in the southern portion of its property.

* * *

The chancellor heard considerable testimony on the issues made by the complaint and the answer and, as noted, entered a temporary injunction restraining the defendants from continuing with the construction of the addition. His reason for so doing was stated by him, in a memorandum opinion, as follows:

"In granting the temporary injunction in this case the Court wishes to make several things very clear. * * * It is based solely on the proposition that no one has a right to use his property to the injury of another. In this case it is clear from the evidence that the proposed use by the Fontainebleau will materially damage the Eden Roc. There is evidence indicating that the construction of the proposed annex by the Fontainebleau is malicious or deliberate for the purpose of injuring the Eden Roc, but it is scarcely sufficient, standing alone, to afford a basis for equitable relief."

This is indeed a novel application of the maxim *sic utere tuo ut alienum non laedas*. This maxim does not mean that one must never use his own property in such a way as to do any injury to his neighbor. It means only that one must use his property so as not to injure the lawful *rights* of another. In Reaver v. Martin Theatres, under this maxim, it was stated that "it is well settled that a property owner may put his own property to any reasonable and lawful use, so long as he does not thereby deprive the adjoining landowner of any right of enjoyment of his property *which is recognized and protected by law, and so long as his use is not such a one as the law will pronounce a nuisance.*" [Emphasis supplied by this Court.]

No American decision has been cited, and independent research has revealed none, in which it has been held that—in the absence of some contractual or statutory obligation—a landowner has a legal right to the free flow of light and air across the adjoining land of his neighbor. * * *

There being, then, no legal right to the free flow of light and air from the adjoining land, it is universally held that where a structure serves a useful and beneficial purpose, it does not give rise to a cause of action, either for damages or for an injunction under the maxim *sic utere tuo ut alienum non laedas,* even though it causes injury to another by cutting off the light and air and interfering with the view that would otherwise be available over adjoining land in its natural state, regardless of the fact that the structure may have been erected partly for spite.

We see no reason for departing from this universal rule. * * *

Since it affirmatively appears that the plaintiff has not established a cause of action against the defendants by reason of the structure here in question, the order granting a temporary injunction should be and it is hereby reversed with directions to dismiss the complaint.

### *Notes and Questions*

1. Nowhere in its discussion of the parties' relative rights does the court in *Fontainebleau* consider whether the Eden Roc's sunny swimming pool or the Fontainebleau's 14-story addition was more valuable. Finding no precedent for giving a landowner a legal right to the flow of sunlight across a neighbor's adjoining land, the Florida Court of Appeals resolved the issue without considering which use was more valuable. A court determined to allocate resources to their most valuable uses would have to

acknowledge that sometimes the right to sunlight is valuable, especially to Miami Beach hotels.

The facts of *Fontainebleau* provide an opportunity to illustrate the Coase Theorem that, absent impediments to exchange, the court's initial allocation of the right will not affect the ultimate efficiency of resource use. The mere existence of damage to the Eden Roc does not mean that the addition to the Fontainebleau was not the more valuable use. If the addition added $1,000,000 annually to the Fontainebleau's profits while reducing the Eden Roc's profits by only $500,000 annually, then using the land for the addition increased the value of beachfront property in Miami Beach. If these values are correct, then the court reached an efficient result, without explicitly attempting to do so.

*Questions:* If the court had come out the other way, had granted an injunction halting the construction, would the Eden Roc have enforced the injunction or would the owners of the Fontainebleau have paid the Eden Roc to allow them to build? How much would the Fontainebleau be willing to pay annually?

2. Suppose that the tower would damage the Eden Roc ($750,000 in lost profits annually) more than it would aid the Fontainebleau ($500,000 additional annual profits).

*Questions:* If the parties could bargain freely, would the Eden Roc's owners be willing and able to pay more to stop the construction than the Fontainebleau would gain by having the construction? Would bargaining lead to an efficient allocation of resources? If the court enjoined construction under these facts, what result would the Fontainebleau's bargaining produce?

3. Reexamine Sturges v. Bridgman and Bryant v. Lefever. According to Coase, the possibility of bargaining eliminates the need for the court to find whose land use is more valuable.

*Question:* Would bargaining have ensured that the most valuable use prevailed in each of those cases regardless of how the court ruled?

## PRAH v. MARETTI

Supreme Court of Wisconsin, 1982.
108 Wis.2d 223, 321 N.W.2d 182.

ABRAHAMSON, JUSTICE.

\* \* \*

According to the complaint, the plaintiff is the owner of a residence which was constructed during the years 1978–1979. The complaint alleges that the residence has a solar system which includes collectors on the roof to supply energy for heat and hot water and that after the plaintiff built his solar-heated house, the defendant purchased the lot adjacent to and immediately to the south of the plaintiff's lot and commenced planning construction of a home. The complaint further states that when the plaintiff learned of defendant's plans to build the house he advised the defendant that if the house were built at the proposed location, defendant's house would substantially and adversely affect the integrity of plaintiff's solar system and could cause plaintiff other damage. Nevertheless, the defendant began construction. The complaint further alleges that the plaintiff is entitled to "unrestricted use of the sun and its solar power" and demands judgment for injunctive relief and damages.

\* \* \*

This court's reluctance in the nineteenth and early part of the twentieth century to provide broader protection for a landowner's access to sunlight was premised on three policy considerations. First, the right of landowners to use their property as they wished, as long as they did not cause physical damage to a neighbor, was jealously guarded.

Second, sunlight was valued only for aesthetic enjoyment or as illumination. Since artificial light could be used for illumination, loss of sunlight was at most a personal annoyance which was given little, if any, weight by society.

Third, society had a significant interest in not restricting or impeding land development. This court repeatedly emphasized that in the growth period of the nineteenth and early twentieth centuries change is to be expected and is essential to property and that recognition of a right to sunlight would hinder property development. \* \* \*

Considering these three policies, this court concluded that in the absence of an express agreement granting access to sunlight, a landowner's obstruction of another's access to sunlight was not actionable. These three policies are no longer fully accepted or applicable. They reflect factual circumstances and social priorities that are now obsolete.

First, society has increasingly regulated the use of land by the landowner for the general welfare.

Second, access to sunlight has taken on a new significance in recent years. In this case the plaintiff seeks to protect access to sunlight, not for aesthetic reasons or as a source of illumination but as a source of energy. Access to sunlight as an energy source is of significance both to the landowner who invests in solar collectors and to a society which has an interest in developing alternative sources of energy.

Third, the policy of favoring unhindered private development in an expanding economy is no longer in harmony with the realities of our society. The need for easy and rapid development is not as great today as it once was, while our perception of the value of sunlight as a source of energy has increased significantly.

Courts should not implement obsolete policies that have lost their vigor over the course of the years. The law of private nuisance is better suited to resolve landowners' disputes about property development in the 1980's than is a rigid rule which does not recognize a landowner's interest in access to sunlight. \* \* \*

\* \* \* Recognition of a nuisance claim for unreasonable obstruction of access to sunlight will not prevent land development or unduly hinder the use of adjoining land. It will promote the reasonable use and enjoyment of land in a manner suitable to the 1980's. That obstruction of access to light might be found to constitute a nuisance in certain circumstances does not mean that it will be or must be found to constitute a nuisance under all circumstances. The result in each case depends on whether the conduct complained of is unreasonable.

Accordingly we hold that the plaintiff in this case has stated a claim under which relief can be granted.

## Notes and Questions

1. Assuming that there are no impediments to bargaining between Prah and Maretti, the Coase Theorem states that bargaining will inevitably produce an efficient allocation of sunlight, whether to Maretti's house or to Prah's solar collectors. The failure to halt construction of the hotel addition in *Fontainebleau* meant that the plaintiff would have to take the initiative in bargaining with the defendant. It might appear that the only consequence of the Wisconsin Supreme Court recognizing that blocking sunlight could be a nuisance in *Prah* is that in Wisconsin the defendant would have to take the initiative in bargaining with the plaintiff. Ronald Coase believed that: "[W]ithout the establishment of [an] initial delimitation of rights there can be no market transactions to transfer and recombine them." In other words, the courts' only role is to ensure that rights are clearly assigned to *someone*. If the initial allocation is clear, the parties are in a position to discuss a reallocation.

*Question:* Justice Abrahamson apparently believed that recognizing a right to sunlight would promote the development of alternative energy sources. If the Coase Theorem is correct can Justice Abrahamson also be correct?

2. *The Invariance Hypothesis:* According to the Coase Theorem, if building the new home is worth more to the Marettis than the sunlight is worth to Prah, the new home will be built so long as the Marettis have enough funds to bribe Prah into allowing it. If sunlight is more valuable to Prah than the new construction is to the Marettis, the Marettis will not build their home so long as Prah has sufficient funds to bribe them not to. The court's decision is irrelevant to the efficient allocation of resources and what the court does appears to have no effect on the property's ultimate use. In other words, rights will end up with the party willing to pay the most for them, and the court's original allocation of right has no effect on that willingness to pay.

This interpretation of the Coase Theorem is referred to as the "Invariance Hypothesis" or the "Strong Version" of the Coase Theorem. The Invariance Hypothesis posits that as long as no obstacles to transactions exist between affected parties, the allocation of resources will be efficient *and* that efficient allocation of resources will be the same regardless of how property rights are initially assigned.

The Invariance Hypothesis is derived from an example involving a cattle raiser and a neighboring farmer developed by Coase to explain his theory. To simplify Coase's example somewhat, assume that the cattle raiser's cow is worth $5 and can be expected to stray and damage $10 of the farmer's crops. To appreciate the possibility that the allocation of resources does not depend on the rights assignment, consider three allocation questions:

a. Will the rights assignment affect whether the rancher keeps the cow? If the rancher has the right to let her cow trample the farmer's crops, the farmer has an incentive to offer the rancher a payment in return for the rancher getting rid of the cow. The farmer would pay up to $10 to avoid the damage from the cow. This is more than the cow is worth, so a rational rancher is likely to allow herself to be bribed, for some amount between $5 and $10, to get rid of the cow. But if the rancher does not have the right to trample the farmer's crops, the rancher will also get rid of the cow, preferring to get rid of a $5 cow rather than pay $10 for the damage it causes.

b. Will the rights assignment affect whether a fence is built to contain the cow? Perhaps the cow could be prevented from trampling the crops by building a fence between the two properties. Assume that the cost of the fence would be $3. If the rancher has the right to let her cow trample the farmer's crop, the farmer will build the $3 fence—this is cheaper than either suffering $10 in crop damage, or giving the rancher a bribe between $5 and $10 to get rid of the cow. And once again, if the rancher does not have the right to trample the farmer's crops, the rancher will build the fence. A $3 fence is cheaper than either paying $10 in damages or getting rid of a $5 cow. Either way, the fence gets built.

c. Will the rights assignment affect whether the farmer plants crops? Suppose that the cow destroyed crops worth $10, but which cost $8 to grow. If the rancher has the right to let her cow trample the farmer's crops, the farmer will stop growing crops altogether. The farmer is unwilling to pay more than $2—the net value of the destroyed crops—as a bribe to the rancher, and the rancher will not accept such a small amount to get rid of a $5 cow. Similarly, if the rancher does not have the right to trample the farmer's crops, the rancher will pay the farmer a bribe not to plant. After all, if the crops are planted the rancher will either have to pay $10 in damages or get rid of a $5 cow; it is less expensive to pay the farmer a bribe between $2 and $5 not to plant. Once again, whether the right is assigned to the farmer or the rancher, no crops are planted.

Part of the symmetry in outcomes is explained by the fact that the potential for exchange appears to internalize otherwise-external costs completely. For the rancher, the damage done by the cow is a cost whether she has to compensate the farmer for his loss, or simply give up the opportunity to get a payment from the farmer by keeping the cow. Similarly, if the farmer has the right to exclude the cow, excluding it is a cost because he gives up the opportunity to get a payment. If the farmer does not have the right, then excluding the cow costs him the amount of the payment he must make. The assignment of rights determines who receives and who pays bribes, but the allocation of resources to crops, cattle, and fences does not vary.

Coase's version of these hypothetical situations is only slightly more complicated. He assumed that the increased crop damage as the herd got larger was as shown below:

| Size of Herd (No. of Cows) | Annual Crop Loss (in dollars) |
|---|---|
| 1 | 1 |
| 2 | 3 |
| 3 | 6 |
| 4 | 10 |

If the cattle raiser has the right to trample the farmer's crop, the farmer has an incentive to bargain with her to keep the size of the herd relatively small. The farmer is willing to pay an amount equal to the damage done by a cow to prevent the cattle raiser from increasing her herd size. Thus, the farmer would pay up to one dollar to avoid the damage from the first cow, two dollars (the *additional* damage done) to prevent the herd from increasing from one to two cows, three dollars (the *additional* damage done by adding the third cow) to prevent the herd from expanding from two cows to three, and four dollars (the *additional* damage done by adding the fourth cow) to prevent expansion from three to four. The cattle raiser will decide how large a herd to have depending on the bribe the farmer is willing to pay and how much each cow is worth in the market for beef. If each cow is worth enough, no bribe that the farmer is willing to pay will reduce the herd size, but if each cow is worth $3.50 as beef, then the cattle raiser would rather take a bribe greater than $3.50 not to add the cow to her herd. Since the farmer is willing to pay an amount up to four dollars, the bribe is likely to occur if there are no obstacles to bargaining.

If the cattle raiser has no right to trample the farmer's crops, the cattle raiser has an incentive to bargain with the farmer to allow her cattle to trample. The cattle raiser is willing to pay an amount no greater than the value of each cow to have trampling rights. Once again, if each cow is worth $3.50, the cattle raiser will have a herd of three, because she will not be able to strike a bargain for rights to the fourth, which would add an additional four dollars in crop loss to the farmer, more than that cow is worth to the cattle raiser.

3. Limitations on the Invariance Hypothesis: Those challenging the Invariance Hypothesis generally focus on the conclusion that the allocation of resources is unaffected by the assignment of rights rather than the conclusion that the allocation will be efficient. The most obvious problem with the Invariance Hypothesis involves the parties' relative willingness and ability to buy rights. The initial assignment of rights *does* affect the parties' relative wealth. Since a party's willingness and ability to pay are affected by wealth, the assignment of a right to one party may determine the outcome in terms of the actual uses to which resources are put.

To understand the wealth effects of the rights assignment, consider how a rancher's valuation of her pet dog depends on how rights are assigned. Suppose that the rancher's dog can be expected to stray and kill $10 of a neighboring farmer's chickens. The dog could be restrained with a $3 fence. If the rancher had the right to let her dog roam free, the farmer would be willing to build the $3 fence to avoid the $10 in lost chickens. But if the rancher must pay for the dog's damage, and if the rancher is too poor to build a $3 fence—the dog must go. Implicit in the farmer's willingness to build the fence is the assumption that the rancher was unwilling to accept less than $3 to get rid of the dog. If the rancher must pay for the damage, however, and is poor, the rancher may not be willing and able to pay $3 to build the fence. The result in both cases is efficient. However, the initial allocation of the rights, by affecting the parties' willingness and ability to pay, has changed which outcome is efficient. The rancher valued the dog at more than $3 when assigned the right to let it roam free, so building a $3 fence made economic sense to the farmer. When forced to pay for its damage, the rancher valued the dog at less than $3, so building a $3 fence did not make economic sense to her.

The limitations of the Invariance Hypothesis have led many economists to adopt the version of the Coase Theorem with which this section started: As long as there are no obstacles to transactions between affected parties, the resources will be allocated efficiently regardless of how property rights are initially assigned.

*Questions:* The discussion of the invariance of the allocative efficiency that would result from bargaining in *Prah* in Question 2 above included two qualifications: "so long as the Marettis have enough funds to bribe Prah" and "so long as Prah has sufficient funds to bribe the Marettis." How is the wealth of Prah and the Marettis affected by the assignment of rights? Might the distribution of wealth affect whether the residence gets built or whether the solar collectors continue to receive sunlight?

4. *Partial Equilibrium Analysis:* If the use of solar collectors is widespread, recognizing the right to bring a nuisance action for blocking sunlight will have effects beyond parties to the suit and beyond bargains between future adjacent landowners whose uses conflict. Among those effects is a decrease in the value of undeveloped land located near homes with solar collectors. The use to which such land can be put is diminished by recognizing the right and so the land's value is diminished; the portions of the land on which large homes can be built are limited. Recognizing the right will also affect the market for undeveloped land and will have corresponding distributional effects, benefitting those who already have already built homes and harming those who would like to develop property. Those effects are externalities, harms and benefits resulting from the assignment of rights that are not taken into account in the process of assigning the right.

When determining whether a reallocation is efficient, economists frequently ignore external effects, such as price changes in a market other than the one under consideration, and wealth redistribution effects. These effects may be significant. Analysis focuses on the allocation of resources in a single market after bargaining has taken place, when the market is in *equilibrium*. Economists often ignore distributional effects or effects on the allocation of other resources, referring to them as secondary or "second order" effects. Examining effects in one market at a time simplifies analysis that otherwise would be too complicated. Sometimes it is necessary to focus on just part of a question, do a *partial* analysis, in order to gain any useful answer at all. Recognizing that the analysis of a single market in equilibrium is only part of the larger picture, economists describe such analysis as *partial equilibrium analysis.*

The analysis of each of the cases thus far has been partial equilibrium analysis that ignores many effects of property rights assignments on wealth distribution and on markets for other resources. While partial equilibrium analysis is useful, many apparently efficient bargains between individuals have effects other than those considered in the partial analysis.

5. *General Equilibrium Analysis:* An assignment of rights has effects that ripple out beyond a single market. A *general equilibrium analysis* considers the wealth effects of a property rights assignment in numerous markets. Even if changes in the parties' wealth resulting from being assigned or denied the property right are not sufficiently large to influence the final allocation of the resource in question, those changes still affect the parties' purchasing habits in two ways. First, since a wealth transfer between parties occurred, the winner now has command over resources that formerly the loser commanded. If the winner and loser spend their money differently, the allocation of other resources shifts in favor of those the winner values. The allocation is still efficient, but who is valuing those uses has changed. If winner and loser have different values, different preferences, the allocation of resources will change.

In addition, the winner's increase in wealth may alter the winner's preferences. Wealthy people are more likely to acquire yachts than are poor people. A poor person must satisfy her nautical desires by renting rowboats. As an individual becomes wealthier, she may be willing and able to devote more resources to luxuries than to basics. The winner's demand for fine wine increases while her demand for jug wine decreases. The loser's altered preferences may exactly compensate for the changes in the winner's tastes, but an exact match is extremely unlikely.

Thus, from both general and partial equilibrium perspectives, the ultimate allocations of resources resulting from alternative property rights assignments will all be efficient (assuming there are no transaction costs) but the allocations may be different.

6. Reexamine Sturges v. Bridgman and Bryant v. Lefever in light of the Coase Theorem, recognizing the limitations of the Invariance Hypothesis. The possibility of bargaining eliminates the need for the court to find who is the best cost avoider of the injuries. Whoever is assigned liability for injuries caused by the conflicting land use will negotiate with the other to find who could avoid the injury at least cost and then pay that person (if it is the other party) to take the appropriate precautions. Where bargaining is possible, the bargaining rather than the court determines the best cost avoider of the injury.

*Questions:* Would bargaining have ensured that the most valuable use prevailed in each of those cases regardless of how the court ruled? Assume that the plaintiff in *Bryant,* the owner of the fireplace, was poor. Would his ultimate ability to use the fireplace depend on whether he was granted the injunction? Would the character of the ultimate use have been invariant regardless of how the court ruled?

## E. TRESPASS AND NUISANCE: TRANSACTION COSTS AND IMPEDIMENTS TO BARGAINING

### 1. TRESPASS, THE COASE THEOREM, AND TRANSACTION COSTS

The Coase Theorem states that as long as there are no obstacles to transactions between affected parties, bargaining will ensure an efficient allocation of resources regardless of how property rights are initially assigned. The key to appreciating the Coase Theorem is understanding the implications of the assumption that there are no obstacles to transactions between affected parties. The following cases examine when obstacles to bargaining arise, the efficiency implications of those transaction costs, and legal mechanisms for promoting allocative efficiency when transaction costs are substantial. They involve the tort of trespass, an invasion of an individual's right to exclusive possession of his property. Ordinarily, an actor's intentional invasion of this right will subject the actor to liability for damages for invasion of the rights that are presumed without proof of actual harm ("nominal" damages) as well as "actual" damages for harms the plaintiff can prove he has suffered. A corollary of the right to damages is the limited right to eject trespassers. Under circumstances described in the following cases, however, the normal rules are modified reflecting the difficulties inherent in bargaining during emergencies.

### PLOOF v. PUTNAM
Supreme Court of Vermont, 1908.
81 Vt. 471, 71 A. 188.

Munson, J.

It is alleged as the ground of recovery that on the 13th day of November, 1904, the defendant was the owner of a certain island in Lake Champlain, and of a certain dock attached thereto, which island and dock were then in charge of the defendant's servant; that the plaintiff was then possessed of and sailing upon said lake a certain loaded sloop, on which were the plaintiff and his wife and two minor children; that there then arose a sudden and violent tempest, whereby the sloop and the property and persons therein were placed in great danger of destruction; that, to save these from destruction, or injury, the plaintiff was compelled to, and did, moor the sloop to defendant's dock; that the defendant, by his servant, unmoored the sloop, whereupon it was driven upon the shore by the tempest, without the plaintiff's fault; and that the sloop and its contents were thereby destroyed, and the plaintiff and his wife and children cast into the lake and upon the shore, receiving injuries. This claim is set forth in two counts * * * charging that the defendant by his servant * * * willingly and designedly unmoored the sloop [and] alleging that it was the duty of the defendant by his servant to permit the plaintiff to moor his sloop to the dock, and to permit it to remain so moored during the continuance of the tempest, but that the defendant by his servant, in disregard of this duty, negligently, carelessly, and wrongfully unmoored the sloop. [The defendant objected to both claims on the grounds that he had the right to eject trespassers from his property.]

There are many cases in the books which hold that necessity, as an inability to control movements inaugurated in the proper exercise of a strict right, will justify entries upon land and interferences with personal property that would otherwise have been trespasses. * * *

This doctrine of necessity applies with special force to the preservation of human life. One assaulted and in peril of his life may run through the close of another to escape from his assailant. One may sacrifice the personal property of another to save his life or the lives of his fellows. * * *

It is clear that an entry upon the land of another may be justified by necessity, and that the declaration before us discloses a necessity for mooring the sloop. But the defendant questions the sufficiency of the counts because they do not negative the existence of natural objects to which the plaintiff could have moored with equal safety. The allegations are, in substance, that the stress of a sudden and violent tempest compelled the plaintiff to moor to defendant's dock to save his sloop and the people on it. The averment of necessity is complete, for it covers not only the necessity of mooring, but the necessity of mooring to the dock * * * .

[The judgment of the trial court denying the defendant's motion for summary judgment on the grounds that the allegations were insufficient to state a cause of action was affirmed.]

### *Notes and Questions*

1. *Ploof* presents another case of conflicting uses of resources—in this instance, the defendant's dock. Mr. Putnam, through his servant, was protecting his right to exclusive possession of the land and dock. The plaintiff, Mr. Ploof, valued the dock as a means of preventing harm to his family and boat. Property owners like Mr. Putnam are normally protected against interference with their right to exclusive possession by the law of trespass. Under the doctrine of trespass by necessity, however, Mr. Ploof's intrusion is not only allowed but protected; Ploof was awarded damages because his sloop was unmoored from defendant Putnam's dock. The court permitted the plaintiff to use the dock, in furtherance of a public policy valuing human life more than the right to exclusive possession of property.

Applying the private necessity doctrine involved the court in the question of which party's use of the dock is more valuable. As the Coase Theorem suggests, it may have been necessary for the law to assign the right to one of the parties so that they would have a reference point for bargaining about departures from that assignment of rights. This does not explain why the law should recognize a private necessity defense.

*Questions:* If the defendant has a right to exclusive possession, would bargaining between the parties lead to an efficient outcome? What are the transaction costs in private necessity cases generally?

2. To arrange a mutually beneficial exchange of rights, parties must become aware of the potential gains of exchange, identify the other party with whom they hope to exchange, establish communication with that party, negotiate the terms of the exchange, and then perform the exchange. At each stage, impediments may arise and costs may be incurred.

When discussing the court's opinion in *Sturges,* Coase argued that "[i]t was of course the view of the judges that they were affecting the working of the economic system—and in a desirable direction. * * * The judges' view that they were settling how the land was to be used would be true only in the case in which the costs of carrying out the necessary market transactions exceeded the gains which might be achieved by any rearrangement of rights." Coase recognized that sometimes the costs of bargaining to reallocate rights exceed the efficiency benefits of reallocation. In such a case, the least expensive course of action is to suffer the inefficiency, unless rights can be redefined to facilitate bargaining or an efficient outcome.

In reality, market transactions almost always involve some costs, and sometimes substantial ones. In many factual circumstances like the one in *Ploof,* transaction costs prevent the efficient reallocation of rights through bargaining and the initial allocation of rights made by the court may be the final allocation. In such cases, the court's decision matters very much to the efficient allocation of resources.

3. If transaction costs prevent bargaining from allocating resources efficiently, then substitutes for bargaining may maximize societal welfare. One substitute might be legal rules that permit a party who values a resource more highly to take that resource from its owner and pay damages. Another alternative would employ a court or other decisionmaker to allocate the resource directly to those who (the decisionmaker believes) value the resource most highly and forbid bargaining over reallocations. In the following excerpt, Calabresi and Melamed describe rules requiring bargaining before rights can be exchanged as *property rules.* The alternatives are characterized as *liability rules* and *inalienability rules,* respectively. The discussion of Vincent v. Lake Erie Transport Co., which follows the excerpt from Calabresi and Melamed, employs that nomenclature in evaluating the efficiency implications of the private necessity doctrine introduced in *Ploof.*

## CALABRESI AND MELAMED, PROPERTY RULES, LIABILITY RULES, AND INALIENABILITY: ONE VIEW OF THE CATHEDRAL *

85 Harv.L.Rev. 1089, 1092–93, 1105 (1972).

Only rarely are Property and Torts approached from a unified perspective. Recent writings by lawyers concerned with economics and by economists concerned with law suggest, however, that an attempt at integrating the various legal relationships treated by these subjects would be useful both for the beginning student and the sophisticated scholar. By articulating a concept of "entitlements" which are protected by property, liability, or inalienability rules, we present one framework for such an approach. * * *

* * *

An entitlement is protected by a property rule to the extent that someone who wishes to remove the entitlement from its holder must buy it from him in a voluntary transaction in which the value of the entitlement is agreed upon by the seller. * * *

Whenever someone may destroy the entitlement if he is willing to pay an objectively determined value for it, the entitlement is protected by a liability rule. This value may be what it is thought the original holder of the entitlement would have sold it for. But the holder's complaint that he would have demanded more will not avail him once the objectively determined value is set. * * *

An entitlement is inalienable to the extent that its transfer is not permitted between a willing buyer and a willing seller. * * *

It should be clear that most entitlements to most goods are mixed. Taney's house may be protected by a property rule in situations in which Marshall wishes to purchase it, by a liability rule where the government decides to take it by eminent domain, and by a rule of inalienability in situations where Taney is drunk or incompetent. * * *

* * *

Whenever society chooses an initial entitlement it must also determine whether to protect the entitlement by property rules, by liability rules, or by rules of inalienability. In our framework, much of what is generally called private property can be viewed as an entitlement protected by a property rule. No one can take the entitlement to private property from the holder unless the holder sells it willingly and at the price at which he subjectively values the property. Yet a nuisance with sufficient public utility to avoid an injunction has, in effect, the right to take property with compensation. In such a circumstance the entitlement to the property is protected only by what we call a liability rule: an external, objective standard of value used to facili-

* Copyright © (1972) by the Harvard Law Review Association.

tate the transfer of the entitlement from the holder to the nuisance. Finally, in some instances we will not allow the sale of the property at all, that is, we will occasionally make the entitlement inalienable.

## VINCENT v. LAKE ERIE TRANSPORT CO.

Supreme Court of Minnesota, 1910.
109 Minn. 456, 124 N.W. 221.

O'BRIEN, J.

The steamship Reynolds, owned by the defendant, was for the purpose of discharging her cargo on November 27, 1905, moored to plaintiff's dock in Duluth. While the unloading of the boat was taking place a storm from the northeast developed, which at about 10 o'clock p.m., when the unloading was completed, had so grown in violence that the wind was then moving at 50 miles per hour and continued to increase during the night. There is some evidence that one, and perhaps two, boats were able to enter the harbor that night, but it is plain that navigation was practically suspended from the hour mentioned until the morning of the 29th, when the storm abated, and during that time no master would have been justified in attempting to navigate his vessel, if he could avoid doing so. After the discharge of the cargo the Reynolds signaled for a tug to tow her from the dock, but none could be obtained because of the severity of the storm. If the lines holding the ship to the dock had been cast off, she would doubtless have drifted away; but, instead, the lines were kept fast, and as soon as one parted or chafed it was replaced, sometimes with a larger one. The vessel lay upon the outside of the dock, her bow to the east, the wind and waves striking her starboard quarter with such force that she was constantly being lifted and thrown against the dock, resulting in its damage, as found by the jury, to the amount of $500.

We are satisfied that the character of the storm was such that it would have been highly imprudent for the master of the Reynolds to have attempted to leave the dock or to have permitted his vessel to drift a way from it. * * *

The appellant contends * * * that, because its conduct during the storm was rendered necessary by prudence and good seamanship under conditions over which it had no control, it cannot be held liable for any injury resulting to the property of others, and claims that the jury should have been so instructed. An analysis of the charge given by the trial court is not necessary, as in our opinion the only question for the jury was the amount of damages which the plaintiffs were entitled to recover, and no complaint is made upon that score.

The situation was one in which the ordinary rules regulating property rights were suspended by forces beyond human control, and if, without the direct intervention of some act by the one sought to be held liable, the property of another was injured, such injury must be attributed to the act of God, and not to the wrongful act of the person sought to be charged. If during the storm the Reynolds had entered the harbor, and while there had become disabled and been thrown against the plaintiffs' dock, the plaintiffs could not have recovered. Again, if while attempting to hold fast to the dock the lines had parted, without any negligence, and the vessel carried against some other boat or dock in the harbor, there would be no liability upon her owner. But here those in charge of the vessel deliberately and by their direct efforts held her in such a position that the damage to the dock resulted, and, having thus preserved the ship at the expense of the dock, it seems to us that her owners are responsible to the dock owners to the extent of the injury inflicted.

\* \* \*

Theologians hold that a starving man may, without moral guilt, take what is necessary to sustain life; but it could hardly be said that the obligation would not be upon such person to pay the value of the property so taken when he became able to do so. And so public necessity, in times of war or peace, may require the taking of private property for public purposes; but under our system of jurisprudence compensation must be made.

Let us imagine in this case that for the better mooring of the vessel those in charge of her had appropriated a valuable cable lying upon the dock. No matter how justifiable such appropriation might have been, it would not be claimed that, because of the overwhelming necessity of the situation, the owner of the cable could not recover its value.

This is not a case where life or property was menaced by any object or thing belonging to the plaintiff, the destruction of which became necessary to prevent the threatened disaster. Nor is it a case where, because of the act of God, or unavoidable accident, the infliction of the injury was beyond the control of the defendant, but is one where the defendant prudently and advisedly availed itself of the plaintiffs' property for the purpose of preserving its own more valuable property, and the plaintiffs are entitled to compensation for the injury done.

Order affirmed.

Lewis, J.

I dissent. It was assumed on the trial before the lower court that appellant's liability depended on whether the master of the ship might, in the exercise of reasonable care, have sought a place of safety before the storm made it impossible to leave the dock. The majority opinion assumes that the evidence is conclusive that appellant moored its boat at respondent's dock pursuant to contract, and that the vessel was lawfully in position at the time the additional cables were fastened to the dock, and the reasoning of the opinion is that, because appellant made use of the stronger cables to hold the boat in position, it became liable under the rule that it had voluntarily made use of the property of another for the purpose of saving its own.

In my judgment, if the boat was lawfully in position at the time the storm broke, and the master could not, in the exercise of due care, have left that position without subjecting his vessel to the hazards of the storm, then the damage to the dock, caused by the pounding of the boat, was the result of an inevitable accident. If the master was in the exercise of due care, he was not at fault. The reasoning of the opinion admits that if the ropes, or cables, first attached to the dock had not parted, or if, in the first instance, the master had used the stronger cables, there would be no liability. If the master could not, in the exercise of reasonable care, have anticipated the severity of the storm and sought a place of safety before it became impossible, why should he be required to anticipate the severity of the storm, and, in the first instance, use the stronger cables?

I am of the opinion that one who constructs a dock to the navigable line of waters, and enters into contractual relations with the owner of a vessel to moor at the same, takes the risk of damage to his dock by a boat caught there by a storm, which event could not have been avoided in the exercise of due care, and further, that the legal status of the parties in such a case is not changed by renewal of cables to keep the boat from being cast adrift at the mercy of the tempest.

## Notes and Questions

1. *Vincent* establishes that the right to trespass on another's property in a private emergency does not include the right to cause physical damage to the property. According to the majority, the ship owner is liable for actual damages if he acted to save his own property at the expense of another's, regardless of whether it was prudent. He is not liable for nominal damages. Using the terminology of Calabresi and Melamed, in an emergency, the dock owner's right to the dock was protected by a liability rule rather than a property rule. If protected by a property rule, the dock owner would be entitled to forbid any boat from using his dock during a storm. A boat in distress would have to bargain with the dock owner. If protected by a liability rule, the dock owner would not be entitled to forbid any boat owner from tying up at his dock during a storm but would be able to collect from the boat owner any damages to the dock caused by the boat's presence.

> *Questions:* What would it mean to assign the right to the boat owner and protect it by a property or liability rule? What kind of rule was adopted in *Ploof?* To whom was the right assigned and how was it protected in *Vincent?* Are the legal rules in *Ploof* and *Vincent* inconsistent?

2. If no obstacles to bargaining existed between the parties in *Vincent,* the party with the greater willingness and ability to pay to protect his property could exclude the other party. If bargaining cannot occur and there is no obligation to pay damages, one party would be able to impose external costs on the other.

*Questions:* Given the factual circumstances, was there any reason to protect the dock owner's right by a liability rule rather than a property rule? Are the incentives created for the boat owners by making them pay damages likely to lead to an efficient result? In these factual circumstances, are the incentives created by a liability rule more likely to give an efficient result than those created by the property rule?

3. *Vincent* illustrates how, when substantial impediments to bargaining exist between the parties, liability rules may be superior to property rules as a means of internalizing costs that would otherwise be external to one of the decisionmakers. Having decided on a liability rule rather than a property rule, it still must be decided who should be liable to whom. If the dock owner bears the costs of incompatible uses, he will be forced to choose between suffering injury to his dock or setting the boat adrift and risking liability under the rule in *Ploof.* Alternatively, if the boat owner bears the costs of incompatible uses, the boat owner (or captain) must choose between the risks of letting the boat drift and liability for damage to the dock under *Vincent.*

*Question:* Are the two parties in equivalent positions to evaluate the risk or is one party in the better position to evaluate the risks and act so as to minimize the risk?

4. In his dissent, Justice Lewis argued that the situation in *Vincent* differed from the usual emergency because the parties had a contractual relationship. That suggests that they had an opportunity to negotiate the allocation of the risks presented by potential emergencies. He believed that the risk of dock damage was part of the dock owner's cost of doing business.

*Question:* Should the contractual relationship between the parties make any difference to the assignment of liability in this case?

## 2. NUISANCE, IMPEDIMENTS TO BARGAINING, AND THE CHOICE OF REMEDIES

The *Ploof* and *Vincent* cases deal with trespass, a one-time invasion of another's property right to exclusive use of a resource. Those cases illustrated the fact that in some trespasses, the parties have little opportunity to bargain. The trespasser may not have anticipated the trespass, and the person whose resource is invaded frequently is not even present for bargaining when the trespass occurs. Nuisance cases that involve a chronic, continuing invasion of another's right present different problems. The fundamental inquiry, however, is still whether there is any reason why, when one person's enjoyment of her resource is disturbed on a continuing basis by another's noise, vibration, or pollution, the parties cannot get together and bargain themselves into an efficient outcome. The following cases explore various transaction costs that may prevent allocative efficiency and raise questions about the efficiency of alternative remedies available to courts.

## BOOMER v. ATLANTIC CEMENT COMPANY

Court of Appeals of New York, 1970.
26 N.Y.2d 219, 309 N.Y.S.2d 312, 257 N.E.2d 870.

BERGAN, JUDGE.

Defendant operates a large cement plant near Albany. These are actions for injunction and damages by neighboring land owners alleging injury to property from dirt, smoke and vibration emanating from the plant. A nuisance has been found after trial, temporary damages have been allowed; but an injunction has been denied. * * *

* * *

* * * The total damage to plaintiffs' properties is * * * relatively small in comparison with the value of defendant's operation and with the consequences of the injunction which plaintiffs seek.

The ground for the denial of injunction, notwithstanding the finding both that there is a nuisance and that plaintiffs have been damaged substantially, is the large disparity in economic consequences of the nuisance and of the injunction. This theory cannot, however, be sustained without overruling a doctrine which has been consistently reaffirmed in several leading cases in this court and which has never been disavowed here, namely that where a nuisance has been found and where there has been any substantial damage shown by the party complaining an injunction will be granted.

* * *

Although the court at Special Term and the Appellate Division held that injunction should be denied, it was found that plaintiffs had been damaged in various specific amounts up to the time of the trial and damages to the respective plaintiffs were awarded for those amounts. * * *

The court at Special Term also found the amount of permanent damage attributable to each plaintiff, for the guidance of the parties in the event both sides stipulated to the payment and acceptance of such permanent damage as a settlement of all the controversies among the parties. The total of permanent damages to all plaintiffs thus found was $185,000. * * *

This result at Special Term and at the Appellate Division is a departure from a rule that has become settled; but to follow the rule literally in these cases would be to close down the plant at once. This court is fully agreed to avoid that immediately drastic remedy; the difference in view is how best to avoid it. [The defendant's investment in the plant is in excess of $45,000,000. There are over 300 people employed there.]

One alternative is to grant the injunction but postpone its effect to a specified future date to give opportunity for technical advances to permit defendant to eliminate the nuisance; another is to grant the injunction conditioned on the payment of permanent damages to plaintiffs which would compensate them for the total economic loss to their property present and future caused by defendant's operations. For reasons which will be developed the court chooses the latter alternative.

\* \* \*

[T]echniques to eliminate dust and other annoying by-products of cement making are unlikely to be developed by any research the defendant can undertake within any short period, but will depend on the total resources of the cement industry nationwide and throughout the world. The problem is universal wherever cement is made.

For obvious reasons the rate of the research is beyond control of defendant. If at the end of 18 months the whole industry has not found a technical solution a court would be hard put to close down this one cement plant if due regard be given to equitable principles.

On the other hand, to grant the injunction unless defendant pays plaintiffs such permanent damages as may be fixed by the court seems to do justice between the contending parties. All of the attributions of economic loss to the properties on which plaintiffs' complaints are based will have been redressed.

\* \* \*

It seems reasonable to think that the risk of being required to pay permanent damages to injured property owners by cement plant owners would itself be a reasonable effective spur to research for improved techniques to minimize nuisance.

\* \* \*

Thus it seems fair to both sides to grant permanent damages to plaintiffs which will terminate this private litigation. \* \* \*

The judgment, by allowance of permanent damages imposing a servitude on land, which is the basis of the actions, would preclude future recovery by plaintiffs or their grantees.

\* \* \*

The orders should be reversed, without costs, and the cases remitted to Supreme Court, Albany County to grant an injunction which shall be vacated upon payment by defendant of such amounts of permanent damage to the respective plaintiffs as shall for this purpose be determined by the court.

JASEN, JUDGE, dissenting.

\* \* \*

It has long been the rule in this State, as the majority acknowledges, that a nuisance which results in substantial continuing damage to neighbors must be enjoined. To now change the rule to permit the cement company to continue polluting the air indefinitely upon the payment of permanent damages is, in my opinion, compounding the magnitude of a very serious problem in our State and Nation today.

The harmful nature and widespread occurrence of air pollution have been extensively documented. Congressional hearings have revealed that air pollution causes substantial property damage, as well as being a contributing factor to a rising incidence of lung cancer, emphysema, bronchitis and asthma.

\* \* \*

I see grave dangers in overruling our long-established rule of granting an injunction where a nuisance results in substantial continuing damage. In permitting the injunction to become inoperative upon the payment of permanent damages, the majority is, in effect, licensing a continuing wrong. It is the same as saying to the cement company, you may continue to do harm to your neighbors so long as you pay a fee for it. Furthermore, once such permanent damages are assessed and paid, the incentive to alleviate the wrong would be eliminated, thereby continuing air pollution of an area without abatement.

\* \* \*

This kind of inverse condemnation may not be invoked by a private person or corporation for private gain or advantage. Inverse condemnation should only be permitted when the public is primarily served in the taking or impairment of property. The promotion of the interests of the polluting cement company has, in my opinion, no public use or benefit.

\* \* \*

I would enjoin the defendant cement company from continuing the discharge of dust particles upon its neighbors' properties unless, within 18 months, the cement company abated this nuisance.

\* \* \*

## Notes and Questions

1. Prior to *Boomer,* New York law recognized a right to injunction whenever a nuisance imposed significant costs on the plaintiff, without regard to any offsetting benefits from the nuisance-causing activity. Judge Bergan's opinion for the majority focused on the wastefulness of shutting down the defendant's $45 million plant just to avoid $185,000 in damages to the eight plaintiffs involved in this suit. Rather than shut down the plant, the injunction was conditioned upon the payment of damages. In effect, the plaintiff's property right to be free of the polluting nuisance was transformed into a liability right to receive compensation for the injuries caused by the nuisance.

According to the Coase Theorem, if there are no impediments to bargaining between the homeowners and the cement plant, the parties will bargain their way to the efficient allocation no matter where the court initially assigns the right. The Coase Theorem focuses attention on the efficiency justification for a judicial decision that allows a resource, formerly protected by a property right, to be protected now only by a liability right. Suppose the cement plant was worth $45 million as an ongoing business but would be worthless if shut down.

*Questions:* If an injunction had been issued as dissenting Judge Jasen wished, what is the maximum the cement plant's owners would offer to avoid being shut down? What is the minimum the homeowners would demand to allow it to continue operating? Could transaction costs have prevented the plant's owners from successfully bargaining with the plaintiffs to refrain from enforcing the injunction?

2. Because the injunctive remedy is the traditional relief accorded in nuisance cases, courts often focus on a balancing of harms and benefits from shutting down the polluter. For instance, in Koseris v. J.R. Simplot Co., 82 Idaho 263, 352 P.2d 235, 237 (1960), the court found the following evidence relevant to its analysis of whether operation of the defendant's fertilizer plant created a nuisance:

> That in the operation of its fertilizer plant it carries on a leading industry in southeastern Idaho, with a capital investment of approximately $5,500,000; that its investment in inventory at the fertilizer plant in Power County as of November 1, 1957, was $1,627,207; that as of the same date its investment at the Gay Mine * * * exceeded $1,644,000; that payments to local businesses amounted to $1,030,000; that its other purchases and sales exceeded $8,500,000; that for the year 1956 it paid over $130,000 in taxes; that nearly 1,000 employees and their dependents rely for their livelihood upon the operations of the Simplot plant, and that it has an annual payroll of more than $1,242,000.

> That it had spent $223,688.00 for a fume and dust control system which constituted only a part of the total moneys expended in its attempts to control dust and fumes; that only 0.1% of any dust which is emitted from its plant due to its operations is discharged from its stacks.

The plaintiff's injured property contained only an abandoned nightclub, which had been closed in 1951 under order of the sheriff and had been vacant until the time of trial except for the storage of small items. The trial court enjoined continued operation of the plant. The Idaho Supreme Court reversed on appeal, relying on the following policy argument from York v. Stallings, 217 Or. 13, 341 P.2d 529, 534 (1959), where the Supreme Court of Oregon said:

> This court heretofore has accepted the balancing doctrine in cases involving the public convenience. In Fraser v. City of Portland, this court stated: " * * * sometimes a court of equity will decline to raise its restraining arm and refuse to issue an injunction * * * even though an admitted legal right has been violated, when it appears that * * * the issuance of an injunction would cause serious public inconvenience or loss without a correspondingly great advantage to the complainant."

The balancing test applied by the Idaho Supreme Court in *Koseris* appears to encourage judges to reassign property rights to pollute, or to be free from pollution, to the user who values the right most highly (see *Ploof*). If Judge Bergan was certain the economic benefits of cement production outweighed the harms, he could simply have refused to grant an injunction.

*Questions:* What is the justification for awarding damages in *Boomer?* What are the risks of awarding damages instead of granting an injunction? Consider dissenting Judge Jasen's point that pollution not only causes property damage, but also is "a contributing factor to a rising incidence of lung cancer, emphysema, bronchitis and asthma."

3. The previous questions have developed the rationale for selecting a liability rule over a property rule in nuisance cases but have not addressed whether the cement plant or the homeowners should be given the incentive to investigate ways to reduce the costs of pollution.

*Questions:* Is there any efficiency reason to provide this incentive to one party rather than the other in *Boomer?* Does the permanent damages solution provide incentives for finding ways to reduce future pollution?

## SPUR INDUSTRIES, INC. v. DEL E. WEBB DEVELOPMENT CO.

Supreme Court of Arizona, In Banc., 1972.
108 Ariz. 178, 494 P.2d 700.

CAMERON, VICE CHIEF JUSTICE.

From a judgment permanently enjoining the defendant, Spur Industries, Inc., from operating a cattle feedlot near the plaintiff Del E. Webb Development Company's Sun City, Spur appeals. * * *

\* \* \*

In 1956, Spur's predecessors in interest, H. Marion Welborn and the Northside Hay Mill and Trading Company, developed feed-lots, about 1/2 mile south of Olive Avenue, in an area between the confluence of the usually dry Agua Fria and New Rivers. The area is well suited for cattle feeding and in 1959, there were 25 cattle feeding pens or dairy operations within a 7 mile radius of the location developed by Spur's predecessors. In April and May of 1959, the Northside Hay Mill was feeding between 6,000 and 7,000 head of cattle and Welborn approximately 1,500 head on a combined area of 35 acres.

In May of 1959, Del Webb began to plan the development of an urban area to be known as Sun City. For this purpose, the Marinette and the Santa Fe Ranches, some 20,000 acres of farmland, were purchased for $15,000,000 or $750.00 per acre. This price was considerably less than the price of land located near the urban area of Phoenix, and along with the success of Youngtown[, a retirement community nearby,] was a factor influencing the decision to purchase the property in question.

\* \* \*

Accompanied by an extensive advertising campaign, homes were first offered by Del Webb in January 1960 and the first unit to be completed was south of Grand Avenue and approximately 2 1/2 miles north of Spur. By 2 May 1960, there were 450 to 500 houses completed or under construction. At this time, Del Webb did not consider odors from the Spur feed pens a problem and Del Webb continued to develop in a southerly direction, until sales resistance became so great that the parcels were difficult if not impossible to sell. * * *

By December 1967, Del Webb's property had extended south to Olive Avenue and Spur was within 500 feet of Olive Avenue to the north. Del Webb filed its original complaint alleging that in excess of 1,300 lots in the southwest portion were unfit for development for sale as residential lots because of the operation of the Spur feedlot.

Del Webb's suit complained that the Spur feeding operation was a public nuisance because of the flies and the odor which were drifting or being blown by the prevailing south to north wind over the southern portion of Sun City. At the time of the suit, Spur was feeding between 20,000 and 30,000 head of cattle, and the facts amply support the finding of the trial court that the feed pens had become a nuisance to the people who resided in the southern part of Del Webb's development. * * *

* * *

It is clear that as to the citizens of Sun City, the operation of Spur's feedlot was both a public and a private nuisance. They could have successfully maintained an action to abate the nuisance. Del Webb, having shown a special injury in the loss of sales, had a standing to bring suit to enjoin the nuisance. The judgment of the trial court permanently enjoining the operation of the feedlot is affirmed.

* * *

In addition to protecting the public interest, however, courts of equity are concerned with protecting the operator of a lawful, albeit noxious, business from the result of a knowing and willful encroachment by others near his business.

In the so-called "coming to the nuisance" cases, the courts have held that the residential landowner may not have relief if he knowingly came into a neighborhood reserved for industrial or agricultural endeavors and has been damaged thereby. * * *

* * *

There was no indication in the instant case at the time Spur and its predecessors located in western Maricopa County that a new city would spring up, full-blown, alongside the feeding operation and that the developer of that city would ask the court to order Spur to move because of the new city. Spur is required to move not because of any wrongdoing on the part of Spur, but because of a proper and legitimate regard of the courts for the rights and interests of the public.

Del Webb, on the other hand, is entitled to the relief prayed for (a permanent injunction), not because Webb is blameless, but because of the damage to the people who have been encouraged to purchase homes in Sun City. It does not equitable or legally follow, however, that

Webb, being entitled to the injunction, is then free of any liability to Spur if Webb has in fact been the cause of the damage Spur has sustained. It does not seem harsh to require a developer, who has taken advantage of the lesser land values in a rural area as well as the availability of large tracts of land on which to build and develop a new town or city in the area, to indemnify those who are forced to leave as a result.

Having brought people to the nuisance to the foreseeable detriment of Spur, Webb must indemnify Spur for a reasonable amount of the cost of moving or shutting down. * * *

It is therefore the decision of this court that the matter be remanded to the trial court for a hearing upon the damages sustained by the defendant Spur as a reasonably foreseeable and direct result of the granting of the permanent injunction. * * *

## *Notes and Questions*

1. Instead of awarding damages to the land developer who suffered from the nuisance of the feedlot or simply enjoining the feedlot, the court in *Spur* awarded damages to the feedlot company, to compensate it for the expense of moving to a new location. The result has appealing distributional consequences, since the feedlot was doing business in its remote location for years before the Del E. Webb Development Co. decided to develop the area, and to require it to bear the costs of moving seems unfair.

*Question:* Is there any efficiency justification for requiring the plaintiff to pay damages in *Spur*?

2. At first, it might appear that the court in *Spur* assigned the right to receive damages to the wrong party. Certainly Spur would appear to be the party in the best position to control the insects and odors emanating from its feedlot, perhaps through use of pesticides or chlorophyll-impregnated feeds. Del Webb, however, could best evaluate whether it was worthwhile continuing to expand his residential community southward. If the concept of best cost avoider is interpreted a little more broadly, the efficient assignment of liability would consider whether one party is in the best position to avoid a conflict over uses at all, as well as whether one party can best reduce the costs of conflict.

*Question:* Does this interpretation of *best cost avoider* assist in choosing whether to impose liability on Spur or Del Webb?

3. Property rules may fail to allocate resources to their most valuable uses when transaction costs prevent bargaining from transferring a resource from a lower to a higher-valuing user. In such cases, damages determined by a factfinder act as a surrogate for voluntary exchanges between the parties. Rights protected by liability rules, however, also may fail to allocate resources efficiently where there is reason to doubt the judge's or jury's determination of value (i.e, the calculation of damages).

Impediments to bargaining may occasionally be greater in one direction of reallocation between parties than in the other. For example, suppose an injunction had been granted in *Boomer* and the cement plant found itself having to negotiate with the homeowners to purchase the right to pollute. If even one homeowner held out and refused to sell, the plant would have to shut down. If the injunction were denied, however, the homeowners would have to pay the cement plant to either stop production or to develop pollution control devices. If a few homeowners refused to contribute in the hope of "freeriding" on the others' efforts, the cement plant and the remaining homeowners might still reach a mutually satisfactory agreement. Because it is more difficult for the cement plant to bribe the homeowners than vice versa, a court might prefer to award a property right to the cement plant and refuse to enter the injunction.

Similar considerations may influence a court trying to decide which of two parties making competing claims for a resource should pay damages to the other. Calculating one party's damages may be more difficult than calculating the other's. In such a case, a court may wish to allocate the liability right so as to minimize the chance of an inefficient outcome due to inaccurate damage calculations.

*Questions:* In Spur, which damage calculation was more reliable: Spur's claim to expenses incurred in moving the feedlot, or the homeowners' claims for losses due to the insects and odors emanating from the feedlot? How might this affect the court's decision as to which party should be required to pay damages?

4. A private nuisance, as in *Boomer,* interferes with a person's use and enjoyment of his property. While the cement particles falling on the plaintiffs' property may have dirtied their lawns, shrubs, and windows, and made their tennis courts slippery, the nuisance is private because it affected the use and enjoyment of their land. In *Spur* the nuisance of the flies and stenches was both private and public. A public nuisance interferes with a right common to the public, such as health, safety, and convenience, and need not be associated with possession of land. In *Spur,* the flies and stenches affected the use and enjoyment of the land Del Webb was developing and presented a health risk. The effect of a public nuisance is often more intangible, harder to quantify than a private nuisance's effect on the value of land.

*Question:* Should the fact that public nuisances often involve more intangible harms affect the choice of efficient remedies between injunction and damages?

## CARPENTER v. DOUBLE R CATTLE COMPANY, INC.

Court of Appeals of Idaho, 1983.
105 Idaho 320, 669 P.2d 643.

BURNETT, JUDGE.

\* \* \*

This lawsuit was filed by a group of homeowners who alleged that expansion of a nearby cattle feedlot had created a nuisance. The homeowners claimed that operation of the expanded feedlot had caused noxious odors, air and water pollution, noise and pests in the area. The homeowners sought damages and injunctive relief. The issues of damages and injunctive relief were combined in a single trial, conducted before a jury. Apparently it was contemplated that the jury would perform a fact-finding function in determining whether a nuisance existed and whether the homeowners were entitled to damages, but would perform an advisory function on the question of injunctive relief. The district judge gave the jury a unified set of instructions embracing all of these functions. The jury returned a verdict simply finding that no nuisance existed. The court entered judgment for the feedlot proprietors, denying the homeowners any damages or injunctive relief. This appeal followed. For reasons appearing below, we vacate the judgment and remand the case for a new trial.

The homeowners contend that the jury received improper instructions on criteria for determining the existence of a nuisance. The jury was told to weigh the alleged injury to the homeowners against the "social value" of the feedlot, and to consider "the interests of the community as a whole," in determining whether a nuisance existed.
* * *

* * *

The Second Restatement [of Torts] treats such an "intentional" invasion as a nuisance if it is "unreasonable." Section 826 of the Second Restatement now provides two sets of criteria for determining whether this type of nuisance exists:

An intentional invasion of another's interest in the use and enjoyment of land is unreasonable if

(a) the gravity of the harm outweighs the utility of the actor's conduct, or

(b) the harm caused by the conduct is serious and the financial burden of compensating for this and similar harm to others would not make the continuation of the conduct not feasible.

The present version of § 826, unlike its counterpart in the First Restatement, recognizes that liability for damages caused by a nuisance may exist regardless of whether the utility of the offending activity exceeds the gravity of the harm it has created. This fundamental proposition now permeates the entire Second Restatement. The commentary to § 822, which distinguishes between "intentional" and "unintentional" invasions, and which serves as the gateway for all succeeding sections, emphasizes that the test for existence of a nuisance no longer depends solely upon the balance between the gravity of harm and utility of the conduct. Comment d to § 822 states that, for the purpose of determining liability for damages, an invasion may be regarded as unreasonable even though the utility of the conduct is great and the amount of harm is relatively small. Comment g to the same section reemphasizes that damages are appropriate where the harm from the invasion is greater than a party should be required to bear, "at least without compensation."

\* \* \*

Both the Second Restatement and [this Court's opinion in] *Koseris [v. J.R. Simplot]* recognize that utility of the activity alleged to be a nuisance is a proper factor to consider in the context of injunctive relief; but that damages may be awarded regardless of utility. Evidence of utility does not constitute a defense against recovery of damages where the harm is serious and compensation is feasible. Were the law otherwise, a large enterprise, important to the local economy, would have a lesser duty to compensate its neighbors for invasion of their rights than would a smaller business deemed less essential to the community. In our view, this is not, and should not be, the law in Idaho.

\* \* \*

However, our view is not based simply upon general notions of fairness; it is also grounded in economics. The Second Restatement deals effectively with the problem of "externalities" identified in the [proceedings of the American Law Institute (ALI), which drafted the Second Restatement]. Where an enterprise externalizes some burdens upon its neighbors, without compensation, our market system does not reflect the true cost of products or services provided by that enterprise. Externalities distort the price signals essential to the proper functioning of the market.

This problem affects two fundamental objectives of the economic system. The first objective, commonly called "efficiency" in economic theory, is to promote the greatest aggregate surplus of benefits over the costs of economic activity. The second objective, usually termed "equity" or "distributive justice," is to allocate these benefits and costs in accordance with prevailing societal values. The market system best serves the goal of efficiency when prices reflect true costs; and the goal of distributive justice is best achieved when benefits are explicitly identified to the correlative costs.

Although the problem of externalities affects both goals of efficiency and distributive justice, these objectives are conceptually different and may imply different solutions to a given problem. In theory, if there were no societal goal other than efficiency, and if there were no impediments to exchanges of property or property rights, individuals pursuing their economic self-interests might reach the most efficient allocation of costs and benefits by means of exchange, without direction by the courts. However, the real world is not free from impediments to exchanges, and our economic system operates within the constraints of a society which is also concerned with distributive justice. Thus, the courts often are the battlegrounds upon which campaigns for efficiency and distributive justice are waged.

Our historical survey of nuisance law has reflected the differing emphasis upon efficiency and distributive justice. As noted, the English system of property law placed a preeminent value upon property rights. It was thus primarily concerned with distributive justice in accord with those rights. For that reason the English system favored the injunction as a remedy for a nuisance, regardless of disparate economic consequences. However, when the concept of nuisance was incorporated into American law, it encountered a different value system. Respect for property rights came to be tempered by the tort-related concept of fault, and the demands of a developing nation placed greater emphasis upon the economic objective of efficiency relative to the objective of distributive justice. The injunction fell into disfavor. The reaction against the injunction, as embodied in the First Restatement, so narrowed the concept of nuisance itself that it rendered the courts impotent to deal with externalities generated by enterprises of great utility. This reaction was excessive; neither efficiency nor distributive justice has been well served.

In order to address the problem of externalities, the remedies of damages and injunctive relief must be carefully chosen to accommodate the often competing goals of efficiency and distributive justice. *Koseris* and the Second Restatement recognize the complementary functions of injunctions and damages. Section 826(a) of the Second Restatement allows both injunctions and damages to be employed where the harm created by an economic activity exceeds its utility. Section 826(b) allows the more limited remedy of damages alone to be employed where it would not be appropriate to enjoin the activity but the activity is imposing harm upon its neighbors so substantial that they cannot reasonably be expected to bear it without compensation.

\* \* \*

Each of the parties in the present case has viewed the Second Restatement with some apprehension. We now turn to those concerns.

The homeowners, echoing an argument made during the ALI proceedings, have contended that the test of nuisance set forth in § 826 grants large enterprises a form of private eminent domain. They evidently fear that if the utility of a large enterprise exceeds the gravity of the harm it creates—insulating it from an injunction and subjecting it to liability only in damages—the enterprise might interfere at will with the enjoyment and use of neighboring property, upon penalty only of paying compensation from time to time. Such a result might be consistent with the economic goal of efficiency, but it may conflict with the goal of distributive justice insofar as it violates a basic societal value which opposes forced exchanges of property rights.

Even those legal scholars who advocate the most limited role for injunctions as a remedy against nuisances acknowledge that damages may be inadequate, and injunctions may be necessary, where the harm in question relates to personal health and safety, or to one's fundamental freedom of action within the boundaries of his own property. Ordinarily, plaintiffs in such cases would prevail on the test which balances utility against gravity of the harm. Moreover, in the exceptional cases, the offending activity might be modified or eliminated through legislative or administrative controls such as environmental protection laws or zoning. Therefore, we expect that few cases would remain in need of a judicial remedy. However, we do not today close the door on the possibility that an injunction might lie, to protect personal health and safety or fundamental freedoms, in cases missed by the balancing test and by non-judicial controls. To this extent, our adoption of the Second Restatement's test of nuisance stops short of being absolute.

* * *

We conclude that the entire judgment of the district court, entered upon the verdict of a jury which had been improperly instructed, must be vacated. The case must be remanded for a new trial to determine whether a nuisance exists under the full criteria set forth in § 826 of the Second Restatement.

* * *

### Notes and Questions

The trend in modern nuisance law has been to recognize a variety of alternative remedies for nuisance that combine both injunctive and damages components. While damages are typically the only available remedy for injuries already suffered by a plaintiff, the courts may deal with complaints of future harms by four variations of the remedies of damages or injunction:

(1) granting the plaintiff an injunction, which halts the defendant's activity if the plaintiff enforces it;

(2) awarding the plaintiff damages, which requires the defendant to compensate the plaintiff for future harm if the activity continues;

(3) denying the plaintiff an injunction, which allows the defendant's activity to continue unless the plaintiff is willing and able to pay him to stop; or

(4) awarding the defendant damages, which requires the plaintiff to compensate the defendant if the plaintiff wishes to halt the defendant's activity.

The notes and question following the preceding cases in this section have developed reasons why each of these types of remedies might be appropriate.

When devising a systematic outline of when each type is appropriate you will want to take into account the following considerations:

(1) whether we know for certain which is the more valuable use;

(2) whether we can say which of the parties is in the best position to evaluate the costs and benefits of the activities and act accordingly;

(3) what is the magnitude of transaction costs that would interfere with correcting an incorrect assignment of rights protected by property rules;

(4) what is the magnitude of costs associated with errors in damages calculations required by liability rules;

(5) whether transaction costs or damages calculations are likely to be more of a problem for one party than another; and

(6) what distributional concerns are present.

*Questions:* Which of the four remedies is appropriate under the facts of *Carpenter?* Which are consistent with Judge Burnett's opinion?

## F. STRICT LIABILITY

### 1. STRICT LIABILITY AND THE BEST COST AVOIDER

From an economic perspective, liability based on negligence involves establishing, case by case, which parties failed to take cost-justified precautions to avoid accidents. Economic analysis of negligence defenses considers how to assign liability when the fault of several persons coincided to produce an accident. An alternative to the case by case approach is to develop categories of activities in which one type of actor is almost always the best minimizer of primary accident costs. If, after looking at the various factual circumstances giving rise to accidents, some actors could be isolated for special treatment in this way, the liability system could be streamlined. Liability could be imposed on the party who was usually the best cost minimizer without having to go through the cumbersome process of establishing fault or apportioning liability. In the following cases, consider whether people in the position of the defendant are usually in the best position to minimize accident costs.

### SPANO v. PERINI CORPORATION
Court of Appeals of New York, 1969.
25 N.Y.2d 11, 302 N.Y.S.2d 527, 250 N.E.2d 31.

FULD, CHIEF JUDGE.

The principal question posed on this appeal is whether a person who has sustained property damage caused by blasting on nearby property can maintain an action for damages without a showing that the blaster was negligent. Since 1893, when this court decided the case of Booth v. Rome, W. & O.T.R.R. Co., it has been the law of this State that proof of negligence was required unless the blast was accompanied by an actual physical invasion of the damaged property—for example, by rocks or other material being cast upon the premises. We are now asked to reconsider that rule.

The plaintiff Spano is the owner of a garage in Brooklyn which was wrecked by a blast occurring on November 27, 1962. There was then in that garage, for repairs, an automobile owned by the plaintiff Davis which he also claims was damaged by the blasting. Each of the plaintiffs brought suit against the two defendants who, as joint venturers, were engaged in constructing a tunnel in the vicinity pursuant to a contract with the City of New York.

* * *

It is undisputed that, on the day in question (November 27, 1962), the defendants had set off a total of 194 sticks of dynamite at a construction site which was only 125 feet away from the damaged premises. Although both plaintiffs alleged negligence in their complaints, no attempt was made to show that the defendants had failed to exercise reasonable care or to take necessary precautions when they were blasting. Instead, they chose to rely, upon the trial, solely on the principle of absolute liability either on a tort theory or on the basis of their being third-party beneficiaries of the defendants' contract with the city. * * *

In our view, the time has come for this court to * * * declare that one who engages in blasting must assume responsibility, and be liable without fault, for any injury he causes to neighboring property.

* * *

Although the court in *Booth* drew a distinction between a situation * * * where there was "a physical invasion" of, or trespass on, the plaintiff's property and one in which the damage was caused by "setting the air in motion, or in some other unexplained way," it is clear that the court, in the earlier cases, was not concerned with the particular manner by which the damage was caused but by the simple fact that any explosion in a built-up area was likely to cause damage. Thus, in Heeg v. Licht, the court held that there should be absolute liability where the damage was caused by the accidental explosion of stored gunpowder, even in the absence of a physical trespass:

> "The defendant had erected a building and stored materials therein, which from their character were liable to and actually did explode, causing injury to the plaintiff. The fact that the explosion took place tends to establish that the magazine was dangerous and liable to cause damage to the property of persons residing in the vicinity. * * * The fact that the magazine was liable to such a contingency, which could not be guarded against or averted by the greatest degree of care and vigilance, evinces its dangerous character, * * * In such a case, the rule which exonerates a party engaged in a lawful business, when free from negligence, has no application."

Such reasoning should, we venture, have led to the conclusion that the *intentional* setting off of explosives—that is, blasting—in an area in which it was likely to cause harm to neighboring property similarly results in absolute liability. However, the court in the *Booth* case rejected such an extension of the rule for the reason that "(t)o exclude the defendant from blasting to adapt its lot to the contemplated uses, at the instance of the plaintiff, would not be a compromise between conflicting rights, but an extinguishment of the right of the one for the benefit of the other." The court expanded on this by stating, "This sacrifice, we think, the law does not exact. Public policy is sustained by the building up of towns and cities and the improvement of property.

Any unnecessary restraint on freedom of action of a property owner hinders this."

This rationale cannot withstand analysis. The plaintiff in *Booth* was not seeking, as the court implied, to "exclude the defendant from blasting" and thus prevent desirable improvements to the latter's property. Rather, he was merely seeking compensation for the damage which was inflicted upon his own property as a result of that blasting. The question, in other words, was not *whether* it was lawful or proper to engage in blasting but *who* should bear the cost of any resulting damage—the person who engaged in the dangerous activity or the innocent neighbor injured thereby. Viewed in such a light, it clearly appears that *Booth* was wrongly decided and should be forthrightly overruled.

\* \* \*

[The jury verdict awarding Spano $4,400 and Davis $329 was affirmed.]

## Notes and Questions

1. In *Spano,* the court recognized two activities as appropriate candidates for assigning liability without fault: blasting with dynamite and storing gunpowder. The court had found in Heeg v. Licht that the danger presented by the storage of gunpowder "could not be guarded against or averted by the greatest degree of care and vigilance" and in *Spano* suggested that the same was true of blasting, at least near existing structures. This conclusion implies that the burden of eliminating all risks associated with these activities is greater than the associated risks. Because it would be inefficient to take the precautions necessary to avoid the risk that materialized, the defendants were not at fault.

Although not at fault, people who blast with dynamite or store gunpowder may always be better evaluators than potential victims of the risks inherent in those activities and in a better position to take whatever cost-justified precautions are or become available.

*Question:* Given this difference between the plaintiff's position and the defendant's, is any economic purpose served by assigning liability to the defendants in these cases?

2. When liability is based on negligence, a defendant is liable only if he was at fault. If no one was at fault, the plaintiff must bear the costs of the accident. Strict liability shifts this burden to the defendant; even if not at fault, the defendant must pay for the damage suffered by the plaintiff.

*Questions:* When liability is based on negligence and neither party was negligent, does denying recovery to the plaintiff create incentives for her to avoid accidents that are not worth avoiding? Under strict liability, does shifting the burden of liability to the defendant even if he is not negligent create incentives to overinvest in accident avoidance?

3. In Booth v. Rome (overruled by *Spano*) the court applied strict liability only if there was an actual physical invasion of the plaintiff's land.

If the damage from blasting was caused by vibration underground or in the air, the plaintiff was required to prove that the defendant was negligent in order to be awarded damages. While recovery for tort damages usually required proof of negligence, blasting cases fell into the category of the tort of "trespass." Proof of a trespass traditionally required evidence of physical invasion of another's right to exclusive enjoyment of one's land. Because the damage from blasting was often caused by rocks, dust, or other objects physically intruding onto the plaintiff's land, the tort of trespass applied to blasting cases. Recovery of damages for trespass had historically been on a strict liability basis, which is why the *Booth* court required the actual physical invasion.

> *Question:* From an efficiency perspective, should the decision to impose strict liability depend on whether the damage from blasting is caused by rocks flying through the neighbor's garage roof rather than vibration in the earth that caused the garage's foundation to crumble?

4. Under the general tort rule governing liability for injuries caused by domesticated animals, a plaintiff must prove that the animal's owner was negligent in order to recover damages unless the animal had shown, or was known to have, dangerous propensities. A plaintiff seeking damages for a dog bite must ordinarily prove that the dog's owner was negligent in permitting the dog to attack. After the dog has bitten one person, however, the owner will be strictly liable to all future plaintiffs under the "One Bite Rule."

> *Question:* What is the economic justification for applying strict liability in selected domesticated animals cases?

5. Occasionally a plaintiff is injured as a result of another's abnormally dangerous activity and the plaintiff is at fault. Suppose that despite the blaster's clear warnings, an adult sneaks up to the blasting site in order to watch the pyrotechnics and is injured. Prohibiting the defense would turn strict liability into absolute liability, effectively insuring the plaintiff against harms from blasting.

> *Question:* Given the economic justification for holding the blaster strictly liable, should recovery be denied to the careless plaintiff?

## SHAVELL, STRICT LIABILITY VERSUS NEGLIGENCE *
### 9 J. Legal Stud. 1, 2–3 (1980).

\* \* \*

By definition, under the negligence rule all that an injurer needs to do to avoid the possibility of liability is to make sure to exercise due care if he engages in his activity. Consequently *he will not be motivated to consider the effect on accident losses of his choice of whether to engage in his activity or, more generally, of the level at which to engage in his activity;* he will choose his level of activity in accordance only with the personal benefits so derived. But surely any increase in his level of activity will typically raise expected accident losses (holding

---

\* Copyright 1980 by the University of Chicago Law School.

constant the level of care). Thus he will be led to choose too high a level of activity; the negligence rule is not "efficient."

Consider by way of illustration the problem of pedestrian-automobile accidents (and, * * * let us imagine the behavior of pedestrians to be fixed). Suppose that drivers of automobiles find it in their interest to adhere to the standard of due care but that the possibility of accidents is not thereby eliminated. Then, in deciding how much to drive, they will contemplate only the enjoyment they get from doing so. Because (as they exercise due care) they will not be liable for harms suffered by pedestrians, drivers will not take into account that going more miles will mean a higher expected number of accidents. Hence, they will do too much driving; an individual will, for example, decide to go for a drive on a mere whim despite the imposition of a positive expected cost to pedestrians.

However, under a rule of strict liability, the situation is different. Because an injurer must pay for losses whenever he is involved in an accident, he will be induced to consider the effect on accident losses of both his level of care *and* his level of activity. His decisions will therefore be efficient. Because drivers will be liable for losses sustained by pedestrians, they will decide not only to exercise due care in driving but also to drive only when the utility gained from it outweighs expected liability payments to pedestrians.

## *Notes and Questions*

1. To avoid accidents, actors can regulate not only *how* they carry on a particular activity, but also *how often*. A jockey like Judy Casella in *Ordway,* for instance, can reduce the risk of being injured in a horse race by wearing a helmet and protective body armor. Such precautions allow the jockey to ride more safely, assuming she is going to ride at all. Perini Corporation similarly may be able to take steps to minimize damage from blasting, perhaps by careful placement of the dynamite or the use of protective barriers. Such strategies reduce the expected losses from risky activities by increasing the actor's *level of care* in engaging in the activity.

A second strategy for minimizing primary accident costs is to reduce expected losses from risky activities by reducing one's level of participation in the activity. Casella could ride in fewer races or none at all; Perini Corporation could plan to blast less often or dispense with blasting altogether. Automobile drivers can reduce the risk of accidents by driving less, as well as by driving more carefully. In other words, actors can reduce the risks of an activity by reducing their *level of activity* as well as by increasing their level of care when they do act.

Once a defendant decides to pursue an activity that poses a risk of accidents, Learned Hand's "$B < PL$" negligence test requires the defendant to invest in all precautionary measures that could reduce the risk of accidental loss at less cost than the expected cost of the risk. Thus, under the negligence standard, Perini Corporation would be liable only if it failed to undertake preventative measures that cost less than the expected damage from blasting.

But suppose preventative measures are impossible or prohibitively expensive? The court found in Heeg v. Licht that the danger presented in storing gunpowder "could not be guarded against or averted by the greatest degree of care and vigilance." *Spano* suggested that the same might sometimes be true for blasting. Assuming that blasting was to be done, the defendants apparently did it with an appropriate and efficient level of care.

Shavell states that the negligence rule is not efficient because potential injurers will be led to choose too high a level of activity.

*Questions:* How does this argument apply to the Perini Corporation in *Spano?* How does strict liability correct inefficient incentives in *Spano?* How does Shavell's argument apply to primary assumption of the risk cases like *Ordway?*

2. At least in theory, judges measuring "B" while applying the BPL formula can consider the burden to the defendant of preventing the accident by simply forgoing the risk-creating activity. For example, a court might find an automobile driver involved in an accident to be negligent if the driver had gone driving "on a mere whim", where the driver would not be negligent if driving to work or on an important errand.

As Professor Shavell notes in Strict Liability versus Negligence at pp. 22–23:

> A question which is in a sense logically prior to the analysis of this article must be mentioned, namely, *"Why isn't the level of activity usually considered in the formulation of the due care standard?"* After all, the inefficiencies discussed here were viewed in the main as deriving from the fact that in order to avoid being found negligent (or contributorily negligent), parties are not motivated to alter their level of activity. The answer to the question appears to be that the courts would run into difficulty in trying to employ a standard of due care expanded in scope to include the level of activity. In formulating such a broadened due care standard, courts would, by definition, have to decide on the appropriate level of activity, and their competence to do this is problematic. How would courts decide the number of miles an individual ought to drive or how far or how often a pedestrian ought to walk? How would courts decide the level of output an industry—much less a firm within an industry—ought to produce? To decide such matters, a court would likely have to know much more than would normally have to be known to decide whether care, conventionally interpreted, was adequate.

The implication of Professor Shavell's argument is that strict liability may create better incentives for efficient behavior than negligence in circumstances where the defendant is in a better position to evaluate the costs and benefits of a particular *level of activity* than either the plaintiff or the finder of fact.

We have recognized that there might be certain activities where the defendant is clearly the best evaluator of the efficient level of *care.*

*Questions:* Are there activities where the defendant is the best evaluator of the efficient level of *activity?* Are there activities where she is not? If the defendant is always the best evaluator of the efficient level of activity should negligence-based liability be abandoned altogether in favor of strict liability?

3. Blasting and the storage of gunpowder are only two examples of activities that tort law describes as being "abnormally dangerous activities" or "ultrahazardous activities" and for which it imposes strict liability. In *Spano*, the court described this category of activities as those in which the activity was "dangerous and liable to cause damage to the property of persons residing in the vicinity" and in which the dangers "could not be guarded against or averted by the greatest degree of care and vigilance" and "located in an area in which it was likely to cause harm to neighboring property." Most states follow the criteria set out in the Restatement (Second) of Torts, § 520, which characterizes an "abnormally dangerous activity" according to whether certain factors are present. Those factors are:

> (a) the existence of a high degree of risk of some harm to the person, land or chattels of others;
>
> (b) the likelihood that the harm that results from it will be great;
>
> (c) the inability to eliminate the risk by the exercise of reasonable care;
>
> (d) the extent to which the activity is not a matter of common usage;
>
> (e) the inappropriateness of the activity to the place where it is carried on; and
>
> (f) the extent to which its value to the community is outweighed by its dangerous attributes.

As generally applied, no one of these factors is necessarily sufficient of itself and, ordinarily, several of them are required for strict liability. It is not necessary, however, that all of them be present, especially if others weigh heavily. See, Restatement (Second) of Torts, § 520, Comment f. The following types of activities have been characterized as abnormally dangerous: storing large amounts of gasoline in a residential area, operating a nuclear fuel processing plant, storing chemical waste near a community's water source, operating a propane gas storage yard, and maintaining a liquified manure lagoon.

*Question:* Do these seem like the kind of activities in which the defendants are in a better position than the plaintiffs to evaluate how the risks should be avoided and how much they should engage in the activity?

## GREENMAN v. YUBA POWER PRODUCTS, INC.

Supreme Court of California, In Bank, 1962.
59 Cal.2d 57, 27 Cal.Rptr. 697, 377 P.2d 897.

TRAYNOR, JUSTICE.

Plaintiff brought this action for damages against the retailer and the manufacturer of a Shopsmith, a combination power tool that could be used as a saw, drill, and wood lathe. He saw a Shopsmith demonstrated by the retailer and studied a brochure prepared by the manufacturer. He decided he wanted a Shopsmith for his home workshop, and his wife bought and gave him one for Christmas in 1955. In 1957 he bought the necessary attachments to use the Shopsmith as a lathe for turning a large piece of wood he wished to make into a chalice. After he had worked on the piece of wood several times without difficulty, it suddenly flew out of the machine and struck him on the forehead, inflicting serious injuries. * * *

* * * The jury returned a verdict for the retailer against plaintiff and for plaintiff against the manufacturer in the amount of $65,000. * * *

Plaintiff introduced substantial evidence that his injuries were caused by defective design and construction of the Shopsmith. His expert witnesses testified that inadequate set screws were used to hold parts of the machine together so that normal vibration caused the tailstock of the lathe to move away from the piece of wood being turned permitting it to fly out of the lathe. They also testified that there were other more positive ways of fastening the parts of the machine together, the use of which would have prevented the accident. The jury could therefore reasonably have concluded that the manufacturer negligently constructed the Shopsmith. * * *

* * *

* * * A manufacturer is strictly liable in tort when an article he places on the market, knowing that it is to be used without inspection for defects, proves to have a defect that causes injury to a human being. Recognized first in the case of unwholesome food products, such liability has now been extended to a variety of other products that create as great or greater hazards if defective.

* * *

* * * The purpose of such liability is to insure that the costs of injuries resulting from defective products are borne by the manufacturers that put such products on the market rather than by the injured persons who are powerless to protect themselves. * * * To establish the manufacturer's liability it was sufficient that plaintiff proved that he was injured while using the Shopsmith in a way it was intended to be used as a result of a defect in design and manufacture of which plaintiff was not aware that made the Shopsmith unsafe for its intended use.

The judgment is affirmed.

### *Notes and Questions*

1. *Greenman* is one of the early cases holding manufacturers strictly liable for injuries caused by defective products. The purpose of holding manufacturers strictly liable, according to Justice Traynor, "is to insure that the costs of injuries resulting from defective products are borne by the manufacturers that put such products on the market rather than by the injured persons who are powerless to protect themselves." The movement

towards strict products liability extends the application of strict liability from activities that are abnormally dangerous or ultrahazardous, as in *Spano,* to the designing and manufacturing of products.

*Questions:* Is the purpose for the extension of strict liability to products articulated by Justice Traynor consistent with the efficiency justification for strict liability for injuries caused by abnormally dangerous activities? Are manufacturers always the parties in the best position to engage in risk evaluation and avoidance? Are consumers always "powerless to protect themselves?"

2. In *Greenman,* and in products liability generally, there are primarily two types of defects: defects in manufacturing and defects in design.

The workbench bought by Mr. Greenman's wife may have been different from the general run of workbenches produced by Shopsmith; screws inadequate to hold the machinery together were installed during the manufacturing process. If the workbench had been designed to have stronger screws and someone on the assembly line installed the wrong ones, then the error would be a manufacturing error. Evidence of a manufacturing error may include a comparison of the construction of the unit that caused the injury to other units producer by the same manufacturer. Often, as in the case of a half gallon of ice cream containing a machine spring or a ten dollar bill printed on only one side, the product quality is obviously different from the usual output.

If the design of the workbench called for inadequate screws, then there is no error in manufacturing because the assembly line followed the specifications correctly. The defect is in the design process instead. Since the design process inherently requires tradeoffs between cost and quality, proof of a design defect may include evidence of costs of alternative, safer designs and risks presented by the design selected. Courts also accept evidence that the designed produced was more dangerous than a reasonable consumer would expect.

*Question:* Does the conclusion that the manufacturer is usually the best cost avoider for product-related accidents depend on whether the characteristic of the product producing the accident is a design defect or a manufacturing defect?

3. Implicit in Justice Traynor's opinion is the conclusion that products will be safer if manufacturers are liable for the cost of injuries resulting from defective products.

*Question:* Is the substitution of strict liability for liability based on negligence likely to result in safer products?

## 2. STRICT LIABILITY AND ALLOCATIVE EFFICIENCY

### DOE v. MILES LABORATORIES, INC.
United States District Court, District of Maryland, 1987.
675 F.Supp. 1466.

RAMSEY, DISTRICT JUDGE.

A plague inflicts society and this Court is called upon to adjudicate the extent to which the effects will be visited upon its victims. The facts are tragic. In the autumn of 1983, plaintiff Jane Doe, who a week previous had given birth, sought emergency medical treatment for vaginal bleeding. During the course of treatment, the attending physician ordered the administration of 500 units of "Konyne," a blood-coagulation-factor concentrate produced by Cutter Laboratories, a division of Miles. Treatment appeared successful and plaintiff eventually was discharged.

Over the course of the months to follow, plaintiff suffered from a succession of ailments, ultimately being diagnosed as infected by the HTLV–III virus, and as having Acquired Immune–Deficiency Syndrome–Related Complex (ARC), a predecessor of AIDS. On July 6, 1986, plaintiffs Jane and John Doe filed suit, alleging claims for strict liability in tort [among others]. Defendant Miles, following other procedural actions, filed this motion for summary judgment on plaintiffs' counts * * *.

* * *

Implicit in the [justifications] for strict products liability, though perhaps not clearly articulated, is [the argument] that strict products liability can promote the efficient allocation of resources. Society has chosen to allow market forces to set the price for goods and thus to determine their availability and distribution. In some respects the market is very efficient. The price purchasers pay invariably reflects direct costs such as raw products, capital investment, labor, plus a reasonable rate of return. However, in other respects the market is not efficient. Prices often do not reflect indirect costs. These hidden costs can include the effects of pollution or the expenses of accidents, and are what economists refer to as "externalities."

When the price of an item does not reflect both its direct costs and its externalities, the price will be lower than its actual cost. This lower price will stimulate an inefficient allocation of resources, for persons will be encouraged to buy more of the product than they might if they were paying its true price. Society thus may increase the consumption of the very goods that create pollution, and thus have indirect cleanup costs, or that are defective, and thus have indirect accident costs. Strict products liability shifts the cost back to manufacturers, who will then reprice the goods to reflect their actual costs. Strict products liability therefore affords society a mechanism for a rational allocation of resources. Absent it, the costs of externalities are thrust upon victims or upon society through its governmental welfare programs. In essence, without it there is a subsidy given to the polluting or defective products.

* * *

It is argued that providers of blood and blood products are promoting the general welfare by making possible improved health. It is argued that it is a fundamental social policy of the State of Maryland to promote the supply of blood and blood products. And it is argued that to allow strict products liability, which given the wide exposure to AIDS due to transfusions could create potentially substantial liability, would so raise costs of production that the supply of blood could be choked off.

The arguments are unpersuasive. * * * Those who choose to operate in the economic marketplace play by the rules applicable to all.

The arguments in favor of strict products liability apply as persuasively to blood and blood products as they do to any other product. * * * [I]t makes for a more efficient allocation of social resources when the price of a transfusion of blood or blood products reflects its true costs.

Entrepreneurs by their nature are risk taking individuals. To the extent they need an incentive to engage in socially beneficial activities, the law already provides it in the form of a corporate shield on personal liability. To do as defendant argues, and exempt blood from strict liability would be to subsidize the product by forcing either victims or government through its social welfare programs to bear accident costs. In the absence of a clear expression on the part of the legislature of an intent to subsidize a particular product, it is not this Court's role to create the subsidy indirectly by carving out a Judge made exemption to strict products liability.

Accordingly, the Court will deny defendant's motion for summary judgment on plaintiffs' claim for strict products liability.

* * *

## *Notes and Questions*

1. In *Doe,* Judge Ramsey recognized that the failure of an actor to internalize the costs of his activity may result in allocative inefficiency. A manufacturer of products derived from blood charges a price sufficient to cover the costs of supplying that product, including some profit. The sale of this product to a buyer who is willing and able to pay the cost of the resources that went into producing that product is allocatively efficient, because the buyer values the product more highly.

Judge Ramsey considered the injuries resulting from use of the blood coagulant to be part of the cost of manufacturing the product. If the manufacturer is not required to bear all of the costs associated with the product and the price does not reflect that cost, then "[s]ociety cannot make rational decisions concerning the allocation of resources." If the price consumers pay is less than the full social costs then too many resources are allocated to the production of this good. The inefficiency that results is similar to the inefficiency that results when polluters produce an inefficiently large output of their product because they are not forced to take into account the costs they impose on others. By imposing liability on the manufacturers, the cost of accidents becomes a cost they must pass on through higher prices, which discourages buyers and reduces production to the efficient level. (See the discussion following *Orchard Views Farms* in Chapter 1.)

2. The efficiency concern Judge Ramsey identified is ensuring that manufacturers choose the proper level of activity. The activity in which

Miles Laboratories is engaged is producing blood coagulants. By ensuring that the price of blood coagulants includes all of their costs, Judge Ramsey intended to ensure that the efficient quantity of that product is produced.

Generally people buy less of a product when the price rises. However, the amount of decrease in use resulting from a given increase in price varies from product to product. When the quantity demanded varies relatively little in response to a change in price, the demand for that product is said to be *inelastic*. The demand for blood coagulants is likely to be inelastic. Patients in Jane Doe's position may want blood coagulant at any price because without it they may bleed to death. If a price change has a relatively great effect on the quantity people demand, demand for that product is *elastic*. The demand for the Shopsmith in *Greenman* is likely to be more elastic than the demand for coagulants.

*Question:* For which products, those with elastic or those with inelastic demand, does the failure to include in the price the cost of externalities lead to greater inefficiencies?

3. Judge Ramsey argued that strict liability forces manufacturers to internalize all the costs associated with their productive activity and to raise their prices accordingly. If there were no liability for dangerous products, manufacturers could charge lower prices and consumers would buy more. The result is the inefficient overproduction of dangerous products because the manufacturer's prices do not reflect the true social costs.

But why conclude that the risk of injury is a cost of supplying the product? Why isn't it a cost of using the product? Coase's theory of reciprocal causation, discussed in Section D, above, suggests that the risk is associated with both activities. Generally the user can take the risk into account in deciding how much he is willing and able to pay to use a dangerous product, *if he is aware of the risks*. If the user must bear the costs of injury, the risk is reflected in the maximum price he will be willing to pay. The reduced willingness to pay generally results in fewer units of the product being bought, reducing production to an efficient level.

A comparison of the relative abilities of the manufacturer and user may direct the imposition of liability to one or the other. If both the manufacturer and the user have complete information about the risks and are equally able to adjust their behavior to account for the risk, there is no reason to prefer manufacturer liability over no liability. Unless consumers are preferred to manufacturers or vice versa, it does not matter whether the level of activity is reduced to an efficient level by increased prices reflecting greater risks borne by manufacturers or by decreased willingness to pay reflecting the greater risks borne by consumers.

There is reason to believe, however, that manufacturers have a greater ability to evaluate the risks associated with their products and to reflect those costs in their prices accurately. The buyer may investigate carefully every product he buys and still not know as much about it as the manufacturer. The manufacturer is much more likely to know the design characteristics of a product and the probability of a manufacturing defect as a result of repeated, daily experience with the product and its characteristics. After a certain number of defects appear, the manufacturer may be able to project the frequency with which consumers will be injured and reflect potential judgment costs in its prices. The consumer, on the other hand, may have only a single experience with a product, may be unfamiliar with prior defects, and be unable to evaluate how much less he is willing to pay.

> *Questions:* How does the imbalance in the availability of information to consumers and manufacturers affect the choice between no liability and strict liability for product defects? Is fault-based or strict liability a superior method for ensuring that dangerous products are neither over- nor under-produced?

4. Sometimes the injured party is not the purchaser but a third party or bystander. Because these parties do not respond to the price charged for the product, proper incentives for allocatively efficient behavior can be created only by imposing liability on the manufacturer or purchaser. Consider the case of Richman v. Charter Arms Corp., 571 F.Supp. 192 (E.D. La. 1983). The plaintiff was the victim of a shooting by a handgun. Unable to recover her damages from the shooter, the victim sued the manufacturer claiming that the manufacturer should be strictly liable, on the theory that the defendant's activity should be classified as ultrahazardous.

> *Question:* If the price of handguns is to reflect the external costs imposed by their use, should the gun manufacturer be held strictly liable for damages associated with shootings involving its guns?

5. In *Spano,* Chief Judge Fuld overruled the holding of Booth v. Rome, W. & O.T.R. Co., which had limited the liability of blasters. The rationale in *Booth* was that "[p]ublic policy is sustained by the building up of towns and cities and the improvement of property. Any unnecessary restraint on freedom of action of a property owner hinders this."

> *Questions:* Does the imposition of strict liability on blasters interfere with the building up of towns and cities and the improvement of property by making it more expensive? Is interference desirable?

6. In a footnote in *Doe,* Judge Ramsey considered the argument that strict products liability has the potential to drive some manufacturers into bankruptcy, 675 F.Supp. at 1471 n. 3:

> The argument is often made that strict products liability has the potential to bankrupt manufacturers. Such an argument misses the salutary economic role strict products liability plays. Understood properly, it can be seen that strict liability promotes a rational market place. Society cannot make rational decisions concerning the allocation of resources unless the price reflects the true costs. When the price rises greatly, reflecting the fact the product produces either substantial direct costs or creates widespread externalities, it is rational to discourage or even abandon consumption of that product. Strict products liability thus allows the marketplace to make better informed decisions.

> *Question:* When is a manufacturer likely to be driven into bankruptcy as a result of a switch from negligence-based liability to strict products liability? Is it allocatively efficient to eliminate such a manufacturer?

## 3. RISK-AVERSION AND LOSS SPREADING

## ESCOLA v. COCA COLA BOTTLING CO.

Supreme Court of California, 1944.
24 Cal.2d 453, 150 P.2d 436.

GIBSON, CHIEF JUSTICE.

Plaintiff, a waitress in a restaurant, was injured when a bottle of Coca Cola broke in her hand. She alleged that defendant company, which had bottled and delivered the alleged defective bottle to her employer, was negligent in selling "bottles containing said beverage which on account of excessive pressure of gas or by reason of some defect in the bottle was dangerous * * * and likely to explode." This appeal is from a judgment upon a jury verdict in favor of plaintiff.

[The majority of the court affirmed the judgment in favor of the plaintiff concluding that the jury could have reasonably inferred that the defendant was negligent.]

TRAYNOR, JUSTICE, concurring.

I concur in the judgment, but I believe the manufacturer's negligence should no longer be singled out as the basis of a plaintiff's right to recover in cases like the present one. In my opinion it should now be recognized that a manufacturer incurs an absolute liability when an article that he has placed on the market, knowing that it is to be used without inspection, proves to have a defect that causes injury to human beings. * * * Even if there is no negligence * * * public policy demands that responsibility be fixed wherever it will most effectively reduce the hazards to life and health inherent in defective products that reach the market. It is evident that the manufacturer can anticipate some hazards and guard against the recurrence of others, as the public cannot. Those who suffer injury from defective products are unprepared to meet its consequences. The cost of an injury and the loss of time or health may be an overwhelming misfortune to the person injured, and a needless one, for the risk of injury can be insured by the manufacturer and distributed among the public as a cost of doing business. It is to the public interest to discourage the marketing of products having defects that are a menace to the public. If such products nevertheless find their way into the market it is to the public interest to place the responsibility for whatever injury they may cause upon the manufacturer, who, even if he is not negligent in the manufacture of the product, is responsible for its reaching the market. However intermittently such injuries may occur and however haphazardly they may strike, the risk of their occurrence is a constant risk and a general one. Against such a risk there should be general and constant protection and the manufacturer is best situated to afford such protection.

\* \* \*

As handicrafts have been replaced by mass production with its great markets and transportation facilities, the close relationship between the producer and consumer of a product has been altered. Manufacturing processes, frequently valuable secrets, are ordinarily either inaccessible to or beyond the ken of the general public. The consumer no longer has means or skill enough to investigate for himself the soundness of a product, even when it is not contained in a sealed package, and his erstwhile vigilance has been lulled by the steady efforts of manufacturers to build up confidence by advertising and marketing devices such as trade-marks. Consumers no longer approach products warily but accept them on faith, relying on the reputation of the manufacturer or the trade mark. Manufacturers have sought to justify that faith by increasingly high standards of inspection and a readiness to make good on defective products by way of replacements and refunds. The manufacturer's obligation to the consumer must keep pace with the changing relationship between them; it cannot be escaped because the marketing of a product has become so complicated as to require one or more intermediaries. Certainly there is greater reason to impose liability on the manufacturer than on the retailer who is but a conduit of a product that he is not himself able to test.

The manufacturer's liability should, of course, be defined in terms of the safety of the product in normal and proper use, and should not extend to injuries that cannot be traced to the product as it reached the market.

### Notes and Questions

1. One of the arguments raised by Justice Traynor in *Escola* in favor of strict products liability is the ability of manufacturers to "anticipate some hazards and guard against the recurrence of others, as the public cannot." This characteristic of the manufacturer makes it the best minimizer of primary accident costs.

Traynor makes a second argument in favor of strict products liability. He points out that those injured by defective products may find that "[t]he cost of [the] injury and the loss of time or health may be an overwhelming misfortune". If manufacturers pay for such injuries under a strict liability regime, however, "the risk of injury can be insured by the manufacturer and distributed among the public as a cost of doing business." In other words, even if strict liability does not affect the level of primary accident costs society incurs, it changes the *distribution* of those costs in a desirable manner. The costs of accidents are dispersed evenly among consumers in the form of higher product prices, rather than borne entirely by the injured individual. Strict liability thus serves to "spread the losses" associated with injuries from defective products.

2. *Risk-Aversion.* In this context, risk means uncertainty. The study of the implications of "risk-aversion" involves examining how people's distaste for uncertainty affects their behavior. Consider a products liability risk as an example. Suppose that the probability of being injured by a defective bottle of Coca Cola is 1 in 100,000, and that the expected cost of

the injury (if it occurs) is $5,000. Would you rather pay $.05 (.0001 x $5000) more for each bottle of Coca Cola you drink and know that the manufacturer is strictly liable for any injuries, or would you rather pay less and bear the cost of any injury that occurs yourself? The expected loss in each case is five cents per bottle, but the outcome in the second case is more uncertain; you may suffer $5,000 in accident costs or zero accident costs.

If a consumer is *risk-neutral,* she will be indifferent between paying $.05 more per Coca Cola or bearing the probable loss associated with drinking each Coke (also $.05). A risk-neutral individual is indifferent between the sure thing and an uncertain thing with the same probability-discounted outcome: indifferent between receiving $100, or receiving a lottery ticket with a 10% chance of winning $1,000.

But are consumers really risk-neutral? The practice of gambling indicates that some individuals appear to enjoy risk; they are *risk-preferrers.* Still, most people most of the time seem to prefer to avoid risk, whether risky gains or risky losses. People seem to be *risk-averse* rather than risk-neutral. The existence of a large and highly-developed insurance industry may be sufficient proof that people dislike risk and are willing to pay money to avoid it.

3. *The Declining Marginal Utility of Money.* There is a theoretical explanation for risk-aversion. Many economists believe that as an individual becomes wealthier each additional dollar of wealth adds smaller increments to that individual's total utility. In other words, individuals have "declining marginal utility" for extra income. If you doubt this assumption, ask yourself which would mean more to you, the first million dollars you make—or the second?

The declining marginal utility of money works in reverse, as well. As one loses wealth, each additional dollar lost imposes a greater sacrifice. A $50,000 loss resulting from an accident inflicts a harm more than 50,000 times greater than the loss of one dollar.

4. *Products Liability and Risk–Spreading.* The examples in the previous paragraphs address the principle of declining marginal utility of income for a single individual, but extending the theory to numerous individuals is straightforward. If everyone has declining marginal utility of income, then one person's loss of $5000 is quite possibly a greater subjective loss than 5000 people each losing one dollar (though one cannot be certain, since one cannot systematically compare one person's loss in utility to another's). The possibility that individuals are risk-averse suggests that the risk-spreading that results from strict products liability is a significant benefit. People are better off paying slightly higher prices for products under a strict liability regime, than bearing the risk of large, uncompensated losses from defective products. Notice that this is true even if the expected losses from defective products are the same under strict liability as under a rule of negligence.

5. The costs of having and avoiding accidents are primary accident costs and the administrative costs of the tort system are tertiary accident costs. In The Costs of Accidents, p. 27 (1970), Guido Calabresi referred to the dislocation costs incurred when the lives of the parties to an accident

are disrupted, the "societal costs resulting from accidents," as *secondary accident costs*. The distinction between primary and secondary costs is not always clear, but secondary costs are usually associated with two theories of accident cost reduction: The Deep Pocket Theory and the Risk–Spreading Theory. Imposing liability on manufacturers may reduce secondary accident costs in either of two ways. First, it may place liability on the wealthier party, who derives less utility from the money at stake and so suffers a lesser subjective loss than a poorer individual. Second, it distributes the loss as widely as possible, so that many individuals suffer a small loss rather than one victim suffering a large loss.

*The Deep Pocket Theory:* Placing liability on the wealthiest party is justified on more than simply a distributional equity basis that favors the poor or injured over the wealthy. Under the theory of declining marginal utility, a dollar is worth less to a wealthy person than to a poor person. With their first dollars people buy the things that matter most to them; the later dollars are spent on things that matter less. People still value those later dollars, but not so highly as the initial ones.

In cases where there is no foundation for believing that one party is the better minimizer of accident costs, the law must inevitably decide whether the defendant or the victim will bear the costs of an accident that has occurred. If the wealthy manufacturer pays, then the judgment is paid out of dollars that are valued less highly than if the poor victim must pay. Thus, society's total level of well-being declines less if liability is placed on the wealthier party.

This theory has numerous problems. The most obvious one is that manufacturers are not always wealthy. The accumulation of judgments against manufacturers can drive them into bankruptcy. In addition, it is not clear whether a company has any "utility" of its own at all. A corporation is made up of its officers, employees, and stockholders. Any loss to the corporation must be a loss to them and the deep pocket theory says nothing about their level of wealth compared to the victim's. Moreover, we do not know how the loss will be distributed among these constituent groups. These problems make the deep pocket theory the less favored of the two approaches to minimizing secondary accident costs.

*Risk–Spreading and Insurance:* Under this theory of spreading, manufacturers can raise prices so that accidental losses are spread over a larger group. Judge Mentz relied on this argument in Richman v. Charter Arms Corp., 571 F.Supp. 192, 203–04 (E.D. La. 1983), which involved strict liability under the theory of abnormally dangerous activities for damages to a woman who was kidnapped, robbed, raped, and murdered by a man using a handgun manufactured by the defendant:

> Perhaps the most significant fact the defendant ignores is that increased insurance costs can be passed on to consumers in the form of higher prices for handguns. The people who benefit most from marketing practices like the defendant's are handgun manufacturers and handgun purchasers. Innocent victims rarely, if ever, are beneficiaries. Consequently, it hardly seems unfair to require manufacturers and purchasers, rather than innocent victims, to pay for the risks those practices entail. Furthermore, economic efficiency seems to require

the same result. In an important article on ultrahazardous activities and risk allocation, Professor Clarence Morris makes just this point. Morris, "Hazardous Enterprises and Risk Bearing Capacity", 61 Yale L.J. 1172 (1952). In his view, "the avowed goal of the absolute liability approach is allocation of loss to the party better equipped to pass it on to the public: the superior risk bearer." Professor Morris discusses a variety of examples to show that the defendant is not always the superior risk bearer in an ultrahazardous activity case. Here is what he says, however, about bodily injury and risk-bearing capacity:

> The financial burden of disabling personal injury overwhelms most people. While many can bear the cost of minor injury, prolonged infirmity and extended medical expense often exceed the financial competence of common men. Unless [common man] happens to be rich or covered by one of the more generous workmen's compensation plans, he will probably bear the risk less easily than Enterpriser. The preponderant likelihood is that Enterpriser is the better risk bearer of the two.
>
> * * * Thus, both fairness and economic efficiency suggest that the community would be better off if the defendant's marketing practices were classified as ultrahazardous. * * *

The court in *Charter Arms* apparently believed that even if the manufacturer was not the best party to minimize primary accident costs, secondary accident costs would be minimized by requiring the manufacturer to spread the loss through higher prices.

The manufacturer may be able to insure against losses by charging higher prices and holding a reserve against future liability or buying a liability insurance policy. The consumer might also be able to obtain insurance, of course.

*Questions:* Would the consumer's insurance ("first party" insurance) spread the loss just as effectively as imposing liability on the manufacturer? Might there be a difference between the ability of the consumer and the manufacturer to obtain insurance at low cost? If so, what impact should this difference have on the efficiency of strict liability?

## SHEPARD v. SUPERIOR COURT

Court of Appeal, First District, Division 2, 1977.
76 Cal.App.3d 16, 142 Cal.Rptr. 612.

KANE, ASSOCIATE JUSTICE, dissenting.

* * *

* * * To start with, it is noted that the avowed purpose of imposing strict liability upon the manufacturer is twofold: (1) loss-distribution or risk-spreading and (2) injury-reduction by enhanced safety. The first rationale, risk-spreading, holds the manufacturer liable for injuries resulting from the use of his product because he is in the best position to distribute the loss either by insurance or by increasing the price of

his product. As stated in *Greenman v. Yuba Power Products, Inc.*, the purpose of strict tort liability is to insure that the costs of injuries resulting from defective products are borne by the manufacturers who put such products on the market rather than by the injured persons who are powerless to protect themselves. Echoing the same idea, the court in *Vandermark v. Ford Motor Co.* reemphasized that strict liability on the manufacturer affords protection to the injured person and works no injustice because the manufacturers can protect themselves through obtaining insurance and dispersing the cost through the prices of the products. The second rationale, the theory of injury reduction, holds the manufacturer liable because he is in the best position to discover and correct the dangerous aspects of his products before any injury occurs. Again, the manufacturer may pass on to the consumer the increased product costs by incorporating them in the purchase price of the merchandise.

Although since its inception the courts have generally tended to broaden the scope of products liability, there are few cases, if any, which have embarked on a thorough and delicate analysis to explore whether the above stated policy goals are indeed promoted by the ever-expanding scope of enterprise liability. It is time for such an examination.

The basic facts of economy teach us that the fashionable trend of a wholesale extension of strict liability proves to be counterproductive in many instances by hampering and arresting, rather than promoting, the policy objectives underpinning the doctrine. Thus, it requires no special economic expertise to realize that the double demand posed by the law, i. e., to make the product absolutely safe on the one hand, and to spread the cost of the ever increasing insurance premiums together with the expense of safety measures to the consumer on the other, becomes increasingly difficult, if not entirely impossible, to meet. It is well to remember that economic forces do not work in a vacuum, but rather in a strict and realistic economic environment where prices of merchandise are greatly influenced (if not entirely determined) by economic rivalry and competition. Under these circumstances, the fundamental assumption of spreading the risk of the enterprise to the consumers at large cannot be attained and materialized. While some portion of the ever growing safety and insurance cost may pass directly to the consumer by way of a higher dollar price, the remainder will take the form of decreased quality not affecting safety and decreased profits. The decreased profits affect the manufacturers first (among them mainly the large segment of small businessmen with limited or marginal capital who have to shoulder the strict enterprise liability side by side with the huge corporations), then society as a whole. The motion and realistic operation of economic forces have been graphically described by one observer as follows: "Decreased profits, however, do not stop with the manufacturer. He distributes them to the shareholders of his corporation, just as he distributes increased prices to the consumers of his product. Moreover, decreased profits do not stop with the shareholders. *Rather, in more or less attenuated form, they pass on to other, broader classes.* The major distribution of decreased profits occurs when shareholders switch their investment to other, more profitable enterprises. When this happens, the liability-bearing manufacturer's enterprise loses its ability to attract investment capital resulting in decreased industrial activity. *This decreased activity results in losses to several categories. First, the consumer will feel the loss because the manufacturer's ability to produce a better, safer product will diminish. Second, reduced industrial activity will affect labor.* Severely diminished profits may force the manufacturer out of business. Even less drastic reductions, however, could reduce the number of new jobs. *Finally, reduced economic activity will affect the entire society, in a more or less attenuated form, through lower tax revenues, lower wages, and lower profits for distribution.*" (Alden D. Holford, The Limits of Strict Liability for Product Design and Manufacture (1973) 52 Tex.L.Rev. 81, 87, emphasis added.)

Paying heed to economic realities rather than our own fancy, the courts as a matter of judicial policy must stop the further extension of the strict liability of entrepreneurs, at least to areas where, as here, the determination of damages is speculative and conjectural rather than real and definable. In doing so, we are in line with established law which holds that the manufacturer is not an insurer of the product and that the strict liability of entrepreneurs may not be equated with absolute, limitless liability. As has been emphasized time and time again, in determining the parameters of enterprise liability we must draw a proper balance between the need for adequate recovery and the survival of viable enterprises. The guiding principles to achieve these goals are judicial temperance, evenhandedness and, first and foremost, fairness to all.

\* \* \*

## *Notes and Questions*

1. In *Shepard,* Justice Kane's dissent raises the question of who actually bears the costs of liability when strict liability requires the manufacturer to compensate victims without regard to the manufacturer's fault. Several possible candidates exist: consumers, who may pay more for the manufacturer's products; stockholders in the corporation, who may receive a lower return on the investment in the corporation due to lessened profitability; and employees of the corporation, who may be forced to accepted lower wages as a result of the higher costs. Economic theory provides tools for analyzing how these losses are distributed.

It is not usually true that the manufacturer can increase the price of its product dollar for dollar to reflect the increased judgment costs. There are several ways in which increased prices reduce the amount of output the manufacturer can sell. The most obvious are that the price of the product will be too high for some buyers to afford and that some buyers will not be willing and able to buy as much of the product as they did before. As a result the manufacturer will not be able to sell as much as before. The extent to which people curtail their purchases depends, among other things, on how expensive the product is initially and what substitutes there are for the product. The more expensive the product, other things being equal, the greater is the percentage cut in purchases associated with a given percentage price increase. The more desperately people need the product (that is, the fewer the substitutes) the less people will reduce their purchases. The manufacturer may be willing to raise its price by less than the full amount of the increased costs to avoid losing a large volume of sales. This willingness results in a sharing of the increased costs between manufacturer and buyers.

The share of increased costs borne by the manufacturer decreases the profitability of the investment of assets in the corporation. One way to minimize this decrease in profitability is to reduce costs of inputs, such as labor and raw materials. It is not usually true, however, that the manufacturer can reduce the amount it pays for inputs dollar for dollar to reflect its share of increased liability costs. The willingness of employees to take pay cuts is analogous to the willingness of consumers to pay higher prices for the product; it is affected by the size of the pay cut and the other job opportunities available to them. This is also true of the suppliers of other inputs such as raw materials.

After the manufacturer has raised prices as high as it profitably can and reduced the prices it pays for inputs to the production process, there remain the stockholders. To some extent, the manufacturer can reduce the amount it pays to stockholders in return for their investment. Like the other possible sharers of the burden, however, stockholders may have substitute investments available and low rates of return may make raising new capital more difficult or expensive.

Who actually bears the loss is a difficult question. While there is a formal methodology for answering these distributional questions in a systematic way, many related issues are not empirically answerable.

2. To get some idea of how the costs associated with strict liability are distributed, consider the various products involved in the strict liability cases in this chapter.

*Questions:* For which products would the manufacturer be able to pass on the largest percentage of the costs to the customer? In other words, for which products is consumer demand likely to be inelastic?

## 4. STRICT LIABILITY AND DUTY TO RESCUE

### OSTERLIND v. HILL

Supreme Judicial Court of Massachusetts, 1928.
263 Mass. 73, 160 N.E. 301.

BRALEY, J.

This is an action of tort, brought by the plaintiff as administrator of the estate of Albert T. Osterlind to recover damages for the conscious suffering and death of his intestate. There are four counts in the original declaration and five counts in the amended declaration, to each of which the defendant demurred. The first count of the original declaration alleges that, on or about July 4, 1925, the defendant was engaged in the business of letting for hire pleasure boats and canoes to be used on Lake Quannapowitt in the town of Wakefield; that it was the duty of the defendant to have a reasonable regard for the safety of the persons to whom he let boats and canoes; that the defendant, in the early morning of July 4, 1925, in willful, wanton, or reckless disregard of the natural and probable consequences, let for hire, to the intestate and one Ryan, a frail and dangerous canoe, * * * that, in consequence of the defendant's willful, wanton, or reckless disregard of his duties, the intestate and Ryan went out in the canoe, which shortly afterwards was overturned and the intestate, after hanging to it for approximately one-half hour, and making loud calls for assistance, which calls the defendant heard and utterly ignored, was obliged to release his hold, and was drowned; that in consequence of the defendant's willful, wanton, or reckless conduct the intestate endured great conscious mental anguish and great conscious physical suffering from suffocation and drowning. Count 2 differs materially from count 1 only in so far as negligent conduct is alleged as distinguished from willful, wanton, or reckless conduct. In count 3 the acts of the defendant set forth in the previous counts are relied upon as stating a cause of action for death as a result of the defendant's willful, wanton, or reckless conduct. * * *

The trial court sustained demurrers to both the original and amended declarations and reported the case for the determination of this court.

* * * The declaration must set forth facts which, if proved, establish the breach of a legal duty owed by the defendant to the intestate. * * *

In the case at bar, * * * it is alleged in every count of the original and amended declaration that after the canoe was overturned the intestate hung to the canoe for approximately one-half hour and made loud calls for assistance. * * *

* * * The failure of the defendant to respond to the intestate's outcries is immaterial. No legal right of the intestate was infringed. The allegation common to both declarations that the canoe was "frail and dangerous" appears to be a general characterization of canoes. It is not alleged that the canoe was out of repair and unsafe.

It follows that the order sustaining each demurrer is affirmed.

### *Notes and Questions*

1. Apply the Learned Hand "BPL" formula to the conduct of defendant Hill. While Albert Osterlind (who apparently could not swim) was clinging to the overturned canoe and calling for help, the probability of an accident—a drowning—was quite high, unless the defendant came to the plaintiff's rescue. The burden of the rescue seemed quite low, perhaps requiring no greater effort than Hill's simply rowing one of his other canoes out to get the defendant. Since the burden to Hill of rescuing

Osterlind was much lower than the expected loss to Osterlind if Hill did not intervene, one might expect that Hill would be found negligent for his failure to rescue.

*Osterlind* illustrates the common law rule that an individual generally has no duty to rescue another, even when the cost of rescue is negligible and the victim's situation is extremely perilous. The rule against a duty to rescue often is explained as one of causation or responsibility: since the defendant played no part in endangering the plaintiff, the defendant owes no duty to minimize that risk.

> *Questions:* From an economic perspective, is the causal explanation appealing? Does it make sense to hold defendants responsible when their actions impose a harm on plaintiffs, but not when their inaction withholds a potential benefit—rescue?

2. A categorical rule that defendants have no duty to rescue is equivalent to a rule that plaintiffs are strictly liable for their injuries when the defendant did not cause those injuries but simply declined to prevent them. Recasting the rule as one of strict liability may shed some light on its rationale.

> *Questions:* Applying the analysis of strict liability developed in the preceding materials, is there an economic explanation for the common law's failure to impose a duty of rescue? Which party is in the best position to minimize the sum of the costs of accidents and the costs of rescues?

3. The common law recognizes an exception to the general rule of no duty to rescue in cases where the defendant's negligence created the plaintiff's perilous situation. If Hill had been negligently piloting the canoe when it overturned, he would have had a duty to use all reasonable efforts to rescue his passenger, Osterlind.

> *Question:* Is that exception consistent with the economic rationale of the rule against a duty to rescue?

4. Establishing a duty to rescue would affect secondary and tertiary accident costs. When considering the tertiary costs of a duty to rescue consider the application of rule in the following circumstances. If a person on the street tells you that he needs food or will go hungry, do you have a duty to provide him food? If a charitable organization informs you that thousands are starving in another country, must you write a large check? Would a medical doctor violate her duty to rescue if she took the weekend off rather than working in the hospital? It is hard to determine where the duty to rescue stops.

## G. EFFICIENT DEFENSES TO STRICT LIABILITY

### 1. UNFORESEEABLE MISUSE

#### DANIELL v. FORD MOTOR CO.
United States District Court, District of New Mexico, 1984.
581 F.Supp. 728.

BALDOCK, DISTRICT JUDGE.

* * *

In 1980, the plaintiff became locked inside the trunk of a 1973 Ford LTD automobile, where she remained for some nine days. Plaintiff now seeks to recover for psychological and physical injuries arising from that occurrence. She contends that the automobile had a design defect in that the trunk lock or latch did not have an internal release or opening mechanism. * * *

* * *

The overriding factor barring plaintiff's recovery is that she intentionally sought to end her life by crawling into an automobile trunk from which she could not escape. This is not a case where a person inadvertently became trapped inside an automobile trunk. The plaintiff was aware of the natural and probable consequences of her perilous conduct. Not only that, the plaintiff, at least initially, sought those dreadful consequences. Plaintiff, not the manufacturer of the vehicle, is responsible for this unfortunate occurrence.

Recovery under strict products liability and negligence will be discussed first because the concept of duty owned by the manufacturer to the consumer or user is the same under both theories in this case. As a general principle, a design defect is actionable only where the condition of the product is unreasonably dangerous to the user or consumer. Under strict products liability or negligence, a manufacturer has a duty to consider only those risks of injury which are foreseeable. A risk is not foreseeable by a manufacturer where a product is used in a manner which could not reasonably be anticipated by the manufacturer and that use is the cause of the plaintiff's injury. The plaintiff's injury would not be foreseeable by the manufacturer.

The purposes of an automobile trunk are to transport, stow and secure the automobile spare tire, luggage and other goods and to protect those items from elements of the weather. The design features of an automobile make it well near impossible that an adult intentionally would enter the trunk and close the lid. The dimensions of a trunk, the height of its sill and its load floor and the efforts to first lower the trunk lid and then to engage its latch, are among the design features which encourage closing and latching the trunk lid while standing outside the vehicle. The court holds that the plaintiff's use of the trunk compartment as a means to attempt suicide was an unforeseeable use as a matter of law. Therefore, the manufacturer had no duty to design an internal release or opening mechanism that might have prevented this occurrence.

* * *

WHEREFORE,

IT IS ORDERED that the defendant's Motion for Summary Judgment is granted.

### Notes and Questions

1. One of the justifications for imposing strict liability on manufacturers in products cases is that they are usually the party in the best position to minimize primary accident costs and to internalize external costs. The court in *Daniell* held that use of the trunk compartment as a means of attempted suicide was unforeseeable and, therefore, the manufacturer had no duty to design an internal release mechanism. In the law, "unforeseeable" does not mean that people are literally unable to foresee an event. Rather, to be "unforeseeable" in a legal sense, the event must be sufficiently improbable that a reasonable person would not take it into account in his decisions.

*Questions:* What does the foreseeability of someone using the trunk to commit suicide have to do with whether the manufacturer is the best cost avoider for this accident? Does the customary rationale for strict liability support recovery by Ms. Daniell after she locked herself in the trunk of her LTD?

2. The 1973 LTD was a very large car with a big trunk. It is reasonably foreseeable that someone might climb into the trunk to get a small piece of luggage or some groceries that had rolled out of the shopping bag into the back of the trunk, or to fix some wiring, or a hinge.

*Questions:* Is the possibility of the lid accidently closing on such a person so remote that the need to escape from the closed trunk is unforeseeable? If Ms. Daniell had climbed into her trunk to retrieve a grapefruit that had fallen from her shopping bag and the wind had slammed the trunk shut, would holding Ford liable be efficient? Why should this change in facts make a difference?

3. In some states, unforeseeable misuse of a product is a complete defense in a strict products liability action.

*Question:* How does freeing the manufacturer from liability for unforeseeable risks further the goal of minimizing tertiary accident costs?

## CRYTS v. FORD MOTOR COMPANY
Missouri Court of Appeals, St. Louis District, Division Three, 1978.
571 S.W.2d 683.

GUNN, PRESIDING JUDGE.

This appeal arises from a civil action in tort based on a two car collision in which plaintiff, David Cryts, suffered paraplegia. The jury returned a verdict in the amount of $150,000, and the judgment was entered against defendants Ford Motor Company (Ford), the manufacturer of the car plaintiff was driving, and Robert Uttendorfer, the driver of the car with which he collided. Uttendorfer's liability is premised on negligence in the operation of his vehicle, while Ford's liability is premised on strict liability for a defectively designed armrest which caused plaintiff's back to be broken when he was thrown against his door in the collision. Each defendant has appealed. * * *

* * *

Plaintiff predicates his theory of recovery on the principle of strict liability in tort for the defective design and condition of the 1957 Thunderbird armrest as applied in the so-called "second collision" or "injury enhancement" doctrine. * * *

* * * In this case, the second collision was plaintiff's body striking the armrest after the first collision between the Thunderbird and the Uttendorfer vehicle. The second collision doctrine differs from the typical § 402A case, in that the defect would not have produced any injury in the absence of an intervening cause which sets the injury producing cycle into action. The source of the original or intervening cause is irrelevant so long as the plaintiff's particular use of the product is reasonably foreseeable. The Eighth Circuit, in applying Missouri law and in adopting the second collision doctrine, specifically held that a manufacturer could be held liable for injuries shown to have been caused or enhanced by the defective condition of its product which was being used in a manner reasonably anticipated in the course of an accident brought about by an independent cause.

* * *

In this case, plaintiff produced evidence from his expert witness that the 1957 Thunderbird armrest was defective, in that it was constructed of hard plastic with minimal energy-absorbing capacity; that it was lightly padded; and that its pointed shape was such as to concentrate the force of energy absorbed by the body. In light of this evidence the jury could have reasonably found that the armrest was defective and that it was unreasonably dangerous for its anticipated use.

Ford's other arguments that a collision with another vehicle was not an anticipated use * * * [is] not persuasive to the outcome of this case. It has been held that even misuse of a product may be reasonably foreseeable. Further, it has been specifically held that a collision is a foreseeable incident of normal use of a motor vehicle. Ford argues that it built the safest armrest possible under the technology existing in 1957. Such a contention has no bearing on the outcome of a strict liability claim, where the sole subject of inquiry is the defective condition of the product and not the manufacturer's knowledge, negligence or fault. * * *

* * *

Judgment Affirmed.

## *Notes and Questions*

1. In *Cryts,* as in *Daniell,* the consumer was using the product in a manner not intended by the manufacturer. Unlike *Daniell,* the consumer in *Cryts* was using the product in a manner he did not intend and the consumer does not appear to be in a better position than the manufacturer to anticipate the idiosyncratic use. As the majority of courts make clear, however, the manufacturer's liability is not limited to risks resulting from intended uses of the product. See, e.g., Larsen v. General Motors Corp., 391 F.2d 495, 502 (8th Cir. 1968):

> * * * While automobiles are not made for the purpose of colliding with each other, a frequent and inevitable contingency of normal automobile use will result in collisions and injury-producing impacts. No rational basis exists for limiting recovery to situations where the defect in design or manufacture was the causative factor of the accident, as the accident and the resulting injury, usually caused by the so-called "second collision" of the passenger with the interior part of the automobile, all are foreseeable. Where the injuries or enhanced injuries are due to the manufacturer's failure to use reasonable care to avoid subjecting the user of its products to an unreasonable risk of injury, general negligence principles should be applicable. The sole function of an automobile is not just to provide a means of transportation, it is to provide a means of safe transportation or as safe as is reasonably possible under the present state of the art.
>
> We do agree that under the present state of the art an automobile manufacturer is under no duty to design an accident-proof or fool-proof vehicle or even one that floats on water, but such manufacturer is under a duty to use reasonable care in the design of its vehicle to avoid subjecting the user to an unreasonable risk of injury in the event of a collision. Collisions with or without fault of the user are clearly foreseeable by the manufacturer and are statistically inevitable.

2. Suppose that Cryts' injuries had resulted from some intentional, but foreseeable, misuse of the product. For example, Cryts might have lost control of the car while driving in excess of the posted speed limit. Note the language in *Cryts* that "[t]he source of the original or intervening cause [of the plaintiff's injury] is irrelevant so long as the plaintiff's particular use of the product is reasonably foreseeable."

*Question:* Is it efficient for Cryts to be able to recover on the theory that the car he negligently crashed was defectively designed?

3. Like the State of Missouri in *Cryts,* all states but one apply the language of § 402A of the Restatement 2d of Torts in strict products liability cases:

> § 402A. Special Liability of Seller of Product for Physical Harm to User or Consumer
>
> (1) One who sells any product in a defective condition unreasonably dangerous to the user or consumer or to his property is subject to

liability for physical harm thereby caused to the ultimate user or consumer, or to his property, if

 (a) the seller is engaged in the business of selling such a product, and

 (b) it is expected to and does reach the user or consumer without substantial change in the condition in which it is sold.

(2) The rule stated in Subsection (1) applies although

 (a) the seller has exercised all possible care in the preparation and sale of his product, and

 (b) the user or consumer has not bought the product from or entered into any contractual relation with the seller.

## 2. UNREASONABLE ASSUMPTION OF RISK

### WILLIAMS v. BROWN MANUFACTURING COMPANY

Supreme Court of Illinois, 1970.
45 Ill.2d 418, 261 N.E.2d 305, 46 A.L.R.3d 226.

UNDERWOOD, CHIEF JUSTICE.

James Williams was injured while operating a trenching machine manufactured by defendant, Brown Manufacturing Company, Inc. Williams brought an action against defendant under a theory of strict product liability in tort, essentially alleging an unreasonably dangerous design, and was awarded damages in the amount of $40,000 by a Madison County circuit court jury. The judgment was affirmed by the Appellate Court for the Fifth Judicial District, and we granted leave to appeal.

\* \* \*

Plaintiff's recovery was based upon a count alleging that while he was operating the trencher, "the machine bucked and unexpectedly jumped a number of feet to the rear, knocking the plaintiff to the ground and running over him, thereby causing serious and permanent injuries \* \* \*." This count enumerated several respects in which the condition of the trencher was "unreasonably dangerous", alleged that the condition existed when the trencher left defendant's control, and claimed that plaintiff's injuries were a direct and proximate result of the condition. \* \* \* Defendant's answer included two affirmative defenses: the action was barred by the statute of limitations, and plaintiff had "assumed all risk in relation to use and operation" of the trencher. Both defenses were stricken by the trial court on plaintiff's motion because of the court's opinion that the proof was insufficient to support either defense.

\* \* \*

The evidence indicated that, while plaintiff was operating the machine from a position between the handlebars at its rear, the digging teeth of the trencher momentarily caught on an underground pipe; when the teeth suddenly slipped off the pipe, the machine lurched backward. Plaintiff maintained that the power unit should have been equipped with some safety device, such as a "throw out clutch", to prevent such a build-up of force. Alternatively, he argued that the drive-belt should have been easily adjustable to a tension which would allow satisfactory digging normally, but would allow slippage when an obstruction was encountered. * * * An instruction booklet had accompanied the machine, and, though it did not advise as to the proper position for an operator, it did state in the two pages concerned with operation and maintenance:

> "ADJUSTMENTS AND MAINTENANCE
>
> The engine is bolted stationary to the machine, and when the drive belts become loose enough to slip, adjust them by the threaded shaft on the right hand clutch lever. Caution—do not adjust the belts too tight; they must be able to slip under shock load. * * * "

On cross-examination, plaintiff acknowledged having read the manual prior to his injury, although it is unclear how completely he read it. He did admit to reading at least a portion of the maintenance section, in which section the quoted language appeared.

In resolving the case before us the appellate court relied upon § 402A of the Restatement (Second) of Torts, comment (n), which reads as follows: "*n. Contributory negligence.* Since the liability with which this Section deals is not based upon negligence of the seller, but is strict liability, the rule applied to strict liability cases (see § 524) applies. Contributory negligence of the plaintiff is not a defense when such negligence consist merely in a failure to discover the defect in the product, or to guard against the possibility of its existence. On the other hand the form of contributory negligence which consists in voluntarily and unreasonably proceeding to encounter a known danger, and commonly passes under the name of assumption of risk, is a defense under this Section as in other cases of strict liability. If the user or consumer discovers the defect and is aware of the danger, and nevertheless proceeds unreasonably to make use of the product and is injured by it, he is barred from recovery."

* * *

All authorities agree that plaintiffs in tort actions may so conduct themselves as to bar recovery for injuries suffered by them. This recovery-barring conduct, while given different labels, is ofttimes treated within the general concept of "contributory negligence." * * * In determining where the loss should fall as between the nonnegligent manufacturer, distributor or retailer and the less than careful plaintiff, it has generally been recognized in Illinois and elsewhere that plaintiffs who "misuse" a product—use it for a purpose neither intended nor "foreseeable" (objectively reasonable) by the defendant—may be barred from recovery. There is likewise general agreement that a plaintiff who knows a product is in a dangerous condition and proceeds in disregard of this known danger (often termed "assumption of risk") may not recover for resulting injuries.

The question before us is whether, in a strict product liability in tort action, the concept of contributory negligence as it prevails in this State shall bar a plaintiff's recovery, or whether that recovery will be barred only when the nature of plaintiff's misconduct has reached the point at which he has misused the product or has assumed the risk of its use. We are persuaded that the policy considerations which led us to adopt strict tort liability in [Suvada v. White Motor Co.] compel the elimination of "contributory negligence" as a bar to recovery. We also note that all other jurisdictions which have adopted the theory of strict liability have reached substantially the same conclusion, for, even though some of the opinions speak in terms of "contributory negligence", the actual conduct there held to bar recovery would by us be classified as misuse or assumption of risk.

* * *

[S]ubstantial evidence was presented which could reasonably support a jury determination that plaintiff recognized and voluntarily accepted the danger posed by improper drive-belt adjustment. Plaintiff was an experienced "operating engineer", with proficiency in a wide range of machinery; a jury could have believed him aware of the trencher's obvious design features. Indeed, he admittedly "checked out" the new machine to be sure it was in order. Since he was an experienced machinery operator, a jury could reasonably believe that he understood the general characteristics of belt-drive systems, and it was obvious that the trencher utilized such a system. * * *

* * * In any event, plaintiff admits having read, prior to his injury, portions of the manual relating to maintenance. As earlier noted, that was the section of the manual which contained the cautionary instructions relating to the drive-belt. It also appears that plaintiff may have contemplated the possibility of encountering an underground obstruction, but discounted the danger since, as he related on cross-examination, he had understood there was no underground obstruction in the area.

We emphasize that "assumption of risk" is an affirmative defense which does bar recovery, and which may be asserted in a strict liability action notwithstanding the absence of any contractual relationship between the parties. Furthermore, while the test to be applied in determining whether a user has assumed the risk of using a product known to be dangerously defective is fundamentally a subjective test, in the sense that it is *his* knowledge, understanding and appreciation of the danger which must be assessed, rather than that of the reasonably prudent person * * *.

A determination of the propriety of the trial court's action in striking the affirmative defense of assumption of risk must be predicated upon consideration of the totality of the evidence in its aspect most favorable to defendant. Viewed in this light, we cannot say that the evidence as a whole so overwhelmingly favors plaintiff that a jury finding for defendant on this issue could never stand. It is therefore necessary that this cause be remanded for a new trial under proper instructions in accordance with this opinion.

\* \* \*

Reversed and remanded.

### Notes and Questions

1. Unforeseeable misuse cases can be explained by the fact that it is pointless to ask manufacturers to guard against risks that are extremely unlikely to materialize. The plaintiff's injury in *Williams,* however, resulted from a defect reasonably foreseeable to the manufacturer, one addressed in the manufacturer's instruction booklet.

*Questions:* If the manufacturer is aware of and appreciates the risks associated with a defect in the product, why should the plaintiff bear the entire loss resulting from use of the defective product? Does the assumption of the risk defense to products liability resemble the doctrine of last clear chance?

2. Some courts require that the plaintiff's assumption of the risk in products liability cases be *unreasonable* in addition to being knowing and voluntary. Not all jurisdictions add this requirement.

*Questions:* When can a plaintiff "reasonably" assume the risk of using a product with an obvious and known defect? From an efficiency perspective, does the requirement of unreasonableness improve the incentives provided by strict products liability?

## 3. COMPARATIVE NEGLIGENCE

### MURRAY v. FAIRBANKS MORSE

United States Court of Appeals, Third Circuit, 1979.
610 F.2d 149.

ROSENN, CIRCUIT JUDGE.

This appeal raises several issues, including novel and important questions as to whether a comparative negligence statute may be applied and, if so, to what extent, in an action for personal injuries brought under twin theories of strict products liability and common law principles of negligence. The jury returned a verdict in favor of the plaintiff, Norwilton Murray, in the sum of two million dollars against the manufacturer, Beloit Power Systems, Inc. (Beloit). The jury, in response to special interrogatories, found that plaintiff's negligence was a proximate cause of his injuries and that he was at fault to the extent of five percent. The trial judge reduced the verdict accordingly and judgment was thereupon entered for the plaintiff. Beloit's motion for a new trial was denied and it appealed. Murray has also cross-appealed contending that the trial court erred in applying contributory negligence as a defense to a products liability action grounded on section

402A of the Restatement (Second) of Torts and that it should not have reduced his verdict because of his own contributory negligence. We find no error on Beloit's appeal and we reject Murray's cross-appeal. Accordingly, we affirm the judgment of the district court.

\* \* \*

Strict products liability evolved by stripping away certain problems of proof plaintiffs encountered under either negligence or warranty theories. By focusing the legal inquiry on the product defect rather than the defendant's conduct and thereby easing the plaintiff's burden of proof, strict liability theory endeavors to place the risk of economic loss on the manufacturers of defective products, thereby spreading the loss and not saddling it solely on an innocent injured consumer. \* \* \*

The elimination of the need to prove defendant's negligence has led some to view strict products liability as a "no-fault" doctrine to which the application of comparative negligence principles is simply not conceptually feasible. \* \* \*

\* \* \* The key conceptual distinction between strict products liability theory and negligence is that the plaintiff need not prove faulty *conduct* on the part of the defendant in order to recover. The jury is not asked to determine if the defendant deviated from a standard of care in producing his product. There is no proven faulty conduct of the defendant to compare with the faulty conduct of the plaintiff in order to apportion the responsibility for an accident. Although we may term a defective product "faulty," it is qualitatively different from the plaintiff's conduct that contributes to his injury. A comparison of the two is therefore inappropriate. The characterization of both plaintiff's negligent conduct and the defect as faulty may provide a semantic bridge between negligence and strict liability theories, but it provides neither a conceptual nor pragmatic basis for apportioning the loss for a particular injury.

We believe that if the loss for a particular injury is to be apportioned between the product defect and the plaintiff's misconduct, the only conceptual basis for comparison is the causative contribution of each to the particular loss or injury. In apportioning damages we are really asking how much of the injury was caused by the defect in the product versus how much was caused by the plaintiff's own actions.
\* \* \*

\* \* \*

Once a conceptually viable way of apportioning damages in section 402A actions is established, the key inquiry is whether such a system is consistent with the policy goals of strict products liability. As we have indicated already, a central goal of the strict liability action is to relieve the plaintiff of proof problems associated with existing negligence and warranty theories. A system of comparative fault which proceeds to apportion damages on the basis of causation in no way disturbs the plaintiff's burden of proof. The plaintiff still need only prove the existence of a defect causally linked to the injury. The defendant's burden is to prove plaintiff's contributory fault.

A second goal of strict products liability is to place the "burden of loss on manufacturers rather than ... injured persons who are '*powerless to protect themselves* ....' " Under traditional strict products liability law, the ordinary contributory negligence of the plaintiff has been held not to be an available defense. Contributory negligence may occur in two ways in products liability cases. The plaintiff may be negligent in his actual use of the product or he may be negligent in failing to discover the product defect. Because the defendant exposes the plaintiff to a risk of harm by placing a dangerous product on the market, traditional thinking is that he alone should bear the loss despite the presence of such contributory negligence. The rationale is that the manufacturer is in a better position to absorb the economic loss by spreading the risk of loss through the chain of distribution. Eventually the cost is passed on to society as a whole in the form of an increased cost of the product.

The problem with this "deep pocket" rationale is that the manufacturer may be paying for a part of the loss which is attributable not to the product defect, but to plaintiff's conduct. If contributory negligence is ignored in determining the extent of plaintiff's loss, then the future cost of the manufacturer's product will be artificially inflated and will not accurately represent the actual risk posed by the defective product. Although individual plaintiffs may benefit from the immunity currently given for their contributory negligence, the consuming public at large may be adversely affected. If the future cost of a product does not accurately reflect the risk posed, then consumers may actually choose cheaper, less safe products because the cost of the manufacturer's product is artificially high.

The recognition of contributory fault as an absolute bar to recovery would improperly shift the total loss to the plaintiff. Under a system of comparative fault, however, there are good reasons for allowing some form of contributory fault to be considered in reducing damages. When plaintiff's conduct is faulty, *i.e.*, he exposes himself to an unreasonable risk of harm which causes part of his injuries, the manufacturer should not be required to pay that portion of the loss attributable to the plaintiff's fault. Under a comparative system, the future cost of the defendant's product will accurately represent the danger it has caused and not the danger caused by plaintiff's own fault.

\* \* \*

The foregoing analysis leads us to conclude that a system of comparative fault may effectively operate in strict products liability cases and will result in a more equitable apportionment of the loss for product related injuries while furthering the valid policy goals behind the strict products liability action. \* \* \*

\* \* \*

## Notes and Questions

1. States have taken different positions on whether contributory negligence should limit a plaintiff's recovery in strict liability cases. Some states allow only specified types of conduct to be raised as a defense (such as voluntarily and unreasonably proceeding in the face of a known risk) while others consider the full range of plaintiff's conduct. In *Murray,* the product defect was faulty welding of iron bars supporting an electrical control panel. The plaintiff was installing the panel when the accident occurred. His contributory negligence consisted of putting his weight on one of the bars while leaning dangerously over an open space at the bottom of the panel. When the bar gave way, Murray fell ten feet to a concrete floor suffering severe spinal injuries. His negligence consisted of failing to use a safer method of installation, such as a scaffolding, which would have prevented his fall. The court reduced Murray's recovery by 5% ($100,000) to give people in his position an incentive to be more careful. Because the jury found that the defect was 95% responsible for the accident, the manufacturer was liable for $1,900,000.

If contributory negligence completely bars a plaintiff's recovery in a strict liability case, the strict liability system may be characterized as one in which defendants bear the costs of accidents unless they can prove that the plaintiff was negligent. This is the exact reverse of the rule of pure negligence, under which plaintiffs must bear their own losses unless the defendant was negligent. The rule of negligence combined with contributory negligence gives desirable incentives in all categories of cases except Category IIIA.

> *Question:* When is a strict liability system with contributory negligence as a complete bar inefficient?

2. In *Murray,* Judge Rosenn demonstrated his concern for the allocative efficiency of the market for electrical control panels. He reasoned that if consumers do not bear the portion of the risk attributable to their own behavior, they will fail to take efficient precautions and the price of the product must rise to reflect such inefficient losses. But apportioning risk to different parties is an even more conceptually difficult task under strict liability than under a rule of negligence. Because in strict liability there is no "fault" on the part of the manufacturer to balance against the fault of the plaintiff, Judge Rosenn concluded that "the only conceptual basis for comparison is the causative contribution of each to the particular loss or injury."

> *Questions:* If society's goal is to minimize accident costs, does it matter who caused the injury? If society's goal is to ensure that prices properly reflect the risks associated with a product, does it matter who caused the injury?

3. Faced with the problem of allocating risks between two parties each capable of preventing accidents, the court in *Murray* opted for comparative apportioning of damages on the basis of relative causation, as a means of creating incentives for both to minimize primary accident costs. As discussed in the notes following Golden v. McCurry, comparative negligence can lead to duplicative overavoidance or to mutual nonavoidance.

*Question:* Are the factual situations that give rise to those possibilities present in *Murray,* suggesting that apportioning liability in strict liability cases may be inefficient?

## H. PROBLEMS IN CALCULATING DAMAGES

This chapter focuses primarily on the economic analysis of who should be liable for the costs of accidents. This section briefly examines how that liability should be measured, the question of damages.

### 1. THE COLLATERAL SOURCE RULE

#### ANHEUSER–BUSCH, INC. v. STARLEY

Supreme Court of California, in Bank, 1946.
28 Cal.2d 347, 170 P.2d 448.

SCOTT, J.

\* \* \*

Plaintiff appeals from a judgment for defendant entered on a directed verdict.

Denver–Chicago Trucking Company, hereinafter referred to as carrier, was engaged as a common carrier, in the transportation by truck of personal property owned by plaintiff. In the course thereof defendant's car collided with the carrier's truck containing the property, resulting in a partial destruction of the property. Prior to the commencement of this action the carrier paid plaintiff's claim for the damage to the property presumably under the law providing: "Unless the consignor accompanies the freight and retains exclusive control thereof, an inland common carrier of property is liable \* \* \* for the loss or injury thereof from any cause whatever, except: 1. An inherent defect, vice, or weakness, or a spontaneous action, of the property itself; 2. The act of a public enemy of the United States, or of this state; 3. The act of the law; or, 4. Any irresistible superhuman cause." Civ. Code, § 2194. Evidence was adduced that the claim was paid without reference to any negligence or tortious conduct on the part of the carrier. No release was given to the carrier by plaintiff.

In the instant action plaintiff seeks to recover damages to its property flowing from the collision, asserting that defendant's negligence was the cause of it. Defendant's motion for a directed verdict was granted solely upon the ground that plaintiff had been fully compensated for its loss by the carrier and that it was not a proper party plaintiff in this action.

Where a person suffers personal injury or property damage by reason of the wrongful act of another, an action against the wrongdoer for the damages suffered is not precluded nor is the amount of the damages reduced by the receipt by him of payment for his loss from a source wholly independent of the wrongdoer. The rule has been applied where the independent source is pension systems or charity. The most typical case is where the person suffering the damage has procured insurance protecting him against the loss, to which the wrongdoer did not contribute in procuring, and his insurer pays him for the loss suffered. In the insurance cases its application is not prevented by the circumstances that the insurer is subrogated to the rights of the insured person suffering the damage as against the tort feasor. The analogy between that rule and the instant case is close.

The liability of the carrier to the owner for damage to property in transit under the contract to transport is practically absolute. The few exceptions are stated in the statutory law. His liability is that of a limited insurer whether it be said to be contractual (the statute forming part of the contract), statutory or in tort. The recovery of the loss by the owner from the carrier comes from a source wholly independent of the tort feasor whose negligence caused the loss. Therefore under this rule plaintiff's action is not barred unless there are some other factors which compel it.

* * *

The judgment is reversed.

TRAYNOR, JUSTICE, dissenting.

I dissent. In my opinion plaintiff's action is barred on the ground that plaintiff has been fully compensated by the carrier for the injury to its goods and would be unjustly enriched by a double recovery.

"When the plaintiff has accepted satisfaction in full for the injury done him, from whatever source it may come, he is so far affected in equity and good conscience, that the law will not permit him to recover again for the same damages." Whether the persons who are responsible to the plaintiff have acted jointly or separately is immaterial, for the controlling questions are whether the loss for which they are responsible is identical and whether the payment by one of them has fully compensated the plaintiff. * * *

* * *

## Notes and Questions

1. Under applicable California law, the Denver–Chicago Trucking Company as a common carrier had to compensate Anheuser–Busch fully for the merchandise damaged in the accident, even though the Denver–Chicago driver might not have been at fault.

*Questions:* How does such a strict liability provision minimize primary, secondary, and tertiary accident costs? What is the economic effect of the statutory exceptions to carrier strict liability?

2. The "collateral source rule" applied in *Anheuser–Busch* permits plaintiffs to recover damages from defendants even when a third party fully compensated them for their losses.

*Question:* Does allowing the plaintiff to collect double compensation encourage the defendant to invest too much in preventative measures, resulting in inefficient accident avoidance?

3. If she must pay *someone* for the damage she inflicts, the defendant will avoid that damage when doing so is cost-justified. Defendant Maud Starley would have faced the same incentives if, instead of paying damages to plaintiff Anheuser–Busch, she had been required to compensate the carrier, Denver–Chicago Trucking Company, or even to pay a fine to the California Highway Commission in the amount of the cost of the damaged goods.

*Question:* What interests are served by requiring defendants to pay their damages to plaintiffs, rather than to a third party?

4. Suppose that plaintiff Anheuser–Busch could have taken precautionary measures to avoid or reduce the damage to its property in the event of a shipping accident, perhaps by investing in special protective packaging.

*Questions:* In cases where both the plaintiff and the defendant could take cost-justified precautions to minimize accident losses, how does the collateral source rule affect the plaintiff's incentives to take such precautions?

## 2. MEASURING FUTURE LOSSES

If a defendant is to face appropriate incentives for accident avoidance, legal damages must fully and accurately reflect the plaintiff's losses. Many of the losses plaintiffs suffer fall into a category described as "economic" or "pecuniary" loss, losses easily measured in monetary terms. Pecuniary losses include lost earnings, property damage, or medical expenses.

It is relatively easy to measure a plaintiff's pecuniary losses when those losses have already been incurred. Often, however, a seriously injured plaintiff may expect to incur additional medical expenses for years into the future. Similarly, a severe injury may render an individual unable to work and earn wages for a substantial period of time, perhaps for life. How are such future losses measured?

### KACZKOWSKI v. BOLUBASZ

Supreme Court of Pennsylvania, 1980.
491 Pa. 561, 421 A.2d 1027.

Nix, Justice.

Appellant instituted a complaint in trespass in Allegheny County Court of Common Pleas. The suit arose from an automobile accident in which the decedent, Eric K. Kaczkowski, was riding as a passenger in a vehicle operated by appellee. At the original trial of this matter, the jury established the liability of the appellee. Upon appellant's Motion For a New Trial, the case was returned to the trial court for a retrial on the issue of damages.

\* \* \*

\* \* \* [T]he plaintiff relied upon the trial court's charge of impairment of future earning power for the guidance of the jury. The lower court charged the jury to consider the decedent's personal characteristics to: calculate the potential gross earnings of the decedent for the period of decedent's work life expectancy; to determine the maintenance costs of the decedent for the period of decedent's work life expectancy; to deduct the personal maintenance costs from the gross earnings to produce net earnings; and to discount the net earnings to present value by six percent (6%) simple interest. Based upon the judge's instructions, the jury returned a verdict of $30,000. on behalf of the estate of Eric K. Kaczkowski. \* \* \*

The issue raised by appellant is whether the trial court erred in excluding reliable economic testimony showing the impact of inflation and increased productivity[5] on decedent's future earning power. \* \* \*

\* \* \*

Personal injury awards are usually lump-sum payments, and are not paid in weekly or monthly installments. Thus, all damages for personal injuries, including damages expected to accrue in the future, must be proved and calculated at trial. The loss of future wages is discounted to its present value by using the six percent (6%) simple interest figure.[10]

\* \* \*

There are three significant approaches, traditional, middle ground, and evidentiary which the judiciary has adopted in considering the impact of future inflation and productivity on lost future earning capacity. The traditional approach ignores altogether the effects of future productivity and future inflation as being "too speculative." This view was previously adhered to by this Commonwealth, but for reasons stated above, it is hereby rejected.

The middle ground approach is anomalous in that it permits the factfinder to consider the effects of productivity and inflation on lost future earning capacity, but prohibits expert testimony on either of

---

5. Economists recognize that there are at least four major elements which influence the rate of increase of an employee's income. These factors are: (1) the educational attainment of the participant prior to his entry into the labor marker; (2) the influence of age upon the earnings of participants over their life cycle; (3) the significance of productivity and growth; and (4) the impact of inflation. In our analysis, we will isolate the inflation element from the other three factors, collectively called "merit" increases, which are consumed in productivity. \* \* \*

10. The rationale for reducing a lump-sum award to its present value is that: it is assumed that the plaintiff will invest the sum awarded and receive interest thereon. That interest accumulated over the number of relevant years will be available, in addition to the capital, to provide the plaintiff with his future support until the total is exhausted at the end of the period. The projected interest must therefore be allowed in reduction of capital lest it be claimed that the plaintiff is overcompensated. Fleming, Inflation and Tort Compensation, 26 Am. J.Comp.Law 51, 66 (1977).

\* \* \*

these issues. The proponents of this approach argue that expert testimony on future economic trends is "speculative," yet acknowledge that such facts are within the "common experience" of all jurors and, therefore, jurors should not be prohibited from applying their common knowledge in reaching a verdict. However, it has been consistently demonstrated that expert evidence is essential to accurate economic forecasting. Since it is apparent that the middle-ground approach contributes little to the accuracy or predictability of lost future earnings, and paradoxically allows a judge or jury to determine what an acknowledge[d] expert cannot, we decline to adopt it.

The evidentiary approach in its several variants allows the factfinder to consider productivity and inflation in awarding damages. * * * Recognizing that there are myriad of ways to incorporate such economic data we find that there are two versions appropriate for our consideration.

The first of these two variants of the evidentiary approach was developed by the court in Feldman v. Allegheny Airlines. In *Feldman,* a surviving husband brought a wrongful death action as the administrator of his wife's estate. The defendant airline stipulated as to its liability and the trial was confined to the issue of damages. The court assumed that recovery for lost future earnings included the victim's lost earning capacity. In order to demonstrate the bases for the court's conclusions relative to what course the deceased's life probably would have taken, the court extrapolated the evolving pattern of Mrs. Feldman's life. The court detailed the deceased's college grades, her employment history, the opinion of the deceased held by her fellow workers, the expressed employment goals of the deceased and the potential jobs for which the deceased was qualified. The court also examined the employment history of another individual who had remarkably similar credentials as the deceased. The defendant produced one witness who testified as to the decedent's employment prospects. Based upon the above factors, the court predicted the incremental salary (productivity) increases of the decedent over her work-life expectancy.

The court was then faced with the inflation component and the task of discounting the award to its present value. The court developed a formula known as the "offset present value method" in which it subtracted the estimated inflation rate from the discount rate to calculate the inflation adjusted or "real" rate of interest. Each year's earnings were then discounted to present value by this "real" discount rate. The "real" discount rate employed by the court was 1.5%. * * *

The second variant of the evidentiary method was adopted by the Alaska Supreme Court in Beaulieu v. Elliott. * * *

In order to account for the inflationary component's impact on lost future earnings and the effect of future interest rates on lump-sum payment, the Alaska court applied that "total offset method." Under the total offset method, a court does not discount the award to its present value but assumes that the effect of the future inflation rate will completely offset the interest rate, thereby eliminating any need to discount the award to its present value.

* * *

Mindful of our goal that a damage award formula should strive to be efficient, predictable as well as accurate, in computing lost future earning capacity this Commonwealth adopts the *Feldman* court's approach to calculating lost productivity and the Alaska court's total offset approach to inflation and discounting to present value. We believe that this eclectic method best computes a damage award which will fairly compensate a victim to the full extent of his or her injuries and avoids unnecessary complexities likely to produce confusion although in reality contributing little to the degree of accuracy to be obtained. * * * After laying a proper foundation, expert and lay witnesses are called upon to testify as to the victim's past and future employment possibilities. The defense may cross-examine the plaintiff's witnesses and present evidence on their own behalf. Upon a thorough evaluation of all the evidence presented, the factfinder makes an informed estimation of the victim's lost earning capacity. Although this approach may be time consuming, and like all estimations of future events may be subject to a degree of speculation, it is exceedingly more accurate to assume that the future will not remain stagnant with the past.

* * *

In support of our adoption of the "total offset method" in allowing for the inflationary factor, we note that it is no longer legitimate to assume the availability of future interest rates by discounting to present value without also assuming the necessary concomitant of future inflation. * * *

* * *

Since over the long run interest rates, and, therefore, the discount rates, will rise and fall with inflation, we shall exploit this natural adjustment by offsetting the two factors in computing lost future earning capacity. We are satisfied that the total offset method provides at least as much, if not greater, accuracy than an attempt to assign a factor that would reflect the varying changes in the rate of inflation over the years. Our experiences with the use of the six percent discount rate suggest the difficulties inherent in such an approach. As to the concomitant goals of efficiency and predictability, the desirability of the total offset method is obvious. There is no method that can assure absolute accuracy. An additional feature of the total offset method is that where there is a variance, it will be in favor of the innocent victim and not the tortfeasor who caused the loss.

* * *

An additional virtue of the total offset method is its contribution to judicial efficiency. Litigators are freed from introducing and verifying complex economic data. Judge and juries are not burdened with complicated, time consuming economic testimony. Finally, by eliminating the variables of inflation and future interest rates from the damage calculation, the ultimate award is more predictable.

\* \* \*

Henceforth, in this Commonwealth, damages will be awarded for lost future earnings that compensate the victim to the full extent of the injury sustained. Upon proper foundation, the court shall consider the victim's lost future productivity. Moreover, we find as a matter of law that future inflation shall be presumed equal to future interest rates with these factors offsetting. Thus, the courts of this Commonwealth are instructed to abandon the practice of discounting lost future earnings. By this method, we are able to reflect the impact of inflation in these cases without specifically submitting this question to the jury.

In view of the trial court's refusal to permit appellant to introduce evidence relating to a future productivity factor and our formulation of a new standard to be used for accommodating inflation in these cases, we reverse the judgment below and remand the cause for a new trial as to the damage question.

FLAHERTY, JUSTICE, concurring and dissenting.

\* \* \* I must dissent to the majority's adoption of what it calls the "total offset method", a "per se rule" of doubtful validity. True, such an approach is a simple one, but it does not achieve justice, and, has only been adopted in one jurisdiction, i.e., Alaska. We should simply permit expert testimony on the issues of inflation and productivity. Such testimony, on both sides of the issue, is, of course, subject to cross-examination and argument as to its validity and weight. Thus, the jury is free to weigh the evidence before it and render its verdict. This is also simple, and provides justice in accordance with our time honored principles.

### *Notes and Questions*

1. As the Pennsylvania Supreme Court noted in *Kaczkowski*, damages for continuing medical expenses or future lost wages normally take the form of a lump-sum damages award rather than a requirement that the defendant pay the plaintiff damages as long as the plaintiff remains incapacitated.

*Questions:* Is there an economic reason to prefer lump-sum payments? What would be the likely effect on primary and tertiary accident costs of a rule requiring a defendant to pay the plaintiff's lost wages until the plaintiff recovers from his injury?

2. In a wrongful death case like *Kaczkowski*, pecuniary loss normally is measured by the plaintiff's expected future wages less the expected costs of the plaintiff's maintenance (rent, groceries, transportation, and so forth). However, if Kaczkowski had survived and brought an action for lost wages due to personal injury, the defendant would not have been entitled to deduct the cost of the plaintiff's maintenance from lost wages.

*Questions:* Why shouldn't defendants in personal injury cases deduct maintenance costs from lost future wages? What incentives does this aspect of damage law create for defendants?

3. Many jurisdictions require that lost future wages be discounted to their "present value" in damages awards. Discounting allows a defendant to pay an amount of damages that is less than the amount of wages the plaintiff stands to lose in the future.

*Questions:* Why should defendants be able to discount lost future wages to present value? In other words, why might $100 today be full compensation for a loss of $106 next year?

4. As the *Kaczkowski* opinion notes, an individual's salary may rise over his working life for reasons apart from inflation in the general economy. People tend to be paid higher inflation-adjusted salaries later in life. Moreover, the average salaries of American workers have tended to increase over time.

*Question:* What are the causes of productivity increases, both for individual workers and for society as a whole?

5. Inflation requires a defendant to make a larger payment now to give a plaintiff the same purchasing power in the future. Discounting to present value allows a defendant to make a smaller payment now in full compensation for a larger future loss. *Kaczkowski* held that as a matter of Pennsylvania law, the rate of inflation and the discount rate used to reduce future losses to present value would be presumed to be the same, so that the factors of inflation and present value "cancel each other out."

*Question:* Calculate the damage award a defendant must pay under the *Kaczkowski* rule in the following circumstances. The injured plaintiff is a 50–year old plumber currently earning $20,000 who had planned to work fulltime until her retirement at age 65. As a result of her injury the plaintiff is completely incapacitated. Assume that the plumber had no reason to expect her salary to increase other than to keep pace with inflation—in other words, assume no productivity increase. What amount should the defendant pay for lost wages?

6. The Pennsylvania Supreme Court defended the *Kaczkowski* "total offset rule" on the ground that "over the long run interest rates, and, therefore, the discount rates, will rise and fall with inflation." The Court also claimed that "where there is a variance, it will be in favor of the innocent victim and not the tortfeasor."

*Questions:* Is it correct to assume that the interest rate and the discount rate are identical? When would that assumption favor plaintiffs and when would it favor defendants? As a practical matter, which party is most likely to benefit from the total offset rule? What are the rule's advantages?

## 3. VALUING HUMAN LIFE

In addition to past and future pecuniary losses, plaintiffs may suffer physical pain and suffering, mental distress, loss of a spouse's consortium, or even loss of enjoyment of life itself. The problem of attaching monetary values to such non-pecuniary losses raises interesting and perhaps insurmountable questions, some of which are considered below.

## SHERROD v. BERRY

United States District Court, Northern District of Illinois, E.D., 1985.
629 F.Supp. 159.

LEIGHTON, DISTRICT JUDGE.

This civil rights suit was brought by a father to recover for the death of his son who was shot and killed by a City of Joliet police officer. A jury returned verdicts and defendants have filed post-trial motions. One of the issues raised is whether this court erred in admitting evidence which allowed the jury to consider "the hedonic value of a human life" when it decided the damages to be awarded plaintiff for the wrongful death of his son.

An expert in economics was permitted to testify that in determining the value of a human life in such a case, a factor to be considered is the hedonic value which, according to qualified economists, is worth more than the economic value of that person. The jury awarded the father $450,000 for the loss of parental companionship with his son, $300,000 for economic loss to the estate, $1,700 for funeral expenses, and $850,000 for the value of the son's life. Defendants contend they were prejudiced by the testimony of the expert and that consequently, they are entitled either to a judgment notwithstanding the verdict, a remittitur, or a new trial. This court does not agree. When a jury is shown that a person was wrongfully killed, and it is asked to award damages, evidence, including the testimony of an expert, is admissible to enable the jury to consider the hedonic value of the life thus taken.

\* \* \*

At the trial, in order to prove the damages he suffered from the death of his son, Lucien Sherrod called as an expert witness, Stanley Smith, an economist, holder of a master's degree in economics from the University of Chicago. \* \* \*

Accordingly, Smith, after explaining what he did and the information he used, testified to the amount of loss Lucien Sherrod suffered when he was deprived of his son's association and companionship. Smith described and explained how he had calculated the economic loss which Ronald Sherrod's estate incurred from his death. Smith told the jury the basis of his opinions, and the economic theories which supported his conclusions.

Apart from his testimony concerning the economic value of life, he gave the jury some "insight into the guidelines that economists use in looking at how society values what we call the hedonic aspect, the hedonic value of life, separate from economic productive value of an individual." He said there had been studies by economists which "indicate that a human life has value separate from the economic productive value that a human being would have." Of course, Smith said, the economic aspect of life valuation presents what may appear to be imponderable difficulties in those cases when the individual, because of infancy, old age, or physical incapacity, has no measurable economic productivity. These difficulties, however, did not apply to the case before the jury because Ronald Sherrod was gainfully employed up to the day he was killed by Berry.

Smith told the jury that in the last 10 years economic literature showed some 15 studies "with respect to the value of life." There "was a study by Blomquist here in Illinois" which in turn considered all the other studies and found that there was a relationship somewhere in the dimension of three times up to 30 times their economic productive income. Smith expressed agreement with Blomquist's conclusions, considering him an authoritative source of knowledge on the subject of the hedonic value of life. At the end of Smith's testimony, which included extensive direct and intensive crossexamination, this court asked Smith to define for the jury the word "hedonic" as it is used in the expression "the hedonic value of life." Smith said:

> It derives from the word pleasing or pleasure. I believe it is a Greek word. It is distinct from the word economic. So it refers to the larger value of life, the life at the pleasure of society, if you will, the life—the value including economic, including moral, including philosophical, including all the value with which you might hold life, is the meaning of the expression "hedonic value".

\* \* \* A § 1983 action is a suit for tort damages, even though the duty a defendant is alleged to have breached is created by the Constitution or federal law. \* \* \* The basic purpose of a § 1983 damages award should be to compensate persons for injuries caused by the deprivation of constitutional rights.

In this case, Ronald Sherrod's death was caused by the constitutional deprivation for which compensation was sought. Section 1983, and the applicable provisions of the Fourteenth Amendment, protect life. It is well established in this and other circuits that on the facts alleged, and on the evidence the jury heard, the estate of Ronald Sherrod could sue and recover damages for the loss of his life.

"Life," Blackstone has reminded us, "is the immediate gift of God, a right inherent by nature in every individual...." The deprivation of life that is prohibited by the Fourteenth Amendment includes "not only of life [itself], but of whatever God has given to everyone with life for its growth and enjoyment...." In other words, the loss of life means more than being deprived of the right to exist, or of the ability to earn a living; it includes deprivation of the pleasures of life.

This is the point that Smith discussed with the jury when he told them about "the hedonic value of life." As he explained to them, "hedonic" refers "to the larger value of life...." This includes the pleasure of living which is destroyed by the blow that is lethal; in this case, the fatal pistol shot that Berry fired into the temple of Ronald

Sherrod, a mere youth; and thus taking from him what all the wealth in the world could never purchase. Smith's expert testimony enabled the jury to consider this important aspect of injury which the estate of Ronald Sherrod suffered, an aspect they should have considered in the event they determined that Lucien Sherrod, as administrator, was entitled to a judgment against the defendants.

\* \* \*

Contrary to what may be the popular view, the idea that an estate can recover for the hedonic value of the life of the person killed is not new in Anglo American law. In England, for example, hedonic damage awards have been allowed since 1976. Section 1 of the Law Reform (Miscellaneous Provisions) Act of 1934 has been construed by English judges so that the estate of a person killed can recover for "loss of expectation of life." In this country, legal scholars, economists, and social scientists have grappled with the task of formulating a method by which the value of a human life can be measured in terms understood by a jury. Therefore, the concept, although novel, is not unknown. The testimony of Stanley Smith as an expert in economics enabled the jury to perform its function in determining the proper measure of damages in this case. This court's ruling allowing him to testify concerning "the hedonic value of life" was not error.

So ordered.

### Notes and Questions

1. The question of valuing human life often raises an emotional response. Many find the idea that life can be valued repugnant. Some people assert that life is "priceless." On reflection, that cannot be true. If life were truly priceless, no potentially fatal accident would ever be worth risking. People would not fly on airlines, drive cars, or cross the street without a helmet and protective armor. When an individual declines to purchase an airbag for her car because it is "too expensive", she is implicitly saying that she can fix a finite price on the risk of dying prematurely.

*Questions:* If human life cannot, as a practical matter, be treated as priceless, what is the correct price? In *Sherrod*, the jury valued Lucien Sherrod's life at $850,000. Does that figure seem too high? Too low?

2. One way to answer "What is life worth?" is to ask, "What are you willing to pay for it?" At first, a person's ability to pay for life would appear to be limited by his wealth—for the average individual, his earning capacity. Nevertheless, the court in *Sherrod* held that the "hedonic" value of human life can exceed the "economic" value of a person's expected earnings.

Judge Leighton's opinion makes more sense when one considers that most individuals do not attempt to earn as much money as they possibly could if they sacrificed all non-monetary rewards. The average individual does not spend all her waking hours working overtime, taking a second job, and so forth. Many people earn less money than they could because, after they work a forty-hour week, they find that they gain more utility (more "hedonic" pleasure) from using their time for leisure activities instead of working. Others choose lower-paying jobs they enjoy over higher-paid positions that are more unpleasant or stressful.

If an individual knew she was going to be put in the position of having to pay to keep her life (a payment that must be made in dollars, rather than in the utility gained from leisure), she could alter her pattern of employment and work longer and harder hours, or perhaps choose a less-rewarding occupation with a higher salary. Even if life should be valued according to the amount an individual is willing and able to pay to keep it, lost earnings is too low a measure.

3. The hedonic theory of valuing life may raise as many questions as it answers. The fact that most people choose a mixture of leisure and work over constant working suggests that they value their lives more highly than the maximum amount of money they could earn by spending all their waking hours employed at the highest possible salary. But while people may value their lives more highly than the maximum amount they could earn during their lifespans, they can never pay more than that amount because they can never earn more than that amount. There is no convenient way for the individual to "tap into" the value of leisure time, in terms of utility, in offering to pay for life.

When an individual only works forty hours per week and spends the rest of her time on non-paying leisure activities, that decision may indicate a declining marginal utility for money. The money paid in damages may be paid by a tortfeasor out of earnings that still have a high marginal utility to the tortfeasor.

*Question:* Under what circumstances will payment of hedonic damages lead to a decline in total utility?

4. A second approach to valuing life is to focus on how much an individual would be willing to accept in return for her life, instead of asking how much she would be willing to pay to keep it. It should be apparent that the two figures are not identical. An individual's ability to pay for life is limited by her wealth and future income. Presumably, however, only a suicidal person would accept even an infinite amount of money in return for sure death, for after death the money has no value.

*Questions:* Should life be valued according to willingness to pay or willingness to accept? Which criteria more accurately values life?

5. A third approach to valuing life is to shift from an *ex post* evaluation of the loss associated with death to an *ex ante* evaluation of the loss associated with facing a *risk* of death. Even if life is valued according to a willingness to accept criterion, people may be willing to accept a finite amount of money in return for a risk of death because there is a chance of spending the money—money no longer has a zero utility.

*Questions:* Suppose a car buyer declines to purchase an optional airbag for $500 even though the airbag would reduce her lifetime risk of a fatal auto accident from 1 in 5,000 to 1 in 10,000. What implicit cost does the buyer assign to an additional 1 in 5,000 risk of death? What implicit value does she attach to her life? Would she accept half of that amount in return for facing a 50% risk of death? Would she accept the full amount in return for certain death?

6. In a society where people enjoy different levels of wealth and income, valuing life according to economic principles inevitably raises distributional concerns.

*Questions:* What are the distributional implications of both the ability-to-pay and willingness-to-receive-for-risk approaches to valuing life? Are the lives of the rich or the poor likely to be valued more highly under each approach?

### 4. PUNITIVE DAMAGES AND OVERDETERRENCE

To minimize primary accident costs, the defendant must pay an amount at least equal to the loss the plaintiff suffered from the defendant's failure to take preventative measures. Only full compensation ensures that the defendant has completely internalized the otherwise-external costs his conduct imposes on others. What happens if damages not only equal the loss suffered, but exceed it?

### STURM, RUGER & CO., INC. v. DAY

Supreme Court of Alaska, 1979.
594 P.2d 38.

CONNOR, JUSTICE.

\* \* \*

Appellee Michael James Day bought a .41 magnum single action revolver on June 1, 1972. The gun had been manufactured two years before by appellant Sturm, Ruger and Company, in August of 1970, but was purchased new by Day.

On July 30, 1972, Day was sitting in the cab of his small pickup truck with two young friends when he decided to unload his gun. As he was unloading the revolver, the gun slipped out of his hands. When he grabbed for the gun it fired, the bullet striking his leg and causing serious injuries. \* \* \*

Day filed suit against Sturm, Ruger and Company. His second amended complaint \* \* \* included a claim for punitive damages. \* \* \*

The jury returned a verdict for the plaintiff, finding specifically that the revolver was designed defectively and that it had a manufacturing defect as well. The jury awarded $137,750.00 in compensatory damages and $2,895,000.00 in punitive damages to the plaintiff.

\* \* \*

\* \* \* [I]n order to recover punitive or exemplary damages, the plaintiff must prove that the wrongdoer's conduct was "outrageous, such as acts done with malice or bad motives or a reckless indifference to the interests of another." Actual malice need not be proved. Rather, "[r]eckless indifference to the rights of others, and conscious action in deliberate disregard of them ... may provide the necessary state of mind to justify punitive damages."

* * *

* * * Where * * * plaintiff is able to plead and prove that the manufacturer knew that its product was defectively designed and that injuries and deaths had resulted from the design defect, but continued to market the product in reckless disregard of the public's safety, punitive damages may be awarded.

Punitive damages are designed not only to punish the wrongdoer, but also to deter him and others like him from similar wrongdoing in the future. We believe that as a matter of public policy, punitive damages can serve several useful functions in the products liability area. For example, the threat of punitive damages serves a deterrence function in cases in which a product may cause numerous minor injuries for which potential plaintiffs might decline to sue, or in cases in which it would be cheaper for the manufacturer to pay compensatory damages to those who did present claims then it would be to remedy the product's defect. In addition, if punitive damages could not be awarded in the products liability context, a reckless manufacturer might gain an unfair advantage over its more socially responsible competitors. On balance, we find the arguments advanced by appellant in favor of its position to be outweighed by the sound public policy considerations supporting the imposition of punitive damages in appropriate cases. We therefore decline to jettison the doctrine of punitive damages in this area of the law.

We turn next to Sturm, Ruger's claim that there was insufficient evidence to sustain the jury's award of punitive damages. The evidence presented at trial indicated that top officials at Sturm, Ruger knew that the safety and loading notches of their single action revolver presented a danger of accidental discharge because of the propensity of the engaging middle parts to fail or break. The evidence also reflects knowledge on the part of Sturm, Ruger management that serious injuries had resulted from this deficiency, coupled with procrastination in changing the basic design, at an increased cost of $1.93 per gun. Because we find that fair-minded jurors in the exercise of reasonable judgment could differ as to whether Sturm, Ruger's actions amounted to reckless indifference to the rights of others, and conscious action in deliberate disregard of them, thereby evidencing a state of mind which could justify the imposition of punitive damages, we will not upset the jury's conclusions that punitive damages were warranted.

* * *

The compensatory damages awarded to Michael Day and against Sturm, Ruger amounted to $137,750, exclusive of costs, prejudgment interest, and attorney's fees. The punitive damage award of $2,895,000 appears to be so out of proportion to the amount of actual damages as to suggest that the jury's award was the result of passion or prejudice. The jurors apparently responded to an invitation to punish Sturm,

Ruger for all wrongs committed against all purchasers and users of its products, rather than for the wrong done to this particular plaintiff. Under the circumstances, it was a mistake and an abuse of discretion for the trial judge not to have reduced the punitive damages or to have ordered a new trial.

\* \* \*

[The court remanded the case for a new trial with respect to punitive damages as well as a number of other issues.]

BURKE, JUSTICE, dissenting in part.

\* \* \*

The evidence showed that Sturm, Ruger manufactured over 1,501,000 revolvers of the type causing Day's injury. Sturm, Ruger's profit from the manufacture and sale of those firearms alone was enormous, totalling many millions of dollars. At trial, William Ruger, the president and founder of Sturm, Ruger, testified that redesign of the revolver to cure the defect cost approximately $199,000 and that the increased manufacturing cost per revolver was $1.93. The figure agreed upon by the jury as an appropriate award for punitive damages equalled the amount of the increased manufacturing cost per item multiplied by the approximate number of revolvers sold: $1.93 X 1,500,000 = $2,895,000. Thus, the amount of the award is roughly equal to the profit directly attributable to Sturm, Ruger's callous disregard for the safety of its customers. Such being the case, I think there is no merit to the contention that the figure was the result of improper passion or prejudice. Certainly, the amount of the punitive damage award far exceeded Day's actual damages. However, given the purpose of punitive damages, the award was not excessive.

## *Notes and Questions*

1. In *Sturm, Ruger,* the jury required the defendant to pay the plaintiff punitive damages as well as compensatory damages, in order both to punish and deter the defendant's reckless conduct. The gun manufacturer had chosen to accept the known risk of serious injuries with "reckless indifference" and "deliberate disregard" of the consequences. A rational actor engaged in an activity that presents a risk of harm balances the cost of avoiding accidents with the expected cost of letting them occur. Punitive damages increase the defendant's costs of accidents. Adding $2,895,000 to a $137,750 damage award certainly helps to get the attention of an actor considering the primary accident costs associated with his activity.

The jury in *Sturm, Ruger* apparently concluded that the benefits of reduced risk outweighed the costs of redesigning the handgun ($1.93 per gun). Suppose the original unsafe hammer design resulted in injury from one gun out of a thousand, and each injury caused an average of $1000 damage. In that case a prospective defendant would expect to pay $1.00 in compensatory damages for each gun manufactured.

*Questions:* Would expected punitive damages of $25 per gun create incentives for inefficient accident avoidance in that situation? Does the analysis change if average actual damages are $3000 per injury?

2. Awarding punitive damages poses the danger of encouraging accident avoidance when avoidance is inefficient. The likelihood of inefficient accident avoidance depends on the legal standard applied. Although *Sturm, Ruger* was a product liability case, the claim of design defect involves balancing the risks and benefits of alternative designs and resembles the analysis found in negligence cases. Compare the *Sturm, Ruger* test of "reckless indifference" (which follows the Restatement (Second) of Torts § 908) to the test adopted in Reynolds Metals Co. v. Lampert, 316 F.2d 272, 275 (9th Cir. 1963):

> To justify an award of punitive damages, it is not necessary that the act have been done maliciously or with bad motive. Where it has become apparent, as it has here, that compensatory damages alone, while they might compensate the injured party, will not deter the actor from committing similar trespasses in the future, there is ample justification for an award of punitive damages.

*Question:* Which of the two tests creates incentives more likely to minimize primary accident costs?

3. Questions 1 and 2 focus on incentives to engage in the efficient *level of care.* Consider Shavell's argument that internalizing externalities through strict liability also leads to an efficient *level of activity.*

*Question:* What is the impact of punitive damages on gun manufacturers' level of gun production?

4. Justice Connor argues that "the threat of punitive damages serves a deterrence function in cases in which a product may cause numerous minor injuries for which potential plaintiffs might decline to sue." Connor's opinion calls attention to the problem of *underenforcement* of liability rules; not all plaintiffs injured by a negligent tortfeasor bother to sue.

*Questions:* Why might an injured plaintiff decline to sue a negligent defendant? How does potential plaintiffs' failure to sue for their injuries affect defendants' incentives to adopt efficient levels of care and activity? What measure of punitive damages would correct for the problem of underenforcement?

5. Justice Burke supported a measure of punitive damages "roughly equal to the profit directly attributable to the Sturm, Ruger's callous disregard for the safety of its customers." In *Sturm, Ruger,* that amounted to $1.93 x 1,500,000, the savings per gun times the number of guns sold.

*Question:* Which measure of punitive damages—Justice Connor's or Justice Burke's—is more likely to lead to efficient incentives?

6. Under the Learned Hand formula, an injurer is liable to her victim if she failed to take preventative measures that cost less than the expected costs of the accident. Knowing that she will be liable, no rational injurer would ever be negligent. If negligent behavior is inconsistent with rationality, grossly negligent behavior seems even more peculiar.

*Questions:* Why are people grossly negligent? Is gross negligence always irrational? Considering the motivations that may underlie grossly negligent behavior, can punitive damages modify such behavior?

\*

# Index

References are to Pages

**ACCIDENT AVOIDANCE**
See also, Torts
Cooperative precautions, 56, 67
Unilateral precautions, 52, 56, 64

**ADVERSE POSSESSION**
Efficiency characteristics, 77

**ASSUMPTION OF RISK**
Generally, 67–71
Primary, 67–69
Secondary, 67–69, 135–138

**BARGAINING**
Role in maximizing wealth, 5, 20, 78, 81, 88–103
Transaction costs, 88

**BEST COST AVOIDER**
Defined, 75
Property law, 75, 87, 102
Reciprocal causation, 75
Tort law, 46–53, 58, 66–67, 108, 116, 132

**CLASS BIAS**
Efficiency implications, 78

**COASE THEOREM**
Generally, 73–88, 98
Defined, 78
Invariance hypothesis, 83–88
Reciprocal causation, 71–76
Strong version, 83–85
Transaction costs, 88–90
Weak version, 85–86
Wealth effects, 85–86

**DAMAGES**
Collateral source rule, 142–144
Compensation for takings, 13–17
Compensatory, 21–24, 75, 91, 94–108
Earning capacity, 144–149
Nuisance, 95–108
Permanent, 96–100
Punitive, 21–24, 154–157
Torts, 27–35, 142–157
Value of life,
    Generally, 149–154
    Hedonic value, 150–154
    Risk valuation, 153
    Wealth effects, 153–154

**DAMAGES**—Cont'd
Wrongful death,
    Generally, 144–154
    Pecuniary loss, 144–149

**DEEP POCKET THEORY**
Risk spreading, 123–128, 138–140

**DISTRIBUTIONAL CONCERNS**
See also, Deep Pocket Theory
Generally, 17–20
Accident costs, 42, 120
Allocation of resources, 86
Hedonic damages, 154
Nuisance, 102, 105–108
Wealth, 17–20, 75

**DUTY TO RESCUE**
Efficiency of no duty rule, 128–130

**EASEMENTS**
Generally, 76–78
Efficiency, 76
Prescriptive, 77

**EFFICIENCY**
Generally, 4
Allocative efficiency, defined, 6
Fairness compared, 17–20
Level of output, 21–24, 111–114
Relationship to pareto criteria, 15

**EQUILIBRIUM**
General equilibrium analysis, 87
Partial equilibrium analysis, 86

**EQUITY**
See also, Distributional Concerns
Consent, 19–20
Contrasted with efficiency, 17–20
Equality, 19–20
Just desserts, 19–20

**EXTERNALITIES**
External benefit, 22
External cost, 21–26, 84, 95
Internalization,
    Damages, 21–24, 157
    Regulation, 24–26
    Strict liability, 116–120, 132
Nuisance, 104–107
Torts, 32, 38, 116–120

# INDEX
**References are to Pages**

**GROSS DOMESTIC PRODUCT**
As a measure of wealth, 9

**GROSS DOMESTIC VALUATION**
As a measure of well-being, 9

**HEDONIC DAMAGES**
Value of human life, 149–154

**INJUNCTION**
Efficiency of remedy, 29, 96–108

**KALDOR–HICKS CRITERIA**
Potential compensation requirement, 16–17
Relationship to pareto criteria, 16–17

**LAST CLEAR CHANCE**
Generally, 57–60

**LEARNED HAND FORMULA**
Generally, 35–46
Distributional implications, 38
Duty to rescue, 129
Expected (Discounted) Costs, 32
Modern applications, 39–46

**LIABILITY RULES**
See also, Damages
Property rules compared, 91–92
Property law, 91–92
Tort law, 29

**LITIGANT BEHAVIOR**
Decision to sue,
　Punitive damages, 154–157

**NUISANCE**
Best cost avoider, 95–108
Choice of remedy for, 95–108
Coming to nuisance, 100–103
Permanent damages, 96–100
Private, 103
Property law, 71–78, 83, 96–108
Public, 103
Reciprocal causation, 71–76
Right to sunlight, 79–83

**OPPORTUNITY COST**
Defined, 4

**PARETO CRITERIA**
Full compensation requirement, 15
Pareto inferiority, 11
Pareto optimality, 12
Pareto superiority, 11, 14, 23
Property law, 23
Relationship to Kaldor–Hicks criteria, 16
Takings, 15

**POLLUTION**
Air, 21–24, 96–108
Water, 24–26

**PRIVATE NECESSITY**
Defense to Trespass, 89

**PROBLEM OF SOCIAL COST**
Internalizing externalities, 73–88

**PROPERTY LAW**
Adverse possession, 77
Easements, 76
Nuisance, 71–78, 83, 96–108
Trespass, 21–22, 88–90, 109

**PROPERTY RULES**
Liability rules compared, 91–92, 95
Protection of rights in property, 91–92

**RATIONALITY**
Assumption, 3–4
Infants, 4–5

**REALLOCATION OF RESOURCES**
Efficiency, 9
Government coercion, 13

**REGULATION**
See also, Pollution
Internalizing externalities, 24–26

**REMEDIES**
See also, Damages; Injunction
Nuisance, 95–107

**REVEALED PREFERENCES THEORY**
Relationship to wealth maximization, 5

**RISK ALLOCATION**
Loss spreading, 123–128, 138–140

**RISK AVERSION**
Relevance to loss spreading, 121–123

**RISK SPREADING**
See Deep Pocket Theory; Tort Law, Strict Liability

**TAKINGS**
Compensation, 13–17
Efficiency, 13–17

**TORT LAW**
See also, Accident Avoidance; Learned Hand Formula; Nuisance
Defenses to negligence,
　Generally, 46–71
　Assumption of risk, 67–71
　Comparative negligence,
　　Apportioned, 60–65
　　Nonapportioned, 65–67
　Contributory negligence, 34, 48–56
　Last clear chance, 57–60
Defenses to strict liability,
　Generally, 131–142
　Assumption of risk, 135–138
　Comparative negligence, 138–142
　Unforeseeable misuse, 131–135
Duty to rescue, 128–130
Insurance, 124–125
Level of care v. Level of activity,
　Generally, 111–114
　Punitive damages, 157

**TORT LAW**—Cont'd
Primary accident costs, 29, 31, 42, 46, 49, 61, 64–65, 71, 132, 148
Secondary accident costs, 123–125, 130
   *See also,* Deep Pocket Theory
Strict liability,
      Generally, 111–142
      Abnormally dangerous activity, 114
      Allocative efficiency, 116–120
      Blasting, 108–114
      Products liability, 114–142
      Risk spreading, 121–128
Tertiary accident costs, 31–32, 42, 46, 61, 69, 130, 132, 148
Wealth maximization, 29, 32

**TRANSACTION COSTS**
   *See also,* Bargaining
Asymmetric, 102–103, 107
Choice of remedy, 95–108
Coase theorem, 88–95
Exchange of rights, 78, 88–103

**TRESPASS**
   Generally, 1–5
Blasting, 108
Defined, 3
Interpersonal comparisons, 9–10

**TRESPASS**—Cont'd
Maximization, 3–6
Measurement, 6
Private necessity, 89–95
Relationship to pareto criteria, 15
Wealth maximization compared, 11–17

**WEALTH EFFECT**
Coase theorem, 83–86
Efficiency implications, 85–88
Value of life, 152–154
Willingness to pay, 85–86

**WEALTH MAXIMIZATION**
   *See also,* Kaldor–Hicks Criteria; Pareto Criteria
   Generally, 6–11
Auctions, 6–11
Defined, 6–11
Other values, 32
Relationship to pareto criteria, 15
Torts, 29

**WILLINGNESS-TO-PAY**
Bargaining, 95
Bias toward wealthy, 17, 75
Invariance hypothesis, 83–86
Measure of value, 8–11
Relevance to efficiency, 8